ANTHROPOLOGY OF SWEETMEATS

ANTHROPOLOGY OF SWEETMEATS

ANIL KISHORE SINHA

Foreword by:

Jagmohan Negi

GYAN PUBLISHING HOUSE
NEW DELHI-110 002

ANTHROPOLOGY OF SWEETMEATS

(Sociology, Hotel Management, Home Science, Anthropology)

ISBN : 81-212-0665-0

Published in 2000 in India by
Gyan Publishing House
5, Ansari Road, Darya Ganj
New Delhi-110002

Laser Typesetting at: Manas Typesetter
Printed at: Mehra Offset Press

Contents

Foreword

Our modern civilization has made the sweetmeats almost a bane, as the people, nowadays are more and more fitness conscious and very particular about calories they take every day.

However, for most of the Indian folk, sweetmeats form a part of their culture and tradition. There are families who would not allow a single meal to pass without partaking of a sweetmeat. Anthropologically speaking, sweetmeats have an interesting story to tell in a tradition-bound society like ours. It is a common sight to see the signboards of sweetmeat sellers claiming specialization in Bengali and other traditions to catch the eyes of sweet-lovers and passer-by.

It gave me immense pleasure to go through this most fascinating and interesting authored by Dr Anil Kishore Sinha, a social anthropologist, in his own right. Due credit must be given to him for giving an entirely new dimension to the study of sweetmeats. In my assessment the present book practically covers all aspects of it including the traditions connected with it. Their diffusion with special reference to Bihar and West Bengal is excellently depicted in this volume. It is one of the few studies carried out in best tradition of anthropology—diffusion of a cultural trait, the trait being the sweetmeats. Diffusion as a grand theory of anthropology may have had ups and downs but the display of the theory particularly in the concerned area of research has gone beyond recognition. Dr Sinha deserves a special mention for his work.

Besides a befitting introduction, the book starts with the concept of sweetmeat and particularly the Indian sweetmeats, and gives a general background of sweetmeats, its cultural significance and attitude of the Indians in general towards it.

Dr Sinha claims that the sweetmeats which we come across in the present time are generally the evolved form of ancient sweets or sweet dishes. He has discussed in detail about the development of Indian sweetmeats, i.e., from honey to present form of sweetmeats through different phases since Indus Valley Civilization. Sweetmeats have an important place in Indian culture. It is claimed that not only human beings but even gods are fond of sweets. Some gods are also known by their favourite sweetmeats. They play an important role during rituals, festivals, *samaskaras* and social occasions.

Some places are famous for their sweetmeats and known by them only. Besides, several of these sweetmeats have their own 'sweetmeat areas' within which they are quite popular. Some famous sweetmeats of Bihar and West Bengal and their respective places of origin and traditions connected with them have been discussed by the author. In this context he mentions that more than one factor go to explain the popularity of a particular sweetmeat in a particular area. The caste of sweetmeat-makers has also received the author's attention. He has described the problems ventilated by their professional associations.

Sweetmeat, like any other trait of culture, is subject to diffusion. After a sweetmeat is evolved in a particular area, culture or sub-culture, there emerges a tendency for it to be passed on to other cultural or sub-cultural areas. We call it 'diffusion of sweetmeats'. A set of eleven major factors which help in the diffusion of sweetmeats in historical perspective, and various areas and routes of diffusion have been discussed by Dr Sinha in detail with reference to Bihar and West Bengal. Besides, affinity among sweetmeats of different places on the basis of 'W' formula has also been analysed in detail by him which further helps in understanding the diffusion of sweetmeats. That adds a new dimension and beauty to the book.

Social scientists, no doubt, will find in it a veritable mine of information regarding 'sweets'. Dr Sinha's knowledge, experience and expertise, as projected in the book, provide various ideas for an exciting and more exclusive study on the Indian sweetmeats. In my opinion, the study is documentary in nature and may prove to be useful for other researchers working on a similar subject in future.

I am confident that the book is a pleasure to read, for scholars and laymen alike. The book would be a welcome addition to the list of books on social sciences.

Jagmohan Negi

Preface

Sweetmeats in India have a great cultural significance as they are accepted as a mark of hospitality in almost every section of the society. Gift of sweets is considered to be an act of favour and friendliness, which strengthens social bonds between two persons and any warm hospitality cannot be thought of without sweets.

Almost every state or region has its own sweet dishes including sweetmeats and traditions associated with it. The sweetmeats play an important role in Indian culture. Apart from hospitality they are needed during religious performances, festivals and a number of other social occasions. The rapid growth of communication, migration, urbanization and industrialization and other similar factors have led to the diffusion of sweetmeats from one region to other.

It promised an unexplored and rich field of study particularly the diffusion of the cultural traits associated with sweetmeats. The factors and forces which help build up tradition of sweets in a particular area and lead to its diffusion, constitute a significant field of study.

The main objective of the book is to explore the study of sweetmeats which form an integral part of Indian dietary pattern from anthropological point of view. One should know the concept, genesis and development in a historical perspective; cultural significance; some popular sweetmeats of Bihar and West Bengal; cultural traditions; communities traditionally associated with the making of sweetmeats; elaborate the traits connected with sweetmeats, and its diffusion from one region to other; locate the factors and processes involved in the diffusion of traits connected with sweetmeats; significance of sweetmeats as they figure in ancient literature.

This study is confined to two states only, i.e., Bihar and West Bengal, taken for practical purposes as administrative boundary and it has been designed for a comparative study of cultural practices. In Bihar and West Bengal the study of sweetmeats are covered at twenty-three and eighteen places respectively. For collecting field data observation, interview, schedule, generalogical table, photography and case study techniques were employed. To show the affinity among sweetmeats, 'W' formula model was selected. To follows this formula, forty-five sweetmeats traits based on multiple factors were selected. In this formula 'W' stands $\frac{a + d}{a + d + b + c}$ for where a = + +, b = + –, c = – + and d = – –. In other words 'W' is agreement divided by total. The presence (+) or absence (–) of a trait was recorded from 32 places (16 places from Bihar and 16 places from West Bengal) based on the observation.

In this book I have tried to place together the important ideas collected from shreds and patches in different studies and have presented these in a concise and lucid manner for the persons interested in this field.

In the light of the foregoing discussions, the data of the present study have been arranged into ten meaningful chapters.

The opening chapter deals with introduction of sweetmeats, the people connected with it, and research methodology review of literature.

The second chapter deals with the concept of sweetmeats and the Indian sweet. This chapter depicts the differences between a 'sweet-dish' and 'sweetmeat', ingredients, essential criteria of sweetmeats and a functional definition of sweetmeat as used in this study. This chapter also presents an analysis of regional distribution of some popular Indian sweetmeats, their etymological meanings and origin of some important sweetmeats.

The third chapter focuses on genesis of Indian sweetmeats

and development of sweetmeats through different periods of Indian history.

The fourth chapter describes the cultural significance of sweetmeats, i.e., the sweetmeats as favourite offerings to gods, their uses during various festivals, *samaskaras* and on social occasions.

The fifth chapter is divided into five sections. The first section deals with the famous sweetmeats of other zones. The second section deals with the sweets of Bengal as Bengal is madeup of the Indian states of West Bengal and the sovereign country of Bangladesh (formerly East Bengal or East Pakistan). The third section includes the views of tribals on milk and milk products. Regional distribution of some popular Indian sweetmeats and nutritive value of Indian sweetmeats have been given in the fourth and fifth section respectively.

The sixth and seventh chapters attempt to discuss about the sweetmeat areas and their traditions and dietary patterns of Bihar and West Bengal respectively, some popular sweetmeats of these states and their respective places of origin. Traditions connected with such sweetmeats in both the cultural areas and various factors regarding the popularity of sweetmeats have also been dealt with.

The eight chapter deals with sweetmeat-making castes of Bihar and West Bengal and their ethnographic background. It also speaks of the entry of non-sweetmeat making castes in this profession and the sweetmeat maker's associations of all India and State levels of these two states. The problems faced by sweetmeat dealers have also been highlighted.

The ninth chapter discusses in detail the diffusion of some sweetmeats of Bihar and West Bengal, in the other regions of the country and the factors responsible for it.

I hope fervently that this book will elicit the interest of the students and scholars of Anthropology, Sociology, History and Indology and they will be inspired to plan for further researches in theoretical and applied aspects.

In the preparation of this project as a Ph.D. thesis, first of all I owe a deep sense of gratitude to my teacher (supervisor) Dr K.N. Sahay, University Professor, Centre of Advanced

Studies in Anthropology, Ranchi University, Ranchi, who recommended the topic and took a keen and personal interest in my research work. Without his cooperation and valuable help, it would not have been possible for me to complete this gigantic task successfully.

I take great pleasure in recording my gratitude to Prof. Surajit C. Sinha, Prof. Sachchidananda, Late Prof. Makhan Jha, Prof, A.R.N. Srivastava and Prof. B.N. Saraswati who kindly gave me suggestions that proved profitable in course of my study.

I am grateful to Prof. B. G. Banerjee and Prof. R. N. Vashisht of the Department of Anthropology, Panjab University, Chandigarh for helping me in many ways in the preparation of the manuscript to book form. I am also grateful to Dr. Abhik Ghosh for his help.

I am obliged to my mother and brother who have been constant sources of inspiration to me for conducting my studies and helping me to come up to my expectations. I shall be failing in my duty if I do not acknowledge the encouragement and inspiration which I have always received from my father, Late L.N. Ambastha whose dedication and devotion to the cause of my education will always remain with me as a source of inspiration. I am specially thankful to my wife Dr. Anjubala and my daughter, Richa who took utmost care of my needs while I was preparing this book.

Shri Madan Prasad Bezbaruah Secretary, Minister of tourism, Government of India, has been kind in contributing an illuminating foreword to this book.

Finally, Mr. Amit Garg is the key factor in the presentation of this volume in such a nice manner. His profound knowledge and deep interest in the publication work deserves special mention. I am indebted to him as well as his team members in the publication section.

I shall feel grateful if you send your valuable suggestions and criticism for improvement. I will be very happy to incorporate the suggestions and bring out a revised edition of this book.

Anil K. Sinha

1

Introduction

Sweetmeats[1] as a cherished item of food constitute an almost universal phenomenon, though they vary greatly in the dose in which a sweetening agent is used while making a sweetmeat. Somewhere it may be profuse while at other places it may be used in a small quantity so that the sweetmeat has a faint taste of sweetness. The sweets also vary in frequency with which they are used in different communities or classes of people.

In Western countries a sweet dish is generally known as 'dessert'. Desserts usually include a preparation of fruits or a sweet item and are served as the last course of a meal. Here, it is significant to note that their 'food industries' are getting more advanced.

Here, it would not be out of place to mention the names of few varieties of desserts mostly from European countries which are given as follows. The variety of desserts among Anglo-Indians are known as *Mango fod;* in Argentina they are known as *Dulce de Leche;* in Austria as *Green tomato fool;* in

Australia as *Pfann kuchen;* in Brazil they are known as *Banana and cheese, Ovas queimados;* in France as *Atteraux victoria;* in Hawaii as *Orange sweet potato;* in Hungary as *Magyar pancakes;* in Italy as *Bundino di Ricotta, stuffed peaches, Banana cesarino;* in Poland as *Kisiel,* in Portugal as *Rabanadas, Cheese and quince cheese, Pumpkin fruit salad;* in Russia as *Pashka;* in South Africa as *Ananas en surprise, Melktert, Ischin-Tschou;* and in West Indies as *Caribbean Avacado dessert* and *Sweet potato cream.*

Special eating habits of the Nepalese are closely linked with numerous holidays and festivals when the people love to take comparatively expensive food such as sweets made with molasses, sesame and nuts, the most popular of which is called *Yomadhi* made with rice-flour, sugar and sesame. Some other popular Nepalese sweetmeats are the gifts of the Newars. Of these, the sweet called *Punjabi-roti* containing several folds and of the shape of a flat oblong cap is relished by all Nepalese. The traditional Newar sweetmeat which are included under the general appellation of *Lakhamarhi* are of so many varieties that hardly any Non-Newar Nepalese can claim a similar speciality. Among these *Lakhamarhi, gul-marhi, aitha* and *yo-marhi* are items of ceremonial significance.

Sweetmeats in India have a great cultural significance as they have been accepted as a mark of hospitality by almost every section of the society. They are a must during most of the religious performances and social occasions. Gift of sweets is considered to be an act of favour and friendliness which strengthens social bonds between two persons and any warm hospitality cannot be thought of without sweets. It is customary to take sweets to one's kinsmen on certain specific social occasions and one cannot imagine the performance of festivals or ceremonies connected with *rites-de-passage* without sweets as it is a mark of joy and believed to be auspicious. Children are very much fond of sweets and most mothers specially keep or prepare some kind of sweets for their children which is considered as a mark of love and affection. In Braj (UP) any food without sweetmeat is treated as *Bhuta bhojan.*

The Hindu sacred texts speak of the importance of sweetmeats known as '*Naivedya*' and it is one of the essential requisites needed for religious performances. Jaggery, *payasam, ghee, appam, modakam,* curds—all these are to be offered as food (*naivadiyam*) for the gods (Bhagavata Purana).

For thousands of years, Hindus have sought to please the gods and goddesses by showing their devotion through the offerings of sweet things to eat and drink, see, smell and touch. In the sacred scriptures it is said that the gods and goddesses are like children because they take delight in simple offerings, especially sweet ones (*ibid*).

Though particular varieties of sweetmeats may originally be associated with a particular place, the rapid growth of communication, migration, urbanization and industrialization and other similar factors have helped is their diffusion from one place to the other.

In view of this, sweetmeats provide an interesting rich and unexplored field of anthropological study from the point of view of its cultural significance, traditions associated with it, communities connected with sweet making, the different sweetmeat regions and factors responsible for the popularity of a particular sweet in a region and its diffusion.

References of Sweetmeats and their Studies so far

The sweetmeats being an important part of dietary pattern in India with great cultural significance have references found even from ancient times though, sporadic, casual and mostly in the form of brief description or notes. However, one hardly finds any full length study on sweetmeats. No doubt, there have appeared in recent decades some brief studies relating to sweetmeats but these are largely recipes of sweetmeats or write ups on their nutritive value. Sweets have also figured in the writings of a few social scientists but by and large, they have been discussed just as a part of general dietary patterns of the communities under study.

Among religious texts, *Mahabharata, Valmiki Ramayan, Chaitanya Charitamrita, Kabi Kankan Chandi, Chandi Mangal,* references of sweet dishes and sweetmeats in contexts with giving of alms, entertainment during feasts, atonement for taking alms and improper food, *Putreyasti Yajna* and the like, have appeared at several places.

Historians while studying the Indian culture and dietary pattern have also mentioned about sweet dishes and sweetmeats viz.; Agrawala (1953), Chakravarty (1959), Diwakar (1959), Omprakash (1961), Majumdar (1971), Agnihotri (1980) and the like.

Folklorists and poets such as Tripathi (1940, 1952), Archer (1943), Singh (1944), De (1946), Upadhyay (1954, 1957, 1960), Ray (1954), Sriyuta (1957), Prasad (1962), Aryani (1965), Rakesh (1966), Thakur (1969, 1981) while studying the folk culture of Bihar and West Bengal, make references of sweet dishes and sweetmeats in one way or the other.

In Census Reports and District Gazetteers, the authors like Beverly (1872), Gait (1902), O 'Malley (1908, 1910, 1911, 1914), Chaudhury (1957, 1962, 1964, 1965, 1966), Kumar (1970, 1971) make references of traditional communities associated with the making of sweetmeats, and famous sweetmeats of the districts respectively. Besides, the authors like Risley (1891), Russell (1916), Ghurye (1961), Blunt (1969), Cooke (1974), etc., studied, the ethnic background of such castes in detail.

Many people such as Haldar (1926), Maria (1980), Reejhsinghani (1979), Mukhopadhyay (1981), Kumar and Ray (1983) wrote books on recipes of sweetmeats. Besides, Funk and Wagnalls (1955), Helen (1973), Webster (1975), Girling (1978) defined the term 'cookery' and 'sweetmeat'.

Gopalan (1968) and Pasricha (1969) while studying the nutritive value of Indian foods in general also speak of some Indian sweetmeats. The authors like Thakur (1910), Gode (1943) and Ray (1979) wrote some articles exclusively on few sweetmeats.

Generally, on the occasions of Diwali and Bhai Phota there appear a number of articles on the importance of sweetmeats in newspapers such as *Amrita Bazar Patrika, Standard, The Searchlight, Telegraph,* etc. In some periodicals and magazines viz., *Manorama, Saptahika Hindustan, Dharamyuga, Grihsobha, Vama, Desha, Paribartan* and *Femina,* many authors write about the recipes of sweetmeats of different regions. Most of the aforesaid magazines are exclusively meant for women. Besides, in the professional journals connected with sweets such as *Haluwai, Mishtanna Bhojana* published by *Bihar Rajya Mishtanna Bhojana Vikreta Sangh,* one also finds some relevant materials on sweetmeats.

From anthropological point of view Vidyarthi et. al. (1979) in their study 'Changing Dietary Patterns and Habits: A sociocultural Study of Bihar,' deals with indigenous dietary habits and recipes and the dietary pattern and habits of the people of Bihar in the four cultural zones of Bihar mentioned for sweetmeats.

The Sweetmeats and the People Connected with it

It is interesting to note that 'sweetmeats' are known by different names in different regions. In Bihar (except Mithila region) they are known as *Mithai,* in Mithila region as *Madhur*, while in the whole of West Bengal, as *Mishti.*

At every place, one can find varieties of sweetmeats in various shapes and sizes which are generally prepared with basic ingredients such as *Chhena*, *Khoa, Besan* and *Maida*. It is generally called as 'dry sweetmeats' or sweetmeats that are 'hard' in nature. Sweetmeats prepared with gram flour and *Maida* is the characteristic of sweets in Bihar. Similarly, 'syrupy' sweetmeats or those 'soft' in quality generally prepared with *Chhena* are the characteristics of sweets from West Bengal. However, there are some sweetmeats viz., *Rassogolla, Pera, Barfee, Laddu, Jalebi* and the like, which are found in almost all the places.

There are some places from which more than one sweetmeats are popular, whereas there are some other sweetmeats which are popular at more than one place.

As said, there are different varieties of sweets in different regions but some of them have acquired more popularity. The sweetmeats like *Anarsa, Barra, Belgrami, Kala Jamun, Keshariya Pera, Khaza, Laddu, Lai, Lorha-mithai, Pantoa, Pera, Piyao, Raskadam, Rasmalai, Rassogolla, Sohnpapdi* and *Tilkut* are some of the popular sweetmeats of Bihar. Similarly *Adait bhoga, Babarsa, Chhena Barra, Jal bhara sandesh, Kachagulla, Kajusandesh, Kheer-Pantoa, Maicha, Malpua, Manohara, Mihidana, Moa Morabba, Motichur, Nikhuti, Raghavsai, Sandesh, Sarpuriya, Sarbhaja, Sitabhoga and Sponge rassogolla* are some of the popular sweetmeats of West Bengal.

From the point of view of popularity, again, one can think in terms of various 'sweetmeat-areas' in Bihar and West Bengal.

In ancient days, only *Halwai* caste in Bihar and *Marya* one in West Bengal were actively associated with the profession of sweet-making. But with the rapid social change, urbanization and industrialization now, some other castes including even those from whose hands water was not accepted, have become actively associated with this profession.

Research Methodology

When we think of sweetmeat, certain significant things come to mind. Firstly, what is sweetmeat, how to define it as people have been so far using the term in a somewhat loose sense, secondly, one finds a large variety of sweetmeats, with every region of the country having its own sweetmeat, and the number and variety of sweetmeats are still growing very rapidly. It leads us to certain basic questions, whether there were the same variety of sweetmeats in the past? If not, what was the type of sweets later in the past? How did it differ from now? How did such great variety of sweetmeat evolve? Though the present study focuses upon 'sweetmeat' as such it was in the light of the questions just raised that references of the things like honey, jaggery which were the 'Precursors' of sweets', or 'sweet dishes' all of which have been made in several chapters of the present book. It was felt that for a comprehensive understanding of sweetmeat the study of these related aspects was also essential. Thirdly, it leads us to the study of the nature of sweetmeat, traditions connected with it.

the communities associated with sweet-making and distribution of sweetmeats in different regions, Fourthly, these questions have a bearing on the diffusion of sweetmeats or the traits connected with it from one region to the other which also calls for a study of the factors responsible for it. Fifthly, when we know that there are different types of sweetmeats in different regions of the country it is useful to think in terms of 'sweet-areas' and also to compare the sweetmeats of one region with that of the other.

These are some of the considerations which have gone behind the present study. But a researcher has limited time and resources at his disposal and as such, delimitation of the unit of study was another important consideration before this researcher.

In view of it, Bihar and West Bengal were the two regions that were selected for the present study. The reasons behind the selection of these two Sates are as follows :

It was natural for this researcher to select Bihar as he belongs to it. As regards West Bengal, the Bengali sweetmeats are famous all over the country and geographically, it is an adjacent state of Bihar. Besides, the two states which are incidently also two distinct cultural regions, were formerly a single state till 1912 and ther have been large scale migrations both way in course of history. Along with migrations, there have also been the diffusion of sweetmeats or its traits. Hence Bihar and West Bengal formed two convenient, and at the same time, significant units of study.

But as each of the states was itself too large to tackle with, the present researcher selected sixteen places in each of the two states which are famous for particular sweetmeats, or which were situated on the border areas of the two states so that they could give us some idea to the understanding of interactions of the different traditions connected with sweetmeats in these two states.

Selection of the unit of study was followed by initial library work at Ranchi, Patna and Calcutta where he scanned through books, journals, gazetters, census reports and various other literary sources having any sort or relevant information or bearing work was simultaneously combind with field-work among the sweetmeat-makers connected with different sweetmeat shops of the various towns and cities of the two states. It is to be noted here that not only the sweetmeat-makers and sellers were interviewed, but the problem was discussed with several anthropologists, sociologists, and some lady scholars connected with the Departments of Domestic Science at Patna and Calcutta who also encouraged this researcher to go ahead with the study and gave him relevant informations.

For collecting field data the author applied several important anthropological research techniques.

Reference

1. Sweetmeat which is an English term and probably a translation of many Hindi terms like *Mithai*, *Mishti*, etc., seems to have been originally conceived by the Englishmen as some kind of 'meat' that is sweet, hence 'Sweetmeat'

   This term has also been referred to as 'Sweet' the shorter version, at many places in the present study.

2

Concept of Sweetmeats and the Indian Sweets

"The Indians have an unparalleled sweet tooth which, in some parts of India, especially in Gujarat and Maharashtra, is evidenced by the custom of beginning a meal with a sweet. But it is the Bengalis amongst all the communities who beat everybody in consuming sweets. They sometimes take only sweets for a meal. They serve sweets on all important festivals and ceremonies in which sweets are eaten in massive quantities. One can even write a sonnet in praise of the delectable flavour of Bengali sweets. Not only in Bengal, but each community in India has its own special sweets which are a delight to eat and to behold." (Reejhsinghani, 1979).

There are some sweetmeats which are used on festive occasions, e.g., *Rassogolla, Sandesh, Gulab-Jamun* and *Pinni,* while delicious tea-time *Halwa* and sweetmeats like *Peda, Jalebi* and *Barfee* are kept aside for unexpected guests; the simple *Laddu* is for kids. There is an infinite variety of sweetmeats to fascinate both young and old alike. (*ibid*).

Besides sweetmeats there are a number of delightfully delicious sweet dishes which are consumed by the peoples in both villages and sophisticated areas. For many Indians, a meal is not complete until it ends with some sweets. Sweet dishes are also consumed for their nutritional value. It is mostly made with milk, nuts, fresh and dried fruits. The ingredients of all the sweets may not be highly nutritious, but at the same time, they make a dish very satisfying, appetizing and tasty.

As regards the order of taking different items of food, the following direction is given in the *Brihad Dharama Puranam:*

At first, rice mixed with *ghee (a clarified butter),* then vegetables, next soup, etc., and at last rice mixed with milk should be taken. Salt must not be mixed with milk or molasses with sour things. (Upspuranas II. 431) (Majumdar, 1971).

In recent times, taste in food was mainly a contest between bitter and sour tastes and a longing for sweetness. The chief task of sweets is to produce only moderate sweetness in consumption, less than that obtained by dissolving a lump of sugar in the mouth (Ranner, 1944).

It is evident that the larger the quantity of solvent required to dissolve the sugar, the weaker will be the solution and the taste correspondingly less sweet. To make a solid sweet means simply to produce a slowly dissolving sugar. Considering the time factor in the secretion of a quantity of saliva, there will be much less concentration of sugar in the solution than there would be with quickly dissolving cane sugar. The enjoyment of sweetness can only be reached by slow consumption. If the sweets were made in such a way as to yield a more intense sweetness, they would be too sweet and no longer pleasant.

Sweetmeats play an important role in Indian culture. Almost every State or region has its own sweet dishes and traditions associated with it. Apart from hospitality, it is needed during religious performances, festivals and a number of other social occasions. The Hindu sacred texts tells us the importance of sweetmeats known as *naivedya* and it is one of the essential requisites needed for a religious performance. Sweetmeat occupies a privileged place in our social customs and is always associated with a happy occasion or some gay celebration. Our country can boast of many varieties of sweet preparations. Each of these has its own special flavour and taste.

Sweet Dishes and Sweetmeats: A Comparison

Sometimes people confuse with sweet dish and sweet-meat.

In ancient period there was no 'sweetmeat' in modern sense of the term. People used *Kheer* (puddings), *Kasar, Gujia, Payas* (similar to *kheer* of Bihar), and the like, as sweet items of food. But, actually these were not sweetmeats. A sweetmeat has certain essential criteria which have been discussed in later section of this chapter.

Though there is no clear-cut demarcation between the sweet dishes and sweetmeats, for the present study, some differences may be pointed out which are as follows. A sweet dish which has not been fried in *ghee,* cannot be preserved for more than one day, e.g., *Payas, Halwa, Rasia,* so it may not have a market value. Though mixing of a sweetening agent is essential for both, but in some cases a sweetening agent is not mixed in sweet dish. Due to natural sweetness its taste be-comes sweet. But such a condition is not applicable to sweet-meats. People prepare sweet dishes in their houses according to choice and the need of consumption. It may also be said that all sweetmeats may constitute sweet dishes, but all the sweet dishes may not necessarily constitute sweetmeats.

Generally people serve sweet dishes viz., *Kheer, Halwa,* custard, curd and sugar and the like, at the end of a feast. People take it as a symbol for finishing the food. Among these, curd and sugar are very ancient. Puddings, porridge, custard are the most common sweet dishes and people prepare it regularly in their homes. In vegetarian families, preparation of sweet dishes are found frequently.

At the time of worshipping the *Gram Devta* (Home deity) or clan deity, people prepare the offerings in their homes only. Mention may be made of *Roat* (thick bread or thick loaf), *Churma, Rasia* or *Rasawar* (rice cooked in the juice of sugar cane). These are also sweet dishes. It is said that sweet dishes are more pure in comparison to sweetmeats. For this purpose, at first people wash the basic ingredients and dry these in the sun. At this time people take care that these ingredients should not be touched by untouchables or animals or birds. They prepare the flour of such ingredients in a quern at their homes. The utensils for this purpose must be neat and clean and should not be used for daily purposes.

Basic Ingredients of Sweetmeats

Though it is impossible to describe all the ingredients of sweetmeats exhaustively, an attempt is being made here to discuss the basic ingredients of sweetmeats.[1] They are as follows:

Milk

Pure cow's milk is essential for the recipes and is one of the most important constituents of the sweetmeats, being most nourishing in the pure and fresh state. Where milk has to be boiled to become thick, high-fat milk such as from Jersey breed will give a creamier taste and texture. Buffalo's milk is richer in cream and therefore heavy. The products of the former are universally employed for making sweetmeats though those of the latter are preferred in some cases. By special treatment, several important products are obtained from milk, one or the other of which almost invariably enters as a basic ingredient in the composition of sweetmeats.

Kheer and Khoa

Kheer is 'condensed milk' and may be sweetened or unsweetened. *Khoa* is solid milk or 'dried milk' and is unsweetened.

When pure and fresh cow's milk is boiled down until it is of the consistency of viscous liquid, the result is plain *kheer*. When the milk is being boiled, a quarter of its measure of sugar is dissolved in it and the product is sweet *kheer*. If the plain *kheer* is further boiled down completely, i.e., until all the watery portion has been evaporated and only a solid mass (about one-sixth) is left, the residue is known as *khoa*. It is an important ingredient in many of the sweets which enriches it imparts and a creamy taste. *Khoa* may be made from full-cream powdered milk by working one and half tablespoons of hot water into every 2 tablespoons of milk powder to make about 85, gm of *khoa* (Haldar, 1926).

Khoa keeps well for three to four days and even longer. Before use, it is generally pulverised and sifted. Sometimes it is baked on a dry pan or soaked in hot water. It may be partaken of in the raw state with or without the addition of sugar and is extremely nutritious.

Chhena

Chhena (Indian cottage cheese) furnishes the basis of nearly all the important sweetmeats specially of Bengal. *Chhena* of the finest quality is made from pure and fresh cow's milk.

A few crystals of citric acid are dissolved in a tea cup. Later on, this solution is poured on the boiling milk. The whole of the milk will at once curdle and *Chhena* will separate in solid lumps. According to another method, i.e., on commercial scale, the milk is boiled and poured in a vessel. The old whey is thrown into the milk with a ladle. The curdled milk is stirred briskly. In this way the percentage of *Chhena* obtained is larger than usual, is more soggy and therefore remunerative.

The properties of the *Chhena* will, however, differ as it is obtained by either curdling the milk on the fire, or on the ground. In the latter case the *Chhena* will be soft and creamy but at the same time soggy. In the former case the *Chhena* will be firm and compact, and so it need not be pressed subsequently.

The curdled milk has to be strained through a piece of clean cloth. The whey will filter through and may be collected. The *Chhena* remains inside and is drawn together and hung up to drain for a couple of hours. By that time, it loses whatever portion of the liquid it might hold through dripping and becomes a compact mass with uniform texture.

Unlike *khoa, chhena* does not keep even for 24 hours. For good results it is better to prepare *chhena* few hours before the preparation of sweetmeats from it. It may be partaken of in the raw state with or without the addition of sugar. If this *chhena* is pressed with a heavy weight till it hardens, the result is known as *Panir*. *Panir,* like *chhena* is an essential ingredient in certain sweetmeats.

Ghee

Ghee is the traditional cooking medium of India from Vedic times when it was known as *ghrita* in Sanskrit. It is obtained by melting butter in heat until the watery portion contained in it is expelled. The *ghee* solidifies on cooling. Pure cow's *ghee* should have a rich chestnut colour, a uniform granular appearance and its characteristic aroma and flavour. Whereas pure buffalo's *ghee* is white. It is also granular to an extent, but the flavour is not so marked. It is, however, generally employed for frying purposes when it serves the purpose better than cow's *ghee*. Butter, corn, peanut oil may also be used as a substitute.

Sugar

The etymology of the word 'sugar' seems to have been derived from the Sanskrit word *Sarkara* (in the Tabmud), *sakkara* and among the Mahrattas *sakar* (Montagne, 1961). Various forms of brown or white sugar are usually used in making Indian sweets. This ensures that certain colours and flavours are not marred by the strong taste and colour of unrefined sugars or syrups. In most of the recipes, brown or unrefined sugar can be used where healthy nourishment is the prime consideration. Unrefined Indian cane sugar is known as

Gur (jaggery). It has a pleasant individual taste and quality.

Besan (Pulse-flour)

When gram is ground, the flour is known as *besan*. Many other members of the pea and bean family are made into a flour in India for use as ingredients in certain sweets. These flours will be popular with health-food and are also rich in protein. This should be fresh milled, otherwise it becomes musty and clotty.

Rice-flour (Safeda)

This is the meal of the best sunned rice (not parboiled) with its characteristic sweet and delicate aroma and delightful taste. Flour of rice is used in sweets. It may often be substituted for the more lengthy process of grinding rice grains, but this substitution cannot be made where only coarse grinding is called for.

Mewa and Nuts

This term comprises such food-articles as almonds, pistachios, raisins and the like. Before using, they are shelled and steeped in water, then skinned and shredded. If required urgently they may be blanched by scalding in hot water. Raisins are simply picked, washed and stalked.

Where nuts are included they should always be fresh and unsalted. Almonds should be blanched by boiling in a little water for a minute which makes them easy to peel. Where pistachios are used for decoration, as they frequently are, they should be chopped very finely and sprinkled like a powder for their better effect.

Flavouring Agents

Both cardamom major and minor (*Bari elaichi* and *chhoti elaichi*) are used to impart their characteristic flavour to the sweets. Only their seeds are employed either whole or crushed. Camphor, asafoetida, etc., are also used but only in special cases.

Perfuming Agents

Rose water and rose otto are the popular perfuming agents. Mango, ginger, lemon, peel, etc., are employed in special cases. Though introduced by the Mughals, its use is now popular throughout India. Perfuming or flavouring agents are added in very minute doses otherwise the ingredients will be embittered.

Colouring Agents

Saffron *(zafran)* is employed for rich chestnut colour. It is used after blending in warm milk. Genuine unadulterated saffron should be procured. A cheap substitute for saffron is turmeric used for yellow. Cochineal is used for red. Pistachio brayed to a paste with water is used for green. Nowadays, however, cheap vegetable dye-stuffs are employed as colouring agents. Edible colours should always be used.

Soda Bicarb

It is the abbreviation for bicarbonate of sodium. It is added to flour as a softening agent to make the products exceptionally flaky and friable.

Tabqka

The more costly and aristocratic varieties of sweetmeats are often embellished for spectacular effect with rose petals, silver leaf, etc. The metallic leaves are chosen as thick and fine as possible. They may be eaten up without the slightest hesitation.

Hot Spices

Among hot spices are included cardamom minor, cloves, cinnamon and cassia leaves taken collectively. They are preferred for their rich odoriferous properties. They may be either singed whole in *ghee* or oil in which the cooking is to be done subsequently, or stirred in powder form in the cooked product when removed from the fire and covered up. Sometimes the ordinary spices are dried by baking or roasting and then pounded. The 'hot spices' are usually bruised in the mortar.

Essential Criteria of Sweetmeats

After doing extensive fieldwork in Bihar and West Bengal and interviewing several persons connected with this profession, the investigator is able to evolve some essential criteria or pre-conditions of sweetmeats as given below:

Sweetening Agent

Although sweetness is one of the important essential criteria of a sweetmeat, every item that is inherently sweet cannot be called a sweetmeat unless sweetness in the form of sugar or molasses or its substitute like sugar candy., sorbitol and the like, are added to it. For example, dry fruits have sweet taste, but as this is not due to mixing of the sweet raw materials, these items are not called as sweetmeats. Likewise, fragmentary sugar candy is mixed in *keshariya pedha* of Gaya, to develop its taste. It is also interesting to note that, except few sweetmeats, for example, *Sandesh, Chasni* (hot liquid form of sugar) is used in the recipes of almost all the sweetmeats.

Preservation

Preservation is one of the important essential criteria of sweetmeats. There are many sweet items which cannot be preserved even for a few days. So, they cannot be called sweetmeat. For example, pudding, though its taste is sweet and sugar or molasses or its substitute has been added to it, still it cannot be preserved even for one day, it is not a sweetmeat. It might be called a sweet dish. In winter season, sweet dish can be preserved for one or two days, but at that time, other sweetmeats can be preserved for a week or more. Preservation is one of the basic characteristics of a sweetmeat.

Fire Treatment

Without heating, it is impossible to prepare a sweetmeat. Heating process makes the substance easier to eat and improves the taste. Heating process enhances the flavour of a substance and creates a new food. It is difficult to imagine any sweetmeat without undergoing the heating process.

Girling (1978:593) while describing the effects of food preparation on nutrients in food, mentioned that carbohydrates, i.e., sugars do not need cooking to be digested, but are used because of their properties of sweetening and crystallization. The main effects of sugar in cooking are: it decreases the viscosity of starch pastes; resulting in a more transparent and tender jelly; it weakens gluten strands and therefore makes the crumb of cake mixtures tender; it deepens the colour; the crystal size of sugar influences the texture of many sweets and icings; when sugar is creamed with fat, air is more rapidly entangled between the sugar crystals which become surrounded with a layer of fat; caramelization of sugar is widely used for colour and flavour; when sugar is mixed with protein, a golden-brown colour is formed, which gives the characteristic colour to baked products.

Availability in Markets

Besides the above criteria, availability in the market is one of the important essential criteria of a sweetmeat. There are some sweetmeats which are prepared on large-scale according to season, for example, *gond ka laddu* and *tilkut* are available in winter season. Likewise *khobi ka lai* popularly known as *Barh ka lai* and *inarsa* are generally prepared in summer and rainy seasons respectively. However, this does not mean that they are unprepared in other seasons. They may be prepared on a small-scale casually throughout the year.

Manual Preparation

It is obvious that all the Indian sweetmeats are prepared manually. If the sweets are prepared by machine, for example, chocolate, pastries, etc., they do not come under category of Indian sweetmeats. However, nowadays some sweet-makers like K.C. Das (Pvt) Ltd. (Calcutta) and Ganguram & Sons (Calcutta) use machines for preparing some basic ingredients and for some stages of recipes of sweetmeats, i.e., curdling, grinding, mixing of *chhena* and also packing of the sweetmeats in vacuum tins. The scientific development, labour problem, economy of time, uniformity, and improvement in quality of sweets are some important factors which have gone behind the mechanization of the sweet-making. However, even after the mechanization, there is certain process in the sweet-making, i.e., giving of round shape to the sweet which is in raw form can be done by hand only. Besides, the mechanization works only in the making of *rassogolla*. Again in case of Ganguram & Sons, mechanization of sweet is confined to the mixing of *chhena* only.

Definition of Sweetmeat

It would not be insignificant to mention the literal meaning of sweetmeat as given in encyclopaedias and other dictionaries, before giving a functional definition of sweetmeat as used in the present study. There are many terms like 'sweets' (noun), 'confectionery', '*madhur*', (in Mithila region), '*mishtana*', '*modakah*' (in Sanskrit) which are synonyms.

According to *The New Encyclopaedia Britannica Macropaedia* (Helen Hemingway Benton, 1973-74), the application of the terms confectionery and candy varies among English speaking countries. In the United States, candy refers to both chocolate products and sugar based products, and 'flour confectionery' to such products as cakes and pastries.

History

Egyptian hieroglyphics dating back at least 3000 years indicate that the art of sugar confectionery was already established. The confectioner was regarded as a skilled craftsman by the Romans and a confectioner's kitchen excavated at Herculaneum was equipped with pots, pans and other implements similar to those in use today.

Early confectioners, not having sugar, used honey as a sweetener and mixed it with various fruits, nuts, herbs and spices.

During the Middle Ages, the Persians spread sugar cane cultivation, developed refining methods and began to make a sugar based candy. A small amount of sugar was available in Europe during the Middle Ages and was used in the manufacture of the confectionary items prepared and sold mainly by Apothecaries. The Venetians brought about a major change in candy manufacture during the 14th century, when they began to import sugar from Arabia. By the 16th century, confectioners were manufacturing sweets, moulding boiled sugar, with fruits and nuts, into fanciful forms by simple hand method.

The development of candy manufacturing machinery began in the late 18th century, and in the 20th century annual world production had reached many millions of pounds.

Confectionery

Everyman's Encyclopaedia describes confectionery as follows:

(Latin *confectio*, a preparation, from conficare, to make up). Confectionery is of two kinds, sugar and flour. Sugar confectionery means sweets in which sugar is the main ingredient. Either they consist of sugar in very fine crystal form dispersed in a sugar solution and flavoured, such as chocolate creams or fondants, or there may be sugar maintained in a solution of a careful blend of the different types of sugar, i.e., boiled, sweets, toffees, or caramels, fats, milk and nuts are employed to obtain a variety of flavours and textures. Before the 19th century, sweets and candies were the monopoly of apothecaries, who made them to hide the taste of their drugs. Flour confectionery consists of pastries and fancy cakes having flour as their basis but sweetened and mixed with various dairy products such as butter and eggs (J.M. Dent & Sons, 1978).

Oxford English Dictionary describes confectionery as things made or sold by a confectioner, a collective name for sweetmeats and confections; a course of sweetmeats at dinner, the art and business of a confectioner and a confectioners shop. (Clarendon Press, 1933).

The meaning of sweetmeat in this dictionary is as follows:

Sweet food, as sugared cakes or pastry, preserved or candied fruits, sugared nuts, etc., also globules, lozenges, drops or sticks made of sugar with fruit or other flavouring or filling.

Besides, Funk and Wagnalls (1955) gives the meaning of sweetmeat as 'a confection, jelly, preserve or other sweet food or dainty.'

Websters Dictionary (Webster Noah, 1975) of English language mentions sweetmeat as any sweet food or delicacy prepared with sugar or honey, as a cake, confection, preserve, etc., specially, a candy, candied fruit, etc.

Bhattacharya France in her article '*Les mets et la cuisine dans le Candi Mangala*' (The dishes and the cooking in the Candi Mangala) defines sweetmeat as 'small shaped piece of confectionery usually consisting of sugar or chocolate with flavouring or filling or of fruit preserved in sugar'.

Prasad (1964) mentioned that it consists of two words, i.e., *Mishta* (+) *Anna*=*Mishtanna*. *Mishta* means sweet fluid (*madhur-rasa*), so the food-stuff containing sweet fluid is called *mishtanna*.

A Functional Definition as Used in the Study

Though, the meaning and definition of Indian sweetmeat varies as we have seen from the above writings, a functional definition of sweetmeat as used in this study is as follows:

'A sweetmeat is a food item made of cereal or non-cereal, usually small-shaped confectionery prepared manually with sugar, molasses or its substitute with or without flavourings by a specific process and some kind of heat treatment which must have preservability and availability in the market. It may be solid, semi-solid or in syrup.'

Etymology and Origin of Some Important Sweetmeats

It is interesting to note that though being prepared by almost the same ingredients, sweets have different names. In few cases the names of sweetmeats are based on their shape or on the name of their inventor. Nowadays most of the sweetmeat makers slightly change the shape and ingredients of sweetmeats and give attractive names according to their will.

Jalebi

Regarding *jalebi*, Gode (1943) mentioned that Molesworth call *jilabi* or *jililbi* as a 'sweetmeat', but records no details about it in his celebrated dictionary. In the *Hobsen-Jobson* (Yule & Burnell, 1903) we find the following information about this dish:

''Jelaubee S.Hind, Jalebi (which is apparently a corruption of the Arabic *Zalabiya*, P. *Zatabiya* (Steingass in his *Persian-English Dictionary*, notes the word *zatabiya* ā thin pancake). A rich sweetmeat made of sugar and *ghee*, with a little flour, melted and trickled into a pan so as to form a kind of interlaced work, when baked'' (Ibid).

Marathi Dictionary (*Maharashtra Sabdakosa*, *Vibhaga III*, 1934:1309-10) mentioned the following account of *jilabi*:

''जिल (ली) बी - स्त्री. एक मोठें पक्वान्न; मैद्याच्या पिठांत लिंबाचा रस, तूप, उडदाचें पीठ व दहीं मिश्र करून तें मिश्रण दुसऱ्या दिवशीं जिलबीपात्रानें तुपांत तळून साखरेच्या पाकांत टाकून केलेला कडयाच्या आकाराचा वाटोळा पदार्थ. गृ. शि. 1.413 जिलेबी असें जुनें रूप आहे. (हिं. जलेबी जिलेबी)''

(Jila(li)bi)- f.a. rich dish. (An article of diet made of flour, lemon juice, *ghee,* curds, sugar, etc., and having a circular shape). Jilebi is an old form of the word. (Hindustani-*Jalebi*, *Jilebi*).

Regarding the history of *Jalebi* and its introduction in Indian diet, Gode (Ibid) mentioned that 'The Peshwa period of the Maratha history bristles with reference to dinners given to *Brahmins (Bramanna-bhojana)* with *daksina* as enjoined by the Hindu *dharmasastra* and we are likely to get some references of *jillabi* in the accounts and expenditure of these dinners found at times in the records of the Peshwas between A.D. 1700 and say about A.D. 1818, the year which heralded the British advent in India.'

In a Jain work called the *Priyamka-rromrpa-Katha* by Jinasura composed earlier than A.D. 1600 referred a long passage describing a dinner given by a *Sresthi* or a rich merchant. In that dinner reference of Jalebi is also mentioned.

Gode (Ibid) mentioned that 'Jalebi was current in India in the 15th century and has been getting popular in an increasing degree during the last 500 years.'

Regarding etymology of *jalebi*, Thakur (1910 : 69) mentioned that *jalebi* is a Hindustani name. The name of *jalebi* is originated from syrup *(panichasani)*. If *panichasani* is more boiled (in comparison to *panichasani* of *pantowa*), then it is called *jalao chasni* or *jalao ras*. The syrup of *Jalebi* is comparatively more condensed so when we touch its syrup a thread like formation is created. It seems that at first *Jalao* word becomes *Jalebi* and subsequently it becomes *Jalebi*. *Jal dhatu* is the original word of *Jal, Jalao,* etc. Many people called *Jalebi* in Sanskrit as *Jalballi*, but it is not like that.

In Sanskrit language *Jalebi* is called *Kundalini*. It is mentioned that *Kundalini* gives health, beauty and strength. The name *Kundalini* is due to its shape. As it is presented in coiled shape so it is called *Kundalini*.

Pantowa

From the sweetmeat *Pantowa* it apparently means that it is the sweet for *Jalpan* (breakfast) and that is why it is called *Pan* (something to eat) and *Towa* (water). But it is not like that, the fluid substance of *Pantowa* is called *Panichasani* or *Paniras* (syrup) in Hindi. The meaning of '*Paniras*' is, that fluid which is not much boiled and also has much water. As *Pantowa* is dropped into this *Paniras* so it is called *Pantowa*. If cooked-rice is kept in water it is called *Panta* or *Panto Bhat,* similarly due to this, *Pantowa* is named from *Paniras*. The names *Panta, Panto, Pantowa* are almost similar. Generally, Western Indian people like to talk after suffixing the word *Uya* they called *Mor* as

Moroya, Badhu as *Bhadhua* and like. It seems that *Pantowa* is also called so due to the same reason, e.g., suffixing the word '*Uya*' in last. (Ibid).

Barfee

It has originated from the word *Barf* (ice). It seems that the word *Barf* enters into Hindi from Persian. In the process of its preparation, the syrup becomes solid after freezing. So it is called *Barfee.*

Probably, the word *Barf* comes from Sanskrit word *Brish.* It seems that the letter *sh* (ष) of word *Warsh* is changed into *Pha* (फ). At several places it is seen that the Sanskrit word *Śa, Ṣa, Va, Sa* changed into *Pha* (फ) in Persian, for example, Grass word of Sanskrit becomes Grasp, *Grephta* and Griff in English, Parsian and German languages.

The natural characteristics of the ice is to condense that is why the things which have been condensed like ice is called *Barapha.* Due to this, people call them *Kulfi Barpha, Malai Barpha* and also due to this a class of sweetmeat also got the name of *Barfi.*

Though the word *Barf* is Persian, but it is easy to find out its similar word in European languages. In English-Brief, in Parsian *Bref,* and in Latin *Brevis* all comes under the same group (Ibid).

Bundi

It comes from Sanskrit word *Bundi.* As the structure of the food-stuff is much similar to point-like *Bariwindu* so it is called *Bundi.* The meaning of *Bariwindu* is *Bundi.* At some places it is known as *Bundiya.*

Motichur

It is called *Motichur* because its *Bundi* looks like small pearls. The meaning of *Moti* is pearl and *chur* means grains, so it means a substance which looks fine or thin.

Pedha

This name is given due to it's round shape. *Pedha* is a corrupt form of the word *Pinda* which means a round shaped object. This sweetmeat—the structure of which is like a *Pidakriti*— is also known as *Pindika.*

Chandrapuli

As this sweet looks semilunar in shape, so it is called *Chandrapuli, Pupulika, Pulika* and the like, which are the names of sweetmeats in Sanskrit. *Puli* is short form of the word *Pulika.*

Sandesh

The influence that sweets have exercised on the Bengali language can be easily traced. The vernacular word *Sandesh* originally meant 'news', but with long usage it has come to designate primarily 'sweets'. Again whenever one has to enquire about the news of any relative or acquaintance it has become customary to send sweets along with the enquiry. So that the Bengali word *tathya* (enquiry) has come to signify 'presents of sweets' (Haldar, 1926).

Now the question arises as to why people send *sandesh?* Thakur (Ray, 1979) was of the opinion that people liked *Chhena* very much which is the basic ingredient of *Sandesh.* As it is free from the ingredients made of cereals like *Besan, Maida,* Rice-flour which are subject to 'pollution' by lower castes, hence it is free from any sort of pollution and as such can be sent anywhere through any person, whatsoever his caste background may be.

The names of the numerous varieties of *Sandesh* have been derived from all conceivable sources. Primarily the names designated corresponded to accustomed shapes, such as *Gutke* (flat tipped), *Badam Takti* (diamond), *Kasturo,* etc. Latterly they express the delightful feeling associated with *Sandesh* such as *Manoharā* (captivating), *Manoranjan* (pleasing to the mind), *Dilkhosh* (delight of the heart), etc. The analogy with natural objects is another fruitful source, such as *Ata* (custard apple), *Kamranga* (a sour plum), *Talshash* (Palmyra kernel) and so on.

In the selection of fanciful names, however, which are more prolific, imagination is given free play. There are some typical Bengali names the points of which will be well-nigh lost in translation. *Abar Khabo* (Encore), *Phulsayya* (Honeymoon), *Sukhe thako* (God bless you), *Pati param guru* (Husband is wife's master). The purely English names: Good morning, Welcoming, Welcome, 'God save the king', 'Forget-me-not' and the likes are significant of cultural influence.

Rassogolla or (Roshogolla)

Rassogolla means a round shaped substance in syrup. The inventor of this sweetmeat was Nawin Das Moyra of Sutanuti village in Calcutta. Several good qualities of sweetmeats were prepared at his shop. Bhola Moyra (one of the worker of that shop) also prepared puddings. Once a strange idea crossed his mind after curdling the milk. Suddenly, he filtered the whey and made that *chhena* into round shape, after that he left the round shape *chhena* into the syrup of *Jalebi*. This became very tasty after some time. Thus, from that time one new sweetmeat was invented and it was called *Ras-gola*. Later on it became *Rassagulla*.

Belgrami

This sweetmeat of Koath was famous (Rohtas district of Bihar). At present, *Belgrami* is also prepared at Udvantnagar (near Arrah) and Maner. *Belgrami* of Koath is prepared from *Maida* while at Udvantnagar and Maner it is prepared from *Chhena*.

Koath was the residence of well-known Bilgrami family, descendants of Nawab Nurul Hussain Khan, who came from the family home at Bilgram in Oudh after peace had been concluded with Shiya-ud-daula, he received a large *Zamindari*. At the time of migration they had come with their *Pauni* (a lower caste people who get tips on festive occasions). Among *Pauni* Halwai was one of them. At first they prepared this sweetmeat and presented it to the Bilgrami family. Due to this, it is known Belgrami.

Lady Canning

The birth of the *Ladygayni* or *Ladycany* is believed to be from *Lady Canning*. After the police mutiny when Lord Canning came to this country as a Viceroy and succeeded in restoring peace, at that time one business man of Shibpur in Howrah was experimenting on fried *Rasogollas. Rasogollas* easily broke up but though he did not know the actual process of making it, the new product which was born in that laboratory was black to look at and quite fat but was very delicious. Lord Canning in the meantime became very popular with the countrymen as no atrocities were done to the soldiers. As a result, this sweet-meat dealer named his newly invented sweet as *Lady Canning*.This, in course of time, changed and now has become *Lady-gayni*.

Tilkut

The name Tilkut which is a sweet of Gaya district in Bihar, seems to have been derived from the procedure of its making. In preparing *Tilkut*, Til (sesamum seeds) is ground with pestle on stone.

Halwa

Halwa is one of the most nutritious and easily digestible sweets. It is one of the popular sweetmeats among Western people. Sikhs called it *Deoprasad* and treat it as most sacred. It is also known as *Kara Prasad* among the Sikhs as it is cooked in *Karahi* (cauldron). The name *Halwa* has originated from its process of producing. *Halwa* is produced after continuously stirring the ingredients for one hour. In Hindi, stirring the material with ladle is known as *hilana* or *helana*, thus evolving into *Halwa*.

Perakia

This word comes from the word *Petaka*. In Sanskrit the

meaning of word *Petaka* is a box or chest or a collection. As one kept several things inside the *Petaka* similarly *Khoa* or coconut or *Suji* fried in *ghee* with sugar is also kept inside the chest or box made of *maida*. Hence we called this sweetmeat as *Peraki* or *Perakia*.

Chhena

The word *Chhena* is of Sanskrit origin. The Sanskrit *Chhina* (छिन्न) is the root word of *Chhana*. As the word *Chinha* (चिन्ह) gave rise to *Chena*(चेना) likewise *Chhinna* to *Chhena* or *Chhana*. The milk gets curdled torn hence the name *Chhana*. In Sanskrit the meaning of word *Chinna* (छिन्न) is 'to tear' and since the *Chhana* is produced after 'tearing' the milk hence we have been using the Sanskrit term with that connotation. In Bengali, '*Chhana*' is also used to connote a 'new born' and the root also lies in the Sanskrit word *China* (कटा हुआ). The neo-natals come out after tearing the placenta or chord hence '*chhana*' (cheese) also comes out after 'tearing' the milk, so it is called *Chhana* (Thakur, 1910 : 77).

Nutritional and Medicinal Value of Sweets

The food that we eat is assimilated in the body and is used for the growth and maintenance of tissues. Many of our sweets can supplement our diet since all of them are rich in calories and fat while the milk based sweets contain considerable amount of good quality milk protein. Because of the sweet taste, they are very palatable to all age groups, and this makes it easy to find a place in the diet of persons as a source of calorie and protein.

Dietary habits in different regions of the world have been determined, mainly by the local availability of foods and dietary patterns, necessary to sustain reasonably good health and have perhaps been evolved after a good deal of trial and error (Gopalan et. al., 1980). Most people associate nutrition with the food they eat. All the materials needed to make and maintain the body in proper form are usually taken in by mouth in the form of wholesome food. A good diet is merely a combination of foods which supply the materials vital to the body for its maintenance. These dietary essentials are also known as nutrients (Pasricha S. & L.M. Rebello, 1969). Food contains nutrients, and it is for obtaining nutrients which perform various functions in body, that food is consumed daily by any living organism. The nutrients include proteins, fats, carbohydrates, vitamins and mineral salts. They are present in almost all foods in varying proportions and depending on the relative concentrations of the nutrients contained, foods are classified sometimes as protein-rich foods, carbohydrate rich foods, etc. Oils, ghee, etc., provide mostly fat while sugar is purely a source of carbohydrate (Gopalan et.al., 1980).

Proteins, fats and carbohydrates are also sometimes called 'proximate principles'. They are oxidized (burnt) in the body to provide the energy required for the various activities of life. Together with water, which is also a necessary dietary element, proximate principles form the main bulk of foods. Almost all the natural foodstuffs contain a mixture of different nutrients. There is, however, no single food in which all the nutrients are present in quantities sufficient to meet the daily needs of the body. That is why a combination of different kinds of foodstuffs is essential in diet.

A diet should be of sufficient quantity to provide the needed energy and also ensure atleast a minimum supply of the essential nutrients to maintain the life process in proper order.

Sugar and jaggery are used as sweetening agents in beverages and other foods to increase their palatability. They are the main source of energy although jaggery contains in addition iron.

However, depending on the predominant nutrient contained, foodstuffs may be broadly classified under three heads: energy yielding, body building and protective foods (Pasricha S. and L.M. Rebello, 1969).

Besides other food materials, body-building foodstuffs

are also found in milk and milk products. 'Milk products derived from whole milk like curd and *khoa* are equal in nutritive value of milk' (Gopalan and Bela Subramaniam, 1968). Likewise, milk also serves as a protective agent. Sugar is the chief energy yielding nutrient. So, it may be concluded that all the necessary energy levels of balanced diet are present in sweetmeats.

Table 2.1 gives an idea about proximate nutrient level of some basic ingredients of Indian sweetmeats. The table reveals that : (1) Almost all the basic nutritious elements are present in cow's milk. (2) Though the quantity of these elements (except moisture and potassium) are comparatively more in Buffalo's milk but minerals and carotene and vitamin A are minimal. (3) Regarding *khoa,* maximum quantity of protein is found in *khoa* of skimmed buffalo milk, whereas maximum quantity of fat is present in *khoa,* of whole buffalo milk. (4) It is interesting to note that 95.0 gm carbohydrate is found per 100 gms of jaggery, which is followed by honey, but in honey fat is totally absent. (5) Regarding *chhenna* the quantity of calcium is just double in the *chhenna* of buffalo's milk, which is present in *chhenna* of cow's milk.

Here, it would not be out of place to mention that if the sweetmeats are prepared or kept carelessly, then instead of being nutritious it becomes injurious to health. Here a sample report conducted by Railway doctors at several places of Calcutta appearing in the Telegraph dated Septermber 26, 1984 may be quoted :

"The Doctors have revealed dangerous strains of bacteria in sweets like *Rassogolla* and *Sandesh* sold in the city. Food is important as a source of infectious like *E. Coli, Salmonellae, Shigella* and other entero-pathogenic organisms in causing epidemics and also in maintaining endemicity of these infections in the community. Even if the foodstuff is (initially) free from infection, the chance of contamination is high and the moresophisticated or complicated in manipulation to prepare the food, the greater the chance of

TABLE 2.1

Proximate Energy Levels of Some Indian Sweet Ingredients

Per 100 gm. of edible portion

Sl. No.	Name of Foodstuffs	Moisture (g)	Protein (g)	Fat.	Minerals (g)	Other Carbohydrates (g)	Calories	Calcium (mg)	Phosphorous (mg)	Iron (mg.)	Sodium (mg)	Potassium (mg)	Vit.A I U	Carotene & Vit.A I U	Thiamine (mg) (mg.)	Riboflamin (mg)	Nicotinic Acid	Vit.C (mg)
1.	Honey	20.0	0.3	—	0.2	79.5	319	5	16	0.9	—	—	—	—	—	0.04	0.2	4
2.	Jaggery	3.2	0.4	0.1	0.6	95.0	383	80	40	11.4	—	—	—	280	0.02	—	1.0	—
3.	Milk (Cow's)	87.5	3.2	4.1	0.8	4.4	67	149	96	0.2	16.0	140	150	15	0.05	0.18	0.1	2
4.	Milk (Buffalo's)	81.0	4.3	8.8	—	5.1	118	210	130	0.2	19.0	90	160	—	0.04	0.10	0.1	3
5.	Curds	89.1	3.1	4.0	0.8	2.9	60	149	93	0.3	32.0	130	102	—	0.05	0.16	0.1	1
6.	*Chenna* (Cow's milk)	57.1	18.3	20.8	2.6	2.3	270	208	138	—	—	—	365	—	0.07	0.02	—	3
7.	*Chenna* (Buffalo's milk)	54.1	13.4	23.0	1.6	7.9	292	480	277	—	—	—	—	—	—	—	—	—
8.	*Khoa* (whole buffalo's milk)	30.6	14.6	31.2	3.1	20.5	421	650	420	5.8	—	—	—	—	—	—	—	—
9.	*Khoa* (Skimmed buffalo milk)	46.1	22.3	1.6	4.0	24.9	206	990	650	2.7	—	—	—	—	—	—	—	—
10.	*Khoa* (whole cow	25.2	20.1	25.9	0.1	0.5	413	956	613	—	—	—	497	—	0.24	0.41	0.4	—

The basic data of this table has been taken from 'special Report No. 42 of the Department of Nutrition and Biochemistry, Public Health Institute, Patna. To add to that, certain modifications have been made by the investigator.'

contamination.

In the case of dry sweets, a possible source of contamination is the dough kneaded with unclean hands. Usually bacteria lived and multiplied better in sugar containing media. Syrupy sweets in most shops were kept in uncovered trays where flies, a major carrier of germs sit on them."

Table 2.2 substantiates this point and shows different organisms isolated from the sweetmeat samples.

Table 2.2

Different Organisms Isolated from Sweet Sample

Place	*No. of Sample Examined*	*E. coli Enteropathogenic Strains*	*Non-entropathogenic Strains*	*Shigella Sp.*	*Salmonellas Sp.*	*Other Proteins*	*No. Growth*
Sonarpur	8	2	4	3	—	—	2
Garia	8	2	6	2	—	1	—
Dhakuria	4	1	3	1	1	—	—
Jadavpur	4	1	3	2	—	—	—
Ballygange	8	1	5	1	1	—	2
Sealdah	13	1	11	1	—	—	1
Bhowanipur	8	4	4	—	1	—	—
Esplanade	4	2	2	1	—	—	—
Bag Bazar	4	1	3	1	—	—	—
Shyam Bazar	4	2	2	1	1	—	—
Bara Bazar	8	3	5	—	1	—	—
College St.	4	2	2	—	1	—	—
Howrah	23	9	14	5	2	—	—
Total	100	31	64	18	8	1	5

The Report further suggested that the sweetmeat shop-owners should be particular about the cleanliness of their workmen and ensure the maintenance of hygienic and sterile conditions in their kitchens. This would include washing hands before touching the ingredients while making the sweets, washing utensils with hot water and using spoons or tongs while serving.

Anderson (1997 : 87) while describing the traditional medical values of food of China also mentions some properties of sweets like honey, sugar etc. According to him "One other key concept underlies the concepts of cleaning and dispelling, clearing away. In both cases the idea is to get rid of undesirable matter or essences in the body. Cleaning gets rid of waste products and any poisons built up in the system. One clears away excess wetness, "wind", and other parthogenic natural forces that have entered the body. Curing inflammation, edema, and the like involves clearing away the accumulated will humors. Some foods, licorice and honey, for example, free one from poisons. Foods particular good at cleaning are honey, brown sugar, and sugar cane juice, some vegetables, a number of herbs." At another place he mentioned that certain food eaten together, are supposed to react to produce actual, virulent poisons such as garlic and honey.

Sweetmeat is also used by way of indigenous medicines on some occasions. At the time of diarrhoea people take hot *jalebi* with syrup. Regarding the properties of *chhena* (an important ingredient of sweetmeat) Aryuved says that it is *Batagni Grahini Ruksha Durajra Dadhikurchika* (Thakur, 1910 : 76).

Chhena is used as a sort of medicine in rheumatism. Some people say that *chhena* is also used by T. B. patients as a regular diet. Honey and water is used in constipation. The *morabba* which may also be taken as a type of sweet is prescribed by Kaviraj as a medicine in different diseases such as; *Bel ka morabba* for gastric troubles; *Chal kumhra ka morabba* for plethora, worms and constipation; Haritki (yellow myrobalan) *ka morabba* for piles, dysentary and anaemia, *Awala ka morabba* and *satmul* (bulbous root of Dioscoria fasciculata) *ka morabba* for health and nutrition.

3

Genesis and Development of Indian Sweetmeats

Probably, India is the only country in the world where sweets form an integral part of food in most affluent families. They are taken with great relish and have a deep cultural significance. There are variety of sweets in every region, while many of them are basically different from each other. Since ancient times it has been considered auspicious to feed others with sweet items. Sugar is still scattered on ant hills and this act is said to bring a great religious merit. If one wants to please a child, he offers sweets to him or her. The giving of sweets is an act of friendship, affection or love besides being auspicious. In the words of love 'sweetness', stands as the symbol of lover or beloved, their bond itself is considered to be 'sweet' as reflected in the names like 'Sweety', 'Honey', or 'Madhu'.

In India it is not surprising to find a variety of dishes of and traditions associated with sweetmeats. This country itself being the third largest producer of sugar in the world, so it is not surprising if sweet dishes or sweetmeats form part of a meal, being eaten either before or after the main dishes according to the taste of the diners. In many families specially the affluent ones, tasty, nourishing sweets are made regularly and kept in the store, especially for children and guests. They are ideally suited when one wants to take just a little quantity of food which could serve as a source of energy and nourishment as well.

The Hindus every now and then had to provide all kinds of feasts to Brahmins, neighbours and kinsmen in which sweets are a must. This is more prevalent in close knit societies, more so, in towns and villages and is soon becoming a tradition of the past times. No doubt, they have to perform numerous rituals and ceremonies relating to life-cycle and almost all the ceremonies are followed by feast.

Genesis of Indian Sweetmeats

Honey was probably, the earliest sweet thing that the Indians knew of. In Rigvedic period, Aryans drank honey mixed with *Soma.*

मध्वः पिबतं मधुपेभिरासभिरूतं प्रियं मधुने युञ्जाथां रथम्।

आ वर्तनिं मधुना जिन्वथस्पथो दृतिं बहेथे मधुमन्तमश्विना।।

ऋग्वेद *4.45.3*

(They would drive their chariot around and in a leisurely manner while drinking honey, listening to the beautiful hummings of bees and riding on chariot also humming like bees and drinking *Somras* mixed in honey.)

They used honey as sweet. The *Asvalayana Griha Sutra* says: By Aryans, honey was invariably used in welcoming guests, the common preparation used for this purpose being a mixture of honey with curds and ghee known as *Madhuparka.*

दधनि मध्वानीय सर्पिर्वा मध्वलाभे।

आश्वलायनगृह्यसूत्रे, *1.21.5*

According to Panini (4.3.118) honey made of small fly is known as *Bharamer*. According to *Jaataka* (154, 334) (Buddhistic tales narrating incidents of Buddha's previous birth) honey is simple sweet for Aryans. According to *Patanjali* (1.3.25; 7.1.51) at that time, honey was such a favourite that the people felt an ardent desire for it. A special process was used to get the honey, called *Madhu Madhusyati*. Being collected by bees (*Makshika*) the honey was also called *Maakshika* or *Sarath*. According to Kautilya, honey is of two types, i.e., *Ksaudara* (collection by fly) and *Madwirka* (made of the syrup of pulse and Raisin):

क्षौद्रं मार्द्वीकं च मधु

कौटिल्य, अर्थशास्त्र 2.15.16

In *Saundarkand* (11.29) it is mentioned that honey was used in making sweetmeat. It is also mixed in bitter medicines.

In the *Ramayana* it is mentioned that honey was used in welcoming guests at the hermitage of Vashistha and Bhardwaj (*Valmiki Ramayana* 2.36.6). King Dashrath had hoped that Ram would be so much engrossed in hunting in the forest, viewing different rivers, and taking wild honey, that he would settle there and lead a charming life instead of caring for his kingdom. It is mentioned at one place that honey was one of the common drinks of monkeys (*Hanumans*) and *Nishad* (primitive non-Aryan tribe of India). Hanuman used honey as a drink at the time of going to Lanka in search of Sita. (Ibid, 4.37.7.8; 6.4.27). *Hanuman* went to Southern side in search of Sita, after searching her, he along with his subordinates had honey voluntarily (Ibid, 5.61.10). The people also drank wine made of honey. For intoxication, honey was fermented.[1] Intoxicating honey was called *Madhurasa* (Ibid, 5.11.32) or *Madhvik* (Ibid, 4.11.23).

According to *Charak* (Agnihotri, 1980: 166) honey was used as a medicine (Charaksutra, 27.239). According to Sushruta, honey was of eight types viz., *Maksik, Bharamer, Ksaudra, Pautik, Chhata, Aadhrya, Audalak* and *Dal*.

पौत्तिकं भ्रामरं क्षौद्रं माक्षिकं छात्रमेव च।
आर्ध्यमौद्दालकं दालमित्यष्टौ मधुजातयः।।

सुश्रुतसूत्र, *45.133*

According to *Charak*, honey was essential to use in rainy season for the benefit of health. It is also mentioned in *Bhelsanhita* (Bhelsanhita, p. 25). In *Vishnu Puranam* (4.24,95) it is mentioned that use of honey was essential.

Charak mentioned the properties of honey as follows:

वातलं गुरू शीतं च रक्तपित्तकफापहम्।

संधातृच्छेदनं रूक्षं कषायमधुरं मधु।।

चरक सूत्र, *28.242*

According to *Charak* honey cures many diseases. Taking of honey cures *Raktpita* (defect of blood and bile) and cough. It increases govt, rich, cold and capable of uniting fractures, dry, bitter sweet in taste. Sushruta mentioned it as a destroyer of ailments (cough, wind and bile). If honey is used in a reasonable way, it is very useful for health and also destroys several diseases, as honey is a mixture of several things. But if honey is used in improper way it becomes poison. In *Asatang Hridaya* (5, 51-52) and *Asatan Sangrah* it is mentioned that honey is useful for eye and is an exportant of several diseases such as thirst, phlegm, poison-hiccup, plethora, leprosy, diabetes, worms, vomiting, respiration, cough, diarrhoea and *Madhu sharkara* (sugar which is prepared from honey) is as affective as honey.

Sugar Cane

Iksu (sugar cane) is not expressly mentioned in the *Rigveda*. However according to Majumdar *Kusara* (Rigveda 1,191,3) refers to sugar cane. The word is still used for sugar cane in Bengal.

शरासः कुशरासो दर्भासः सैर्याउत।
मौञ्चा अदृष्टा वैरिणाः सर्वे साकं न्यलिप्सत।।

ऋग्वेद *1.191.3*

But sugar cane is found in all other *Samhitas* such as *Atharvaveda* 1, 34, 5; xii, 2, 54, 100, 277; *Maitrayane Samhita* 111, 79, IV, 2.9; *Vajasaneyi Samhita XXV, 1; Taittiriya Samhita* 111, 8. Chewing of sugar cane is referred to in the *Atharvaveda.*[2] "It seems that Proto-Australoid people knew about the preparation of *Guda* and the Aryans learnt it from the Proto-Australoid." (Dikhitar, in *Prehistoric South India*). The reference of field of sugar cane is referred in the eighteenth chapter of Panini and was called *Iksuvana.* The sugar cane juice is boiled for making *Guda*. The condensed boiled juice of sugar cane in which small particles appeared known as *Rab* (molasses). In Sanskrit it is called *Phanita.* Sugar is made from *Phanita.*

The reference of *Iksugriha* at *Dashpur* (Mandsaur) is found in *Uttaradhyayana Tika*. Jain Sadhus were supposed to stay at that house. After cutting the sugar cane from the fields, barks of sugar cane were removed and cut into several round pieces and then they used to eat. Sugar viz. *Matsyandika, Pushpotar* and *Padmotar* are also referred. At that time, people had the juice of sugar cane and the sweetmeat made of it. People used sweetmeat made of *ghee,* milk and juice of sugar cane (Saundarkand, 9.31).

In *Patanjali* it is mentioned that the people of that time freely ate *Guda. Guda* was made of *Iksu* and the *Iksu* in which the excess quantity of *Guda* is extracted is called *Gaudik Iksu.* The reference of *Gudodak* is found in *Bhashya.* The drink made of *Guda* is called *Gododak.* In *Kautilya* the reference of *Rab* (molasses), *Guda, Khar* (unrefined sugar) and *Shakkar* are found which are made of sugar cane.

फाणितगुडमत्स्यण्डिकाखण्डशर्कराः क्षार वर्गः ।

कौटिल्य, अर्थशास्त्र, 2.15.14

(Fermented jaggery, eggs of fish, powder of *Shakkar* (molasses) come under corrosive substance).

The reference of *Iksu* is found in *Anushasana Parva* of the *Mahabharat*. In the *Ramayana* (Valmiki Ramayana, 1.53.4) it is mentioned that *Guda* was made of the juice of sugar cane and different types of sweetmeats were prepared from *Guda.* At one place it is mentioned that molasses was prepared from sugar cane, (Ibid, 2.19.73). *Khandaw* was also prepared from sugar cane and it was keenly taken by the people. (*Mahabharat, Anushasan Parva,* 53.18). It is known from *Rajatarangini* (974) that the juice of sugar was used in abundance by that time and the sugar was first produced in India.

According to *Charak, Shusruta* (45.158) *Asatang-Hridayam* (5.42) and *Asatang-Sangrah* (6.81), the juice of sugar cane which is chewable by teeth are *Viryavardhak* (strength giving), cool, calm, *snigdha, brihana delicious* and cough exportant and juice extracted by *Kolhu* creates a burning sensation in the body of a person.[3] According to *Astang Sangrah*

सोऽग्रे सलवणो दन्तपीडितः शर्करासमः।

अष्टाङ्ग संग्रह 6.82

Anterior part of the sugar cane contains *Isat Lavan* and sucking by teeth is equivalent to the properties of molasses. At the time of Shudrak and Kalidasa, *Iskupan* (drinking the juice of sugar cane) and all materials were used as food. Pulse, rice, millet, milk, *ghee,* sweetmeat and molasses are the food of Indians since very ancient periods (Raghuvansh, 4.20).

In *Rigveda* it is mentioned that—

यस्ते द्रय वृणवदभद्रेशोचेऽपूपं देव घृतवन्तमग्ने।

ऋग्वेद 10.45.9

(Sweetmeat of Aryans was *Apupa* and they ate it with full appetite. They prepared it by mixing water and *ghee* in flour and cooked it in mild flame). According to Panini, *Guda, Phanita* and molasses were important part of the economy of the villagers. In *Satpath Brahmana* (2.2.3.13) reference of *Apupa* are found. At the time of *Jatak, Khaja* (a kind of light sweetmeat like pie-crust) has very important place. Generally kings ate *Khaja* and *Yawagu* was given to *Rishis* (Jatak, 336).

Reference of *Kṣair* (the milk) is found in Patanjali. *Payasa* was cooked in *Kṣair*. The people who drank *Payasa* were called *Payasik.*

At the period of the *Ramayana* and *Mahabharata* following sweetmeats were famous viz., *Apupa, Peya* (cooked by mixing *Kheer,* milk and rice), *Krisara* (rice cooked with sesamum) and *Modaka, Khandawa,* etc.

Therefore it seems that the prevalence of honey in sweets were found and used as sweet, because before the development of civilization, the Aryans did not know the other sweetmeats except honey but due to development in civilization they produced sugar cane and made *Guda* and molasses from the juice of sugar cane. They also cooked other sweetmeats from *Guda* and molasses.

Development of Sweetmeats Through Different Periods of Indian History

Now it would be relevant to discuss the development of sweetmeats through different periods of Indian history.

The Indus Valley Civilization (C. 3000 B.C.)

During this period besides wheat, barley, and rice, milk (including sweet dishes) too must have been an important item of food (Pusalkar, 1951).

Vedic Period (1600 B.C.)

In this period honey was taken out from two kinds of bees, one big *Arangara* and the other small *Saragha.*[4] The latter kind was considered better than the former.[5] It was used to sweeten food articles such as *apupas.*[6]

Sugar cane (*Iksu*) is not expressly mentioned in the *Rigveda* but is found in all other *Samhitas.* Chewing of sugar cane is referred to in the Atharvaveda.[7]

Apupa was a round cake of barley[8] meal or rice-flour[9] baked in clarified butter[10] on slow fire.[11] Honey was added to sweeten it. It is, probably, the earliest sweet preparation known to us (Om Prakash, 1961).

Milk and its products were the most important articles of food. There is mention about 'mess of grain cooked with milk' and of a kind of cheese. Cake of rice or barley was eaten mixed with *ghee* (Vidyarthi, 1952).

The principal sweets of Vedic Indians consisted of :

Apupa—a kind of cake which might be made of *Vrihi* (rice), or of *Yava* (barley), and mixed with *ghee.*[12]

Odana—a mess usually of grain cooked with milk; its varieties are : *Ksiraudana,*[13] *mudgandana* (cooked with beans)[14] and *tilandana;*[15] and Pakri-Cake.[16]

In the time of Aryans, honey was also commonly used. Cakes were made of wheat and barley.

Later Vedic Period

In this period, sweets found at the age of Rik Samhita, Upanishads and Sutras, Later Samhitas, Epics, Panini, Vinaya, Vatsyayana, Susruta Samhita are discussed.

Rik-Samhita

Milk and its products, chiefly *ghrita* (clarified butter) formed the principal ingredient of food. Grain (*yava*) was parched or ground into flour with a mill-stone and then mixed with milk or butter, and finally made into cakes. Milk, drunk warm as it came from the cow, was a favourite drink. *Madhu,* though often used to denote *Soma* or milk or any sweet food or drink, has also the sense of "honey" in the Rigveda (Apte, 1951).

Upanishads and Sutras

In this period milk and its products were very liberally used. The various forms of butter (due to its varying temperature) were distinguished for purposes of the ritual as clarified (*sarpis*), melted (*ajya*) and solid (*ghrita*) butter. Among other esculent things may be mentioned honey and *Kshara lavana* (saline food), which is supposed to be an irritant and an excitant, and therefore, to be eschewed in the interest of celibacy.

The culinary art was fairly well developed. The preparation of a *Purodasa* (sacrificial cake) implied great skill in baking as it was baked on a pan with varying number of hollows (resembling saucers) which gave a variety of forms to it. An *apupa* was a cake baked on a flat vessel. Boiled rice (*odana*) eaten with *ghee*, milk rice (*payasa*) which seems to be a preparation very much akin to *dudha-paka Krisara* (boiled rice mixed with sesamum seeds), *dadhimantha* and *madhu-mantha* (cooked ground grains mixed with curd and honey respectively), and rice and barley gruel are other preparations known (Ibid).

Later Samhitas

Various eatables are mentioned in the texts of this period. The *apupa* is a cake mixed with *ghee* or made of rice or barley; *Odana* is a mess, generally of grain, cooked with milk. Special varieties are those made with water, milk, curds or *ghee* and beans, sesame or meat, and named approximately, such as *tilandana,* etc. A porridge made of grain, barley or sesame unhusked, slightly parched and kneeded is called *Karambha.* Rice cooked with milk and with beans is mentioned in the *Satapatha Brahmana* and the *Vajasaneyi Samhita. Payasa* is one of the chief products of milk.

Epic Period (B.C. 1200-800 B.C.)

Now we come to discuss the references of sweet dishes and sweetmeats found in epics mainly in the *Mahabharat* and the *Valmiki Ramayana.*

Mahabharata : The *Mahabharata* has references to milk and its various kinds of preparations. The references of sweet dishes and sweetmeats like honey, *kheer, halwa, Pua, Laddu, Khandwa, Rasala* and the likes are found in the Sabha Parwa, Shanti Parwa, Anushasan Parwa, Ashwamedhik Parwa of the *Mahabharata.*

In Sabha Parwa, it is mentioned that honey was used in milk rice.[17]

Chapter 36 of Shanti Parwa deals with the form of religion, atonement of sin, description of forbidden food and discussion of people unworthy of alms according to Sawaymabhuwa Manu (the first Manu who was born to the God Brahma).

Regarding forbidden food, Pitamah (an epithet of Bhishma) explain to Yudhistir,

पायसं कृसरे मांसगपूपाश्च वृथा कृताः।

अपेयाश्चाप्य भक्ष्याश्च ब्राहाणैर्गृहमेधिभिः।।

महाभारत, शांतिपर्व 36.33

(Things like Kheer, Khichari, pulp of fruits and *Pua* if not prepared with the intention of offering it to God, are not fit for consumption of Brahman householders.)

Chapter 53 of Anushasan Parwa deals with the patience test of King Kaushik and queen by Chayawan Muni and giving of blessings after he was pleased by their services. While Chayawan Muni tests the patience of King Kaushik and his wife, he is served with sweet dishes as described by the following verse:

रसालापूपकाश्चित्रान् मोदकानथ खाण्डवान्।

रसान् नानाप्रकारश्च वन्यं च मुनिभोजनम्।।

महाभारत, अनुशासन पर्व, 53.18

(Kings arranged the tasteful *Pua,* conspicuous *Laddu, Khandwa* and juice of various kinds, fearing the curse of the hermits.)

Chapter 65 of the Anushasan Parwa deals with the importance of giving alms of gold and water. In this chapter Bhishma narrated the importance of giving alms of several things. Regarding giving of *Kheer* as alms he says:

पायसं सर्पिषा मित्रं द्विजेभ्यो यः प्रबुध ति।

गृहं तस्य न रक्षांसि घर्षश्यन्ति कदाचन।।

वही, 65.11

(who ever gives *Kheer* mixed with clarified butter to Brahman the demon does not attempt their house.)

Chapter 136 of the Anushasan Parwa deals with the atonement for taking alms and improper food. In this connection Bhishma Pitamah tells Yudhistir:

ब्राहौ पुष्पे फले चैव जले पिष्टमेय तथा।
यावके दधि दुग्धे च सावित्री शतशोडन्विलाम्।।

वही, 136.9

(After taking the alms of paddy, flower, fruit, water, *Puu, Lapsee* (porridge of barley), curd and milk, one should make one hundred *Japa* (silent recitations) of Gayatri Mantras).

Chapter 162 of Anushasan Parwa deals with the advantages of religious rites, characteristics of saints and wicked person and description of good manners. Describing the quality of worthy persons, Pitamah tells *Yudhistir*:

संस्कृतं पायसं नित्यं यवांग कृसरं हविः।
अष्टका पितृदैवत्या ग्रहाणामभिपूजनम।।

वही, 162.50

(One should perform the *Sradh* on the eighth day of the Gods and manes by offering well-cooked *kheer, halwa, khichari* and the materials of *Haurishya* (fire). The nine *grahas* should also worshipped).

In Chapter 65 of Ashwamedhik Parwa, after hearing the version of Brahmin, King Yudhistir offered ceremonially to Lord Shankar the following things:

स गृहीत्वा सुमनसो मन्त्रपूता जनायिप
मोदकः पायसनाथ मांसेश्चोपाहरद बलिम।।

महाभारत, आश्वमेधिक पर्व 65.4

(By taking flower charged with spell, they offered the presents of sweetmeat, *Kheer,* pulp of fruit, conspicuous flower, *lawa* (parched rice) and various things.)

Chapter 89 of Ashwamedhik Parwa deals with the giving alms to Brahmins and presentations to kings and leave-taking by Yudhistir. The description of that piece run as follows:

भक्ष्य रवाण्डवरागाणां क्रियतां भुज्यतां तथा।
पूशूनां बध्यता चैव नान्तं दहशिरे जनाः।।

वही, 89.41

(The people of that place could not imagine the limit of the quantity in which the non-exhaustive eatable things and *Khandwarag*[18] are prepared and eaten and the number of beasts chained there).

Valmiki Ramayan

In this period besides foodgrains, milk formed an important item of food. Milk-rice continued to be a favourite preparation. Honey was used to sweeten it and clarified butter to make it more tasteful. The references of sweet dishes and sweetmeats are as follows:

The sixteenth chapter of Balakanda of the *Valmiki Ramayana* mentions about the appearance of Prajapatya Purush from the fire pit in the Putreyasti Yajna (a sacrifice performed for the sake of obtaining children) of King Dashratha who holds a pot of Kheer in his hand:

दिवाकरसमाकारं दीप्तानलशिखोपमम् ।

तप्तजाम्बूनदभर्या राजतान्तपरिच्छादाम् ।। 14 ।।

दिव्यपाससम्पूर्णा पातीं पत्नीमिव प्रियाम् ।

प्रगृहा विपुलां दोर्भ्यां स्वयं मायामयीमिव ।। 15 ।।

वाल्मीकि रामायण, बालकांड, 16, 14-15

(His form was brilliant and was lustrous like the flame of fire. He was holding a *Parāt* in his hand which was made up of *Jambunad* gold and covered with silver lid. That dish was very big and full of divine *Kheer*. He was holding that *Parat* in such a manner just as a lover taking his beloved wife in lap. He seemed conspicuous but mysterious).

Regarding this context, the reference of *Kheer* is also found in the sloka numbers 19, 20, 23, 26-29 and 31.

Chapter 53 of Balakanda deals with the satisfaction of Vishwamitra with his troops by the best food with the help of Kamdhenu. The couplets given below describe the menu of food:

इक्षून मधूंस्था लाजान् मेरेयांश्च वरासवान्।
पानानि च महार्हाणि भक्ष्यांचोच्चाक्चानपि।।

बालकांड, 53.2

(He arranged the sugar cane, honey, *Lawa, Maireya,* best *Aaswa* (intoxicating liquor distilled from sugar and molasses), *Panak* juice and various kinds of costly eatable things).

Similarly,

नानास्वदुरसानां च खाण्डवानां तथैव च।
भोजनानि सुपूर्णानि गौडानि च सहस्त्रशः।।

(Arranged thousands of silver dishes which were full of several types of delicious juices, *Khandwa* and various kinds of food.)

Chapter 75 of Ayodhya Kanda deals with the taking of oath by Bharat in front of Kaushalaya. After hearing the several rough versions by Kaushalaya, Bharat fell down on her feet and said to the lamenting Kaushalya:

पायसं कृसरं छात्रं वृथा सोडश्नातु निधृर्णः।
गुरूंश्चाप्यवजानातु यस्यार्योडनुमते गतः।।

अयोध्याकांड, 75.30

(By which consent Ramchandra went to jungle, it is useless for him to eat the *Kheer, Khichari* and goat's milk without offerings to God.)

Chapter 91 of Ayodhya Kanda deals with the great reception of Bharat and his troops by Bhardwaj Muni. The reference of various kinds of sweet dishes in their reception are as follows:

Firstly,

सुरां सुरापाः पिबत पायसं च बुभुक्षिताः।
मांसानि च सुमेध्यानि भक्ष्यन्तां यो यदिच्छति।।

वही, 91.52

(They would call the soldiers of Bharat several times and say, O! drinkers of honey, take and drink the honey. Those of you, who feel hungry, eat this *Kheer* and pulp of sacred fruits available before you. Taste it. You are free to eat, whatever you like.)

Secondly,

इक्षंश्च मधुलाजांश्च भोजयन्ति स्म वाहनान्।

इक्ष्वाकुवरयोधानां चोदयन्तो महाबलाः।।

वही, 91.56

(Those coming in the vehicles of the superior warriors of *Ekshwa Kukul,* the mighty guards of vehicles (who were appointed for such services by the Maharshi) would inspire and feed them with the pieces of sugar cane and parched rice mixed in honey).

Chapter 128 of Yudha Kanda deals with the returning of royal throne by Bharat to Rama, entrance of Rama to Ayodhya, coronation ceremony, farewell of *Banars* and importance of texts. While Rama entered into the Ayodhya.

अक्षतं जातरूपं च गावः कन्याः सहद्विजाः।

नरा मोदकहस्ताश्च रामस्य पुरतो ययुः।।

वही, युद्धकांड, 128.38

(Many people and maidens taking utensils full of *Akshta* and gold and sweetmeats (*Laddu*) in their hands, were escorted by Sri Rama).

Chapter 92 of Uttarakanda deals with importance of giving alms in Ashwamedhik Yagna by Rama. Regarding this Yagna following verse has been referred:

ईहशं राजसिंहस्य यज्ञप्रवरमुत्तमम्।

नान्या शब्दोडभवत् तत्र हयमेधे महात्मनः।।

छदन्तो देहि देहीति यावत् तुष्यन्ति याचकाः।

तावत् सर्वाणि दत्तानि क्रतुमख्ये महात्मनः।।

विबिधानि च गौडानि खाण्डवानि तथैव च।

वही, उत्तरखंड, 92.10-11-1/2-

(The Yagna of Sri Raghunath Jee (who is brave like a lion

among all kings) had been started in a superior way. Only following verse was heard in that Yagna, "whenever the suitor was not satisfied, till that time supplied all things to them according to their wish". So, the eatable things prepared in molasses and *Khandaw* were regularly supplied to them still they did not stop it after being fully satisfied.)

Sutra Period

Honey was extensively used in many ceremonies in the Sutra period[19] and was invariably used in welcoming guests, and common preparation used for the purpose being a mixture of honey with curds or *ghee* (*Madhuparka*).[20]

Besides honey, another source of sweet ingredients was sugar cane.[21] *Guda* inspissated juice of sugar cane boiled to thick consistency (*Phanita*) and probably sugar were prepared from it.[22] The old preparations in common use were *Apupa, Krsara, Payasa.* Among new sweet preparations *Palala* was prepared with sesamum and *guda* or sugar and *saniyava* (*churma*) with wheat flour fried in clarified butter, and mixed with milk and *guda.* Sometimes cardamom, pepper and ginger were added to make it tastier. Ears of barley or wheat were parched and beaten with a pestle and after being cleaned were mixed with *guda* to make *abhyusa*,[23] sweets called *Svastika, Modaka* and *Nandyavarta* are also mentioned.[24]

The Time of Panini (B.C. 8th century)

Panini was the greatest grammarian of ancient India whose work on the Sanskrit language has up to the present day remained the standard of Sanskrit grammar.

The *Ashtadhyayi* is full of interesting details regarding the social life, manners and customs of its time. It contains material for an important chapter on the history of food and drinks in ancient India.

According to Kasikas gloss on VI.2.154 (*Misrani Chanupasargam asandhan*) *guda, tila* and *ghrita* are examples of *misra* articles. It follows that for improving the taste, it was permissible to have any suitable combination with the principal *bhakshya* food. The process of *misrikarana* (mixing there-with), is the same as Sanisrishta (IV.4.22).

A list of the sweetmeats and their preparation mentioned in the *Ashtadhyayi* are as follows:

A. Cooked Foods (Kritanna)

Yavaka (V.4.29) : According to Patanjali, *Yavaka* was made by pounding barley with pestle and mortar to remove the chaff, and then boiling its pearl, grain in water or in milk with sugar added to it.[25] Charaka calls *Yavaka* a steamed food.[26] The *Arthashastra* lays down that prepared *Yavaka* must weigh twice the original quantity of barley cooked (Arth. Text.11.15).

Pishtaka (IV-3.147) : *Pishta* (IV.3.146) denotes the ground paste of any grain. Articles prepared by mixing *Pishta* were generally called *Pishtamayam-pishtaka* on the other hand was a special preparation, probably the cakes made of powdered rice. Susruta counts *piṣhṭaka* among cooked delicacies (Kritanna Varga).[27]

Samyava (III.3.23) : Kulluka explains *Samyava* as a sweet preparation made with *ghrita,* milk, *guda* and wheat flour (Manu., V. 7) almost the same as modern *churma.* Susruta also includes it with confectioneries.[28]

Apupa (V.1.4) : Sweet cakes made of wheat flour and *ghrita* a dainty confectionery prepared even now. The Kasika mentions oven-baked *apupas* (IV.2.16). The Chandra Vritti and the Kasika read *abhyusha* (variant form abhyosha) in the Apupadigana.[29] It must have been an ancient food since the *Kamasutra* also mentions *Abhyusha-khadika* as a sport in which boys and girls took part by eating the *abhyusha* (parched grain) (Kamasutra, Ch. IV).

Palava (VI.2.128) : A sweetmeat made of pounded sesamum and sugar or *guda* as illustrated by Kasika, *gudena misrani palalani guda palalani* (VI.2.128) and *tila-palalani* (VI.2.135). Its modern equivalent is *tila-kuta.*

Churma (IV.4.23) : It means wheat-flour mixed on a pan and mixed with *ghee* and sugar. In this form it was put inside the cakes or *apupas,* which in Panini's time were called *Churninap apupah* (Kasika, corresponding to modern *gunjha* or *gunjhiya*).

B. Sweets :

Panini mentions the following sweets:

Madhu (honey) : Madhu from which is derived the general term *madhura* (V.2.107) denoting all confectioneries. Honey prepared by the common bee is referred to as *Khhandra* (IV.3.118) treated as a samjna word.

Guda (IV.4.103) : Molasses is a universal product of sugar cane juice. Paninis phrase excellent for making *guda* (*gude sadhu*) refers to some special variety of sugar cane yielding better quality of *guda*. Panini refers to vast cane plantations or forests of sugar cane in *ikshu-vana* (VIII.4.5.).

Phanita : It implied as a counter example in Sutra VII.2.18 which mentions *phanta phanita* denotes inspissated juice of sugar cane boiled down to a thick consistency, a preparation now called *rab* from which after crystallization sugar is prepared.

Sarkara : Granulated sugar prepared from sugar cane.

C. *Milk products*: Milk products are called *gavya* and *Payasya* (IV.3.160) of which curds, milk and butter-milk IV.2.18; *dadhi-payasi* II.4.14) are mentioned as important food articles. *Phanta* as given in Sutra VII.2.18 has the sense of 'made without effort' (*anāyāsa*). The *Kasika* understands it as a hot decoction but the epithet *anayas* points to its old meaning of butter produced from the cream of the day's milk[30] as opposed to *navanita* churned from curds of the previous day's milk for which a new classical word, *haiyanigavina* (V.2.23) had come into use in Panini's time. (Agarwala, 1953)

Sweets at the Time of Vinaya

In Buddha's times peripathetic association of spiritual students round famous teachers were common. The Vinaya, came to represent the wisdom of the Buddha modified and augmented by the collective experience of the Sangha evolving in the course of a century. It affords thus a rare glimpse into the social history of the sixth, fifth and fourth centuries B.C. (Misra, 1969).

Dairy products formed the chief item of the food and the monks were also permitted to take it. Of the milk products, the chief were *dadhi* (curds), *takka* (butter-milk), *navanita* (butter) and *sappi* (*ghee*). Another article made from milk and said to have been used in gastric troubles is *lonasoviraka* or curds made very thin by mixing water in it. The Acaranga Sutra mentions a favourite dish *Sikharini* being prepared from curds mixed with sugar crystal and some pungent spices.

There are also some special articles and sweet-dishes mentioned in the *Vinaya*. *Puva* (a sweet-dish) was one favourite dish which, as it was custom not to send the daughter empty-handed, is recorded to have been sent with the girl when she was going to her husband's home. *Madhupindika* and *madhugolaka* were two other sweet-dishes. *Khajja* or *Khajjaka* is another special article offered for the proper distribution among the monks, the appointment of *Khajja-Kabhajaka* is laid down. The Cullavagga mentions *tiiasangulika* which, as the name proposes, was prepared by sesamum in combination with treacle syrup thumped together with the help of fingers (Ibid).

Sugar cane: The Vinaya references point to a profound knowledge of the people about sugar cane. It is put in the *phalabija* class of plants, i.e., those propagated from joint. At one place *Phanita* (treacle or molasses) is said to be a product prepared out of it. The Mahavagga speaks of the preparation of *gula* (*gulakarnam*) wherein flour (*pittam*) and ashes (*charikam*) are mixed with it so that it is well-lumped together. It also refers to one Belattha-kaccana travelling with 500 carts, all filled with vessels of *gula* (Ibid.).

Sweets at the Time of Vatsyayana

Vatsyayana notes two meals for men, viz., one in the forenoon, and one in the afternoon (*purvalmaparahnayor-*

bhojanam). As for the articles of food, he mentions rice, wheat, barley, pulses, a large number of vegetables, and sweets, such as *guda, sarkara* (*iksurasah*) and sweetmeat (*Khanda Khadyani*) (Majumdar, 1935).

The list of food stuffs cultivated at the time of the authors of the *Arthashastra, Sukraniti*[31] and *Kamasutra* also mentioned about sugar cane.

Sugar cane : As the source of granulated sugar and sugar candy.

Sweets at the Time of Susruta Samhita

The Susruta Samhita sets forth the following diet for men and women for good health. The principal meal should consist of five courses in the following order, namely: sweet dishes, sour, saline and pungent and other ones at the close of the meal. At the forepart of a meal, such fruits as the pomegranates, etc., should be eaten, after that *peyas* and boiled rice and prepared dishes as well as confectionery. Sweet food eaten with a relish pleasurably affects the mind, brings joy, energy, strength and happiness.

The following confectioneries have been recommended and their preparations described: *Ksira-bhaksyas* (a milk preparation); *ghritapuras* (variety treated with *ghee*), *gandikas* (prepared with treacle and corn-flour), *madhu-mastakas, sanyavas* and *pupas, modakas, sattakas, visyandana smita, phenaka* (Khaja of present day), cake with *mudga, vesavaras* (containing minced and pasted meat) *palalas* (containing treacle, sesame and corn-flour, *saskulio* (*luchis* and *kachuris* of present day), *pistakas* (cakes of powdered rice), confectionery made of *vaidalas* (pulses, fruit, meat, etc. (Ibid.).

Sweets

Sarakara, palm sugar, sugarcandy and *madhu,* granulated sugar from sugar cane juice and sugar candy, are both mentioned in the Atharvaveda (XV.94). It also mentions grape juice along with honey of the bee as *Madhu.* In the Vinaya texts

(M.VI.16.1) mention of sugar factory was found, where it is also said that flour and cane dust were put into molasses to make it firm. In another place (Ch.X.I, 6) destruction of sugar canes in cultivation by 'blight' is mentioned.

The institutes of Manu and Greek writers make undoubted references to cane sugar, as well as palm sugar, honey and other saccharine substances.

Twelve varieties of sugar mentioned by Sanskrit writers[32] are as follows:

(i) *Iksurasa* (sugar cane juice)

(ii) *Phanita* (sugar cane juice boiled down to one fourth; it can be drawn out in threads)

(iii) *Guda* (treacle)

(iv) *Matsandika* (sugar cane juice boiled down to a solid consistence, but which excludes a little fluid on drawing)

(v) *Khanda* (candied in white sand-like grain)

(vi) *Sarkara* (white sugar)

(vii) *Sitopala* (sugar candy)

(viii) *Gaudi* (fermented liquor obtained from treacle)

(ix) *Sindu* (fermented liquor obtained from sugar cane juice), and

(x-xii) Varieties of above.

Sweetmeats

They form the last course of an Indian dish (*madhurena samapayet*). *Pistakas* (cakes) and *pāyasa* (milk porridge of rice) form the last course of a Hindu meal. Modern *sandes* and *rasagollas* are preparations of *chhana* (casein) and sugar; *sandes* has many varieties, some of which are shaped and named after the shape of particular fruits such as *talsans* (kernel of the toddy palm seed), *kamranga* (fruits of this plant), *aam* (mango fruit), *ataphal* (custard apple), *Kamlanebu sandes* is coloured and smelled like oranges, and so on (Ibid., pp. 417-18).

Sweets at the time of early Buddhist and Jain (500 BC)

In this period honey was in common use.[33] It had three varieties from which it was drawn: of small bees, of big bees and of a third variety called *Kuttiya*.[34] But sugar cane was the most important source of sweet ingredients.[35] Juice of sugar cane was also extracted with a machine and was used in plenty.[36] *Pundra-vardhana* was noted for its sugar cane crop.[37] Flour and ashes of dried sugar cane were used in preparing *guda* from the juice of sugar cane.[38] It was so important an article of food that even the Buddha included it among the food articles which he allowed to his followers.[39] *Phanita* and sugar were other important products of sugar cane which were in common use.[40] Sugar candy (*Matsyandika*) is also mentioned in the Jain canon.[41]

Of the sweet preparations, *Madhutaja* (sweet fried rice and *Madhugolaka* or *Modaka*[42] were in common use. In the Jain works some five sweets such as *Mandaka* (cakes stuffed with molasses and *ghee), Madhusirsaka* (also a kind of sweet cake), *Gulalavaniya, Ghayapunna* (the modern *ghevara), sihakesara* and *morandaka* (sweets prepared from inspissated milk and shaped like the eggs of peacock).[43] Some of these may however, be later preparations as they are neither mentioned in the early Jain canons nor in the contemporary Brahmanical or Buddhist literature (Om Prakash, 1961).

Maurya and Sunga Period (C. 325 BC – C. 75 AD)

During Maurya and Sunga period, honey was in common use[44] but the products of sugar cane such as inspissated juice of sugar cane, *guda,* raw sugar, sugar candy and refined sugar were quite popular.[45] Even Megasthenes speaks very highly of Indian sugar.[46] Besides the old sweets such as *Apupa, Saskute* and *Palala, Patanjali* mentions *Modakas*[47] (Ibid.).

Honey continued to be used specially with parched rice[48]. Sugar cane was used in making *guda* which was used in the preparation of many sweets.[49] Another product of sugar cane juice in common use was sugar both clarified and raw.[50] Common sweets were *apupa, payasa, samyava, krsara, madhulajah* and *modakas*.[51] *Modakas* were generally prepared with rice or wheat-flour fried in clarified butter mixed with sugar, some aromatic spices and thin slices of the kernel of coconut. Some good quality sweets are called *Khandava* and *Uccavacabhaksya* in the epics[52] (Ibid).

Manu

Preparations constituting the dietary were of barley, wheat (Yavagodhumajam V.25), milk and rice (*Payasa*), honey, curds, sesame, Masha, fruits and vegetables including many varieties of hard and soft food (Pinyaka, yavagu, etc.). At the expiry of meals a mess preparation (*Sarva-varnika-mannadhyam* III.244) was scattered before the *Pankti* to serve the purpose of desert. (Agarwala, 1970).

Patanjali

The evidence adducted by *Patanjali* on the subject of 'food and drinks' is exhaustive. The vegetarian menu included many other items, some of which were meant for breakfast, or afternoon nourishment such as *Krsara*,[53] a mixture of sesamum and rice, *saktu* groats mixed with molasses or *dodhi* (curd). Sweets and sweet cakes included *saskuli* made of ground rice, sugar and sesamum and cooked in oil; pupa of apua mixed with *ghee* (*ghrtavant*) or made of rice and barley; *Pisapindi*[54] a flour cake, and *Palala*[55] a kind of sweetmeat made of *guda*, sesamum and sugar and cooked. The substances used in making sweet preparations were *madhu*[56] or honey, *guda*[57] molasses produced from sugar cane juice and *sarkara*[58] or crystal sugar. The sweet balls probably known as *modaka*[59] were liked by children. Certain cold drinks soothed the wearied people in summer, as for example, *gudodaka*,[60] a thin liquid substance, being a mixture of water and molasses. *Payas*-milk and whey (*mathitani*) were available from shopkeepers known as *mathitika*.[61] *Haiyam-gavina*[62] was clarified butter prepared from last day's milk (Puri, 1957).

Patanjali[63] called *Pistaka* as *Pistapindi*. It was made of flour of rice or powder of any corn. Flour was mixed with molasses or *guda* and cooked in *ghee*. This was called *Pindi* or *Pistapindi*.[64]

Pindi was also made of sesamum seeds. At first sesamum seeds were fried not on oven, but in a closed pot.[65] (Agnihotri, 1980).

The Kusana and Saka Satavahana Period (C.75 AD—C 300 AD)

Honey continued to be widely used and eight varieties of honey are mentioned in the medical works of this period. The eight varieties are *Maksika, Bhramara, Ksawdra, Pauttika, Chatra, Arghya, Auddalika* and *Dala*. Of these, the variety collected by small bees (*maksika*) was considered the best and that by big black bees (*bhramara*) was considered heavy to digest.[66] The consumption of honey was considered particularly useful in the rainy season.[67]

Many varieties of sugar cane are mentioned.[68] Of these the thin reed variety called *vanisaka* was considered the best, while old preparations were made tastier by the addition of some new ingredients. In the preparation of *samyava,* wheat flour, milk, clarified butter, sugar, cardamom, pepper and ginger were used.[69] *Ghrtapura* was also prepared with these substances but thin pieces of kernel of coconut were added to it.[70] *Madhusirsaka* or *Madhukroda* was a sweet which was prepared with wheat flour but had honey or clarified butter inside.[71] *Pupalika* was a small cake of rice or wheat-flour fried in ghee with *guda* inside.[72] Sometimes a stuffing prepared with Mudga pulse was also used.[73] Another sweet preparation with rice-flour, milk, treacle and clarified butter is called Utkarita.[74] Vartika was a similar sweet preparation in the form of a roll,[75] (Ibid).

Period between the End of Maurya Sunga Imperial Rule and Rise of the Glorious Gupta Imperial Dynasty

Milk was also an important item of food of the people. People were, not only taking it in the form of milk but its various products such as *ghee,* curd, *kheer,* butter, *chhena,* etc., were also taken[76] (Prasad, 1970). Auboyer (1965) mentioned that in ancient India (from approximately 200 BC to AD 700), in noble establishments, and at the king's table, a great variety of desserts were offered, including scented curds, creamy cheeses (*Kitata*) and balls of rice or wheat coated with sugar, thin slices of coconut and various spices, these last sweetmeats being either steamboiled or fried in butter. Sweets were made of seeds fried in oil. Sugar cane, refined and moulded into oval loaves, provided the base for sweet-dishes (*modaka*) containing molasses, curds, *ghee* and pepper. These were followed by fruits, curds, whey and salted rice. Milk foods were very popular; for instance, sweetened milk flavoured with spices and camphor, and cooked with ripe bananas. Honey was usually reserved for great occasions. When a guest was expected, the chair which was to be offered to him was got ready, and a special beverage (*Madhuparka*) containing sugar, *ghee*, curds, herbs and honey was prepared. This was a sort of hydromel consumed on great occasions: women were given this to drink when five months pregnant; the eldest son's lips were moistened with it at the time of his birth; the student was offered this when he left his *guru* to become a *snataka;* the suitor just before he went to ask for the hand of a girl in marriage; and the bridegroom when he arrived at the home of his future father-in-law on the morning of the wedding (Ibid).

Sweets in the Gupta Period (C. 300 AD - C. 550 AD)

The four varieties of honey mentioned in the medical works of the earliest period continued to be used in the reception of guests and other festive rites. These were: *bhramara, pauttika, ksaudra* and *maksika*. But all the products of sugar cane were widely used as sweetening ingredients in the food preparations,[77] of these *sarkara* was considered the best and *phanita* the worst.[78] Bana mentions two varieties of sugar, red and white.[79] Sugar was also prepared with a grass called *Yavasa*.[80] Besides the old sweets[81] preparations such as *madhulaja, krsara, modakas, utkarika, samyava, pupa, phenaka, payasa, abhyusa* and *gudaudana*,[82] some new preparations are mentioned. *Morendaka* was a kind of sweet prepared from inspissated milk. The solid part of it was formed into the shape of the eggs of a peacock fried in clarified butter and coated with sugar.[83] *Vimardaka* was preparation of groats and clarified butter[84]

Other sweets mentioned are: *locika, istaka, vitanaka* and *polika*. But as neither Sanskrit dictionaries nor books on food and drinks enlighten us about the way they were prepared, it is difficult to say much about them.[85] (Om Prakash, 1961).

Age of Imperial Unity

In this period, quite a large number of dainties, delicacies and sweetmeats were known. Milk and its products formed part of daily diet, and *ghee* was particularly valued as very substantial and nourishing. An interesting verse Udyoga-parvan says that the food of the middle class was milk and its products.

The Vinaya texts refer to many articles of food such as rice, beans, *tila* seeds, fresh honey, rice-milk, honey-lumps, curries, salt, molasses, oil, pot herbs, fruits, fish, meat and the five products of the cow: milk, curds, *ghee,* butter milk and butter.

The Classical Age

References in the Smritis and the general literature of the period do not indicate any noticeable change in regard to food and drink. The *Lankavatara Sutra* gives, in a list of approved items of food, the names of sali rice, wheat and barley, pulses of three kinds, clarified butter, oils, molasses as well as raw and coarse sugar. Hiuen Tsiang's in the first half of the 7th century, in introducing his general account of India, says that the cakes and parched grain, milk and sugar with their preparations, as well as mustard oil formed the common articles of food (Ghoshal, 1951).

Puranas

The extent which is divided into two parts, i.e., Purva and Uttara contains a good number of chapters on Hindu customs. The chapter seventeen of Uttara deals with edible and non-edible foods. The references of sweet-dishes in this context are as follows:

पायसं स्नेहपवं यत गोरसं चैत्र सक्तवः

कूर्मपुराण, उत्त०, अ० 17.17

(Eating of the food prepared in milk, grains cooked in *ghee* (clarified butter), *Goras* and *Sattu* which are prepared at Sudra's house are not objectionable).

उदुम्बरलाबु च जग्ध्वा पतिति वै द्विजः।

वृथा कृशरसंयावं पायसापूपमेव च।।

वही, 17.21

(Just as on eating Gular and Umbalu, a Brahman becomes degraded, similarly *khichari, oat, kheer* and *apupa* taken at the hands of a Sudra are objectionable.)

अनपाकृतमांसं च देवान्निानि हर्वीषि च।।

यवांगू मातुलिंगझमत्स्यानप्यनुपाकृतान्।।

वही, 17.22

(Uncooked meal, grains, meant for God for the purpose of *Havan* (fire sacrifice), *kheer, halwa* (porridge), *Matulings* (a kind of fruit) and uncooked fish must not be taken.)

At the Time of Kalidasa

Kalidasa refers to the following items of food:

Yava:[86] or barley including perhaps wheat also, rice of various kinds like the *sali*[87] and the *kalama*,[88] *tila*[89] or seasamum; sugar with its several kinds like the *gudavikara*[90] and *matsyandika*[91] and its sweetmeat preparations of round balls (*modaka*);[92] milk[93] and its various preparations like butter,[94] clarified butter,[95] curds,[96] *khira* or *payascaru*[97] and the like and honey.[98]

Indian food during the time of Kalidasa was nutritious and vigorous, sugar cane produced *guda* and sugar. *Gudavikara* was a particular stage in the preparation of sugar.[99] It was globular in shape like the eggs of fish as the phrase would suggest. Various preparations of sweetmeats (*modaka*) were made with sugar. Apart from its various use in food, it was also used as an antidote for the intoxication from wine.

Sugar and Sweetmeat : *Modaka* was prepared from rice or

wheat-flour stuffed with sugar, thin slices of the kernel of the coconut, together with spices were mixed and then either boiled over steam or fried in clarified butter.[100] It was a round ball and its parts have been supposed to resemble the phases of the moon.[101]

Preparation of Milk: The enormous wealth of cows supplied the people with the vigorous milk, butter (*navanita*), clarified butter (*Ghrita*)and curds (*Dadhee*). Siharini (*sikharini*) as the commentator points out,[102] was prepared from curds mixed with spices like cardamoms, cloves, camphor and other fragrant ingredients and cooked in milk and sugar. Sometimes it was also prepared in milk and ripe plantains and other ingredients enumerated above (without curd) and named *Sikharini.*[103] Honey was another item of food which was also used in the reception of guests[104] and at other festive rites. It was given the name of *madhuparka*[105] and *arghya* and later honey was mixed with rice and *durva* grass.[106]

Post Gupta Period (C.600 AD – C. 1200 AD)

Honey was not so widely used as in the previous period. The Puranas mention *guda* (treacle) and *Sarkara* (raw sugar) and not honey among the sweet things.[107] The Jains avoided the use of honey on the ground that it was pressed out of the young eggs in the womb of bees and resembled the embryo in the first stage of its growth.[108] The Paundra variety of sugar cane was grown near Rajagriha.[109] Sugar is also mentioned as an important article of food in the Ambasamudra Inscription of Varaguna Pandya (ninth century AD) in the Naisadha Carita the whiteness of sugar has been compared to a stream of snow.[110]

The act of preparing sweets is considered an art[111] and many new sweets are mentioned. *Kasara* was a preparation of wheat-flour, milk, clarified butter, crystal sugar, cardamom and black pepper.[112] A preparation of wheat-flour stuffed with *Kasara* was called *udumbara.*[113] A sweet preparation of wheat flour, *guda* and some spices such as black pepper and cardamom was called *murmura.*[114] *Modakas* prepared with rice-flour, sugar and some aromatic spices such as cardamom and camphor were called *varsopalagolakas* because they looked like hail-stones.[115] Sometimes dolls were also made with sugar (*Sarkari putrika*).[116] *Ghrtapura, Phenakas, Khajjakas* and *Laddukas* continued to be popular.[117] Sometimes they were also prepared with rice or *mudga* pulse.[118] In the preparation of *Ksiraprakara,* sour curds were mixed with boiled milk and the solid part of curds was separated from the liquid one. The solid curds were mixed with rice flour and sweets were prepared in different shapes. Possibly they were same as modern *chamcham* and *rasogullas.*[119] Another sweet prepared with milk was called *Ksirayastika*[120] (Om Prakash, 1961).

Fifteenth Century as Gleaned from Brihadyogata Rangun of Trimala Bhatta

The most important sweetening ingredient from which ordinary sugar, crystal sugar, *phanita* and *guda*[121] were prepared was sugar cane. As many as thirteen varieties of it are mentioned by Bhatta.[122]

In addition to ordinary *phenikas*[123] prepared with wheat flour, which were prepared in earlier periods there were those prepared with the flour of *masa* pulse, *trapabispinosa* and the roots of waterlily.[124] *Mudga* pulse soaked in milk was ground with curds or butter, and formed into balls. These balls fried in clarified butter and coated with a solution of sugar were called *navanitaphonikas.*[125] Similarly when *masa* pulse was used for preparing *phenikas* they were called *masaphenis.*[126] These look like modern *imartis.* In addition to ordinary sweetballs (*laddukas*)[127] prepared with powdered wheat flour formed into the form and threads another variety was prepared by mixing powdered wheat flour with clarified butter and water and frying the cake. It was then ground and crystal sugar and spices and dry fruits were added to it before shaping them into the form of *Ladduka.*[128] *Laddukas* prepared with the paste of *masa* and *mudga* pulse passed through a sieve and fried in clarified butter were also in use.[129] Roots of waterlily were boiled, ground and formed into the shape of threads. These threads were fried in clarified butter and coated with sugar to prepare.[130] *Saluka, Laddukas*[131] and sweet balls were also prepared with small balls of flour of gram pulse fried in clarified butter. Camphor, cardamom and seeds of gourd fried in clarified butter were mixed with it to make it fragrant and tasty.

Lapsi[132] was prepared with wheat-flour after frying it in clarified butter and mixing milk, sugar, cloves, cardamom and pepper to it. Another variety of *Lapsi* is called *chandrahasa.*[133] In preparing it milk was also used.

Another sweet preparation of wheat-flour was called *Bhaimi.*[134] It was stuffed with cardamom, raisins, dates, dry gingers, pepper, camphor and crystal sugar.

Apupas[135] and *Kamsara*[136] continued to be used during this period. *Gunjhiyas* (*Guhyakas*)[137] and sweet cakes with holes called *manthas*[138] were common.

Bhatta mentions six varieties of *ghara* (ghrtapura). Pure (*Suddha*) *ghevara* was prepared with powdered wheat flour. The other five varieties were prepared with kernel of coconut, solidified milk, rice flour mixed with solidified milk, *kaseru* and the juice of ripe mango fruit.

Jalebis (*Kundalika* or *Jalavallika*) were prepared with fermented solution of powdered wheat flour.[139]

Milk products such as cream, curds, butter and clarified butter were all in common use.[140] In addition to milk rice[141] some sweets were prepared with solidified milk.[142] It was mixed with wheat-flour and fried after passing through a sieve. Then the small balls were coated with sugar and formed into *laddukas.* Two other such preparations are called *dugdhamandakas* and *dugdhakaranjika.*[143] Three preparations of insipissated milk were *Ksiravatis,*[144] *Ksigamodakas*[145] and *Ksirasaka.*[146]

Sikharan (*isikharini*)[147] was prepared with curds as before. A variety of *sikharan* was kept in a red hot earthen pot for sometime and then the pot was called *vasavati.*[148]

Sweetballs[149] were prepared with curds from which water

had been separated. The curds were mixed with rice flour and salt and formed into balls before frying. Then they were coated with a solution of sugar. They look like modern *gulab jamuns. Indurasa*[150] was prepared by mixing rice flour with curds and sugar. The mixture was allowed to ferment for one night. Then sesamum seeds were mixed with it and the cakes were fried in clarified butter on a flat pan. To prepare *dedhivatikas,* rice flour was mixed with curds, formed into flat balls and fried in clarified butter. These balls were dipped in a solution of sugar (Om Prakash, 1968).

Sweets at the Time of Mughal Period

The royalty, nobility and aristocracy enjoyed a rich vegetarian diet. Abul Fazal had mentioned nine vegetarian dishes prepared in the royal kitchen. They were: *Zardbriranj, khuskhe, sheerbrinj, chikhee, badanjam, pahet, sag, halwa* and *khichari*. For the preparation of all these dishes ample quantity of *ghee* was indispensable.

Deep-fried things like *puris, kachauris, luchais,* besides rice, vegetables, pulses, sweets, fresh and dry fruits formed the menu in rich people's diets. The contemporary Hindu poets like Sur Das, Parmananda Dasa, Kumbhan Dasa, Nanda Dasa, Malik Mohammed Jayasi[151] and others have furnished us with the detailed items of morning and afternoon breakfast, lunch, and dinner in the houses of these people (Sangar, 1969).

The references of sweets are also found in the text such as *Sri Sri Chaitanaya Charitamrita, Kabi Kankan Chandi,* and *Chandi Mangal* which also comes under this period.

After some advancements in recipes, people prepared sweetmeats by mixing of *chhena* and *khoa*. Though, such sweetmeats are very occasional, this lead to the development of stuffed and sandwich types of sweetmeats. The example of stuffed and sandwich types of sweetmeats are *mitha-singhara, raskadam* and *creamchop, chhena-toast* respectively.

The liking for sweetmeat is so great and so much that it is an inevitable part of our food. On several occasions, the sweet sellers have been compelled to think about the problem of diabetic patients and prepared sweetmeats with the help of 'sorbitol' which is a sweetening agent. Though, a sweetmeat prepared with sorbitol is costlier, it is congineal to diabetic patients.

References

1. शहद की शराब भी बनाकर लोग पीते थे। मादक बनाने के लिए मधु को सड़ाया जाता था। सड़े हुये मधु को मधुरस* या माध्वीक** कहा जाता था। मधु से मधुर्मरये नामक सुरा बनाई जाती थी।

*चन्दनस्य च शीतस्य सीधोर्मधुरसस्य च।
विविधस्य च माल्यस्य प्रस्यस्य विवधस्य च।।

वाल्मीकीय रामायण, 5.11.32

*शर्करासवमाध्वीकाः पुष्पासवफलासवाः।
वासचूर्णैश्च विविधर्मृष्टास्तैस्तैः पृथक्-पृथक्।।

वही, 5.11.23

2. परित्वा परित्लुने क्षुणागाम विद्विषे।
यथा मां कामिन्यसो कथा मन्नापगा असः।

अथर्व वेद 1.34.5

3. वृष्यः शीतः स्थिरः स्निग्धो बृंहणो मधुरो रसः।
श्लेष्मलो भक्षितस्येक्षोर्यान्त्रिकस्तु विदह्यते।।

चरकसूत्र 27.234

4. आरड रेव मध्वेरयेथे सारधेव गवि नीचि नवार।
कीनारेव स्वेदमीसष्विदाना क्षामे वोर्जा सूयवसात सचेथे।

ऋगवेद × 106.10

5. यज्ञो हवै मधु सारघम् (सतपथ ब्राह्मण III.11.3.13)
6. अपूपवान् मधुमांश्चरुरेह सीदतु। (अथर्ववेद 18.4.22)
7. परित्वा परित्लुने क्षुणागाम विद्विषे
यथा मां कामिन्यसो यथा मन्नापगा असः। (अथर्ववेद 1.34.5)
8. यवमयमपूपं कृत्वा यत्राहवनीयमाधास्यन्भवति तन्निदधाति। (शतपथ ब्राह्मण 2.2.3.13)
9. व्रीहिमयमपूपं कृत्वा यत्र गार्हपत्य माधास्यन्भवति तन्निदधाति। (*Ibid*., II. 2.3.12).
10. यस्ते अद्य कृणवद् भद्रशोचेऽपूपं देव घृतवन्तमग्ने।
घृतवन्तम्—in clarified butter.

भद्रशोचे—on slow fire. Rigveda X. 45.9

Rigveda III. 51.1.

11. Satapatha Brahmana IV.2.5.19 (Om Prakash, 1961, pp. 18-19). See Appendix-1 of Om Prakash's book *Food & Drinks in Ancient India, History of Frying in Ancient India* Up to C. 500 A.D. (For details see Appendix-III of this book).
12. Rigveda, i, 26; III. 52.7; X. 45.9.
13. Rigveda, VIII. 69.14; 77.10.
14. Satapatha Brahmana II.5.3.4; XI. 57.5.

    Sankhayana Aranyaka, XII.8.
15. Vedic Index i, p. 124.
16. Rigveda, IV.24.5.7; 25.6.7; VI.29.4.
17. साज्येन पायसेनैव मधुना मिश्रितेन च।

    —महाभारत, सभापर्व 4.2
18. *Khandwarag*: The juice of *Munga* (kidney bean) which is prepared by mixing it with dry ginger and pepper is called *Khandwa.* If Shakker (molasses) is mixed to it, it is called *Khandwarag.*

    According to Gupta (1950:54-55) The *Mahabharat* also gives a vivid picture of a picnic. At rare feasts there were also sweetmeats besides roasted birds, curds, milk, whey, cream, fruits, and other delicacies.
19. Apastamba Dharma Sutra 1.4.6; Manava Grihya Sutra 1.1.12; Baudhayana Grihya Sutra 1.3.23-24; Paraskara Grihya Sutra 11.5.12; Gobhila Grihya Sutra 111.117.19-23.
20. दधनि मध्वानीय सर्पिर्वा् मध्वलाभे।

    Asvalayana Grihya Sutra 1.21.5.
21. Sugar cane plantations (Iksuvana) are mentioned Panini VIII.4.5.
22. Guda-Panini's Astadhyayi IV. 4.103; Baudhayana Grihya Sutra 1.10.11.

    Phanita. Inspissated juice of sugar cane boiled to thick consistency. Apastamba Dharma Sutra 1.5.17.19.
23. Abhyusa is mentioned in the Apupa divarga in Panini.
24. Manava Grihya Sutra 11.6.4.
25. Bhashya, 11.307; Idam tuna Sidhyati autukhalo yavaka iti. . . . . .Na Cha Yavaka utukhatad eva pakrishya abhyava hriyate vasyani randhana devi pratekshyani.
26. Sirnna bhakshya, Sutra-sthana, XXVII. 259.
27. G.P. Majumdar, Food, Indian Culture, 1.413.
28. *Ibid.*, p. 413.

29. Also prithuka boiled rice, crushed and dried (chiruve); cf. Kasika, guda-prithukah, II. 1.35. Amara, Apakvani paulirabhyushah, i.e., half-rice corn fried in fire.
30. Ayatayama, Satapatha Brahmana III.1.8.
31. Arthasastra, XV, 94; Sukraniti, IV, III, 146.
32. Materia Medica of the Hindus, U.C. Datta, p. 266.
33. Vinayapitaka, Mahavagga, IV. 17; Jatakas by Fausboll. I. 154.334.
34. Avasyaka Sutra curni II.319; Acaranga Sutra II.1.4; Uttaradhyayana Sutra XIX. 70.
35. Vinayapitaka IV; Anguttara. III. 76; IV. 179; Milindapanho, 46; Dhamma Tika (commentary) IV. 199; Petavatthu Tika (commentary) 124; Jatakas by Fausboll I. 139, IV, 114, 446; Uttaradhyayana Sutra Tika (commentary) II., p. 23.
36. Jatakas by Fausboll, I.339., II. 240 IV. 160-61, VI. 539 Vinayapitaka Mahavagga VI. 35-6; Brihatkalpa Sutra Bhasya Pi. 575; Bhagavati Sutra XXI.5.
37. Tandula Tika (commentary) p.2 (a) Therefore two kinds of sugar cane, Pundra (pale yellow) and Kajate (dark purple). The former gave its name to Pundradesa (Bengal to the east of the Ganges) and latter to Kajolaka (Bengal to the West of the Ganges).
38. गुले पिट्ठम्पि छारिकम्पि पक्खिपन्ते

    Vinayapitaka Mahavagga VI.16.1. Jatakas by Fausboll I. 123; Avasyaka Sutra curni II. 319; Vinayapitaka Mahavagga VI. 25-27.
39. इमानि खो पंच भेसज्जानि सेय्यथीदम् साप्पिनवनीतम् तेलभ् मधु फाणितम् भेसज्जानि।

    Vinayapitaka Mahavagga VI. 199.

    The Buddha allowed Guda to sick persons and water of Guda to healthy persons. Mahavagga (II) VI. 4-6.
40. Phanita -

    अधम्मिकेसु तेलमधुफाणितादीनिपि वनमूलफलाफलानि पि अमधुरानि होन्ति निरोजानि।

    Jatakas by Fausboll I.334

    Sarkara सप्पिना सार्धम् सक्खरचुण्णम् यावदत्थम् सवादित्वा

    Jatakas by Fausboll 442.
41. जो भिक्खु रण्णो खतियाणां ....खीरं वा दहि वा नवणियं वा सप्पि वा गुलं वा खंड वा सकरं वा मछंडियं वा अण्णतरं वा भोयणं जायं पडिगाहेइ।

    Nisitha Sutra VIII. 18.
42. Vinayapitaka Mahavagga I.43., VI.25.3.
43. Mandaka - Nisicu. II p. 695.

Madhusirsaja - Arya Manjusri mulakalpa, ed. Ganpati Sastri 48.8

Ghayapuma -

घयपुण्णेहि खंडखज्जेहि वा अवसेसं भक्खणविहि पच्चक्खाति

Upasaka Dasanga 1.34

Sihakesara - Antagadodasao, p. 10

Morandaka - Brhatkalpa Sutra Bhasya 1.328.

44. Honey-Strabo. XV. 491; Patanjali I. 1.1, pp. 18-19 Kautilya also mentions honey prepared from grapes:

क्षौद्रं मार्द्वीकं च मधु।

Kauṭ. II. 15.17

45. Sugarcane-Aelian mentions reeds which yielded very sweet milk which did not require honey to be mixed with it. Mc. Crindle, X. 143, Kaut. II, 15.24

फाणितगुडमत्स्यण्डिकाखण्डशर्कराः क्षार वर्गः

Kautiy. II.15.15

Phanita (inspissated juice of sugar cane) Kaut. II.15.15

Guda (molasses) Kaut. Ibid. Patanjali 1.4.49, pp. 333.3

Khanda (raw sugar) - Kaut. *Ibid.*

Sarkara (granulated sugar) Kaut. *Ibid.*, Patanjali IV. 4.83, p. 334.11.

46. Pliny says that the Indian sugar was better than the Arabian sugar (Mc. Crindle. X. 122.) Megasthenes thought that the Indian sugar candy was better than that prepared from figs or honey (Megasthenes XX. Strabo XV. 703).

47. Palala—A kind of sweetmeat made of *guda*, sesamum and sugar. Patanjali I.1.1., p. 38.6. *Modakas* were generally prepared with wheat-flour fried in *ghee* and mixed with sugar. Patanjali. V.1.119, p. 336.9.

48. इक्षून मधूंस्तथा लाजान् मैरेयांश्च वरासवान्।

Ramayana of Valmiki, Bala Kanda 53.2

मांसप्रतिग्रहे चैव मधुनो लवणस्य च।

Mahabharata Anusasana Parva 136.5

49. Isku-Ramayana. Balakanda 53.2; Ayodhya Kanda 91.56;

Mahabharata Anusasana Parva 136.8.

भोजनानि सुपूर्णानि गौडानि च सहस्त्रशः - Ramayana, Balakanda 53.4

विविधानि च गौडानि खाण्डवानि तथैव च Ramayana Uttara-kanda 92.12

50. Sarkara

बभूवुः पयसश्चान्ये शर्कराणां च संचयः

Ramayana Ayodhya kanda 91.73.

51. Modaka

नरा मोदकहस्ताश्च रामस्य पुरतो ययुः

Ramayana Yuddha kanda 131.38

रसालापूपकाश्चित्रान् मोदकानथ खाण्डवान्।

Mahabharata Anusasana Parva 53.18

52. Khandava

नाना स्वादुरसानां च खाण्डावानां तथैव च।

Ramayana Balakanda 53.4

विविधानि च गौडानि खाण्डवानि तथैव च।

Mahabharata Anusasana Parva 53.18

भक्ष्य खाण्डवरागाणां क्रियतां भुज्यतां तथा।

Ibid., 41.89

Uccavacabhaksya -

Ramayana Balakanda 53.2, Ayodhyakanda 61.14, Kishkindhakanda 33.7, 37.7 Sundara.

53. Mahabasya VIII. 3.59, p. 439 L.12.
54. *Ibid*. II. 1.57, p. 399 L.24.
55. *Ibid*. I. i. 1 p. 38 L.6.
56. *Ibid*. I. 1.1 p. 18 L.19.
57. *Ibid*. I.4.49, p. 333 L.3.
58. *Ibid*. IV.4.83, p. 334 L.11.
59. *Ibid*. V.1.119, p. 336 L. 9.
60. *Ibid*. I.4.3, p. 310 L.14.
61. *Ibid*. V.3.83, p. 425. L.18.
62. *Ibid*. V.2.23, p. 375. L.25.
63. Patanjali, 2.1.57.
64. Patanjali 2.1.57.

65. तप्ते भाष्टे तिलाः क्षिष्ता मुहूर्तमपि नावतिष्ठन्ते। *Ibid.*, 1.1.50

66. माक्षिकं भ्रामरं क्षौद्रं पौत्तिकं मधुजातयः।
माक्षिकं प्रवरं तेषां विशषाद् भ्रामरं गुरुः।

Caraka Samhita Sutra 27.242

67. *Caraka Samhita Sutra* 6, Bhela Samhita, p. 25.

68. पौण्ड्रको भीरुकश्चैव वंशकः श्वेतपोरकः।
कान्तारस्तापसेक्षुश्च काण्डेक्षुः सचिपत्रकः।
नैपालो दीर्धपत्रश्च नीलपोरोऽर्थ कोशकृत्।

Susruta Samhita 45.149-150

69. मधुशीर्षकसंयावाः पूपा ये ते विशेषतः *Ibid.*, 46.392
गोधूमसमिता मधु दुग्धेन मोदयित्वा सुशोभनाम्
पचेद् घृत्तोत्तरे खण्डे क्षिपेद् भाण्डे नवे ततः।
संयावोऽसौ युतश्चूर्णैः खण्डैलामरिचार्द्रकैः Dalhana

70. मर्दिताः समिताः क्षीरनालिकेरसितादिभिः।
अवगाह्य घृते पक्वो घृतपूरोऽयमुत्तमः।

Susruta Samhita Su.46.393.

गोधूमपटशूद्विकां क्षीरेण संमर्द्य सर्पिषा विस्तार्य पक्त्वा
सितायुक्तां कुर्याद् इत्येष हविष्पूरः घेवर इतिलोके

Sri Kanthadatta Vrinda Siddhayoga

71. Susruta Samhita Su. 46.395
समितावेष्टिताः पाकघनीभूताः मधुघृतोदराः मधुमस्तकाः
त एव मधुशीर्षकाः। Dalhaṇa
पाकघनीभूतमधुगर्भः गोधूमपिष्टकः वेष्टितः पक्वः सचतुर्जातकादि भक्ष्यविशेषः
मधुमस्तकः। अन्येतु गोधूमसमितां धृतयुक्तां तोयै मर्दयित्वा वृत्तमपूपंकृत्वा
घृतेन पक्त्वा सितायुक्तं कुर्यादित्येष मधमस्तकः।

Sri Kanthadatta Vinda Siddhayoga

72. विमर्द्य समिताचूर्ण मृदुपाकं गुडान्वितम्।
घृतावगाहे गुडिकां वृत्तां पक्वां सकेशराम्।
सौगन्धिकाधिवासांच कुर्यस्पूपलिकां वुधः।

Nala quoted by Cakrapani

73. Mudga Vesavaro - Susruta Samhita Su. 46.399.

74. Utkarika - Caraka, Ci. 2, Sweets prepared with milk treacle and *ghee*.
75. Vartika - Sweets in the form of a roll.
76. Patanjali on Panini 11.1.1. & 111.1. 122.
77. Vagbhata I mentions five varieties of sugar cane:

    Paundraka, Vamsika, Sataparvaka, Kantara and Naipala and considers the juice extracted with the help of a machine unwholesome.

    Astanga Samgraha Su. VI. 83-85.

    Phanita-Angavijja, p. 182, Amarakosa II. 9.43

    Astanga Samgraha VI.86

    Guda - Angavijja, p. 181, Vayu Purana 105.34, Astanga Samgraha Su. VI.88,

    Matsyaudika - Angajja, p. 181, Amarkosa-II.9.43, Astanga Samgraha Su. VI. 88, Malavikagnimitra II, p. 42.

    Astanga Hridaya V.49.

    Khanda - Astanga Samgraha VI. 88, Vayu Purana 105.34

    Sarkara - Angavijja, p. 181, Kurma Purana 25, Amarkosa II.9.43 Harsacarita, p. 156.

    Sita (sugar candy) - Amarkosa II.9.43, Astanga Hridaya V.49.
78. शकरेक्षु विकाराणां फाणितं च वरावरे।

    Astanga Samgraha Su. VI.98
79. Palala Sarkara (red sugar)

    Karka Sarkara - white sugar, Harsacarita, p.156.
80. Astanga Hridaya V.50.
81. *Gudavikara* denotes all sweets prepared with guda (Rtusamhara V.16) and Khandakhadyaka, those with unrefined sugar.

    जलानुपानं वा खण्डखाद्यकमन्यद्धा प्रकृतिसात्म्य युक्तमुभावप्युपयु ञ्जीयाताम्।

    Kamasutra IV. 10.16.
82. Madhulajah - Kamandaka VII.52

    Krsara-Matsya-Puranam 268.6.30

    Modakas (sweet balls) - were generally prepared with rice or wheat-flour mixed with sugar, some spices and slices of kernel of coconuts-Vikram. III.65.75;

    Angavijja Mrcchakatika V.98;

    Malavika, p. 81; Abhijnana Sakuntalam, p.62; Matsya Purana-268.6.30

Samyava-Kurma Purana II.17

Phenaka-Angavijja 182: Fine sweet cakes prepared with powdered wheat-flour.

Payasa-Mateya Purana. 268.6-30, Raghuvamsa X.51.54

Ghritapura - Vayu Purana 80.47

Abnyusa - Amarakosa II.9.47

Gudaudana - Mrcchakatika 1.8, Matsya Purana 268.6-30.

Utkarika was a sweet preparation with rice flour, milk, treacle and clarified butter.

Angavijja 182, Natyasastra III.36-39. Divyavadana 500-23.

83. Morendaka-Angavijja, p. 182.

84. घृत सक्तुकान्वितम् द्रव्यम् विमर्दकम्

Astanga Hridaya. Uttaradhyayana Sutra. 39.

85. Locika - Natya Sastra III. 36-39

Istaka भक्ष्यान् वक्ष्ये करम्भञ्च इष्टका घृतपूरकाः।

A *Vayapurana 80.47*

Vitanaka-Matsya Purana 268.6.30

Polika - *Ibid.*

86. यवॉकुरैः Raghuvamsam IX.43; *Ibid.*, VII.27.

87. Rtusamhara III. 1.10.16, IV. 1, 8, 18, V.1, 16, Raghuvamsam XV. 78, XVII.53.

88. Raghuvamsam IV.37; Kumarasambhavam V.47.

89. Sak. p. 94.

90. Rtusamhara V.16.

91. एदं खु सीहुपाणुव्बेजिदस्स मच्छण्डिआ उवणदा

Malavikagnimitra, p.48.

92. मोदक Vikramonase, p. 75; मोदखण्डिआए

Malavikagnimitra, p. 81, मोदखण्डिआए Sak, p. 62;

खण्डमोदअसरिसोअ Vikramorvase, p. 65.

93. Raghuvamsam II.63.

94. नवनीत Malavikagnimitra, p. 57

95. हैयंगवीन Raghuvamsam I.45.

96. सिहरिणी Vikramonasii, p. 71.

97. Raghuvamsam, X. 51.54.

98. Kumarasambhavam VIII.72
99. मत्स्यण्डिका नाम शर्कराविशेष Malavikagnimitra p. 42.
100. M.R. Kale : Malavikagnimitra, notes.
101. Vik., p. 65.
102. एलालवंगकर्पूरादिसुरभिद्रव्यमिश्रितं दुग्धेन सह गलितं सिलासंगलं दधिशिखरिणी त्युच्यते, Vik., p. 71.
103. दध्यतिरिक्त पर्वोक्तद्रव्यमिश्रितः पक्वकदलीफ्लान्तः सरोडपि तत्पदैवाच्यः *Ibid.*
104. Ku. VII. 72.
105. Raghu. XI.69, Ku.VI.50.
106. Ku. VII.72.
107. मृतश्च पञ्चमादूर्ध्वमव्रतः सव्रतोडपिवा।
पायसेन गुडेनापि पिण्डान् दद्याद् दशक्रमात्।

Garuda Purana 10.96

गुडाद्यं शान्तिमाप्नोति क्षीरेण च तथायुतम्।
पद्मरागसमं वर्ण चांशुमत्याः प्रजायते।

Vishnudharmottara Purana II.63.8

गुडशर्करमत्स्यण्ड्यो देयं फाण्तिमुर्मुरम्।
गव्यं पयो दधि घृतं तैलञ्च तिलसंभवम्।

Brahma Purana

108. मक्षिकागर्भसंभूतबालाण्डविनिपीडनात्।
जातं मधुकथंसन्तः सेवन्ते कललाकृतिः।

Yasatilaka, p.331.

109. Ravisena - Jaina Padma Purana Ch. II.
110. अमीभिराकण्ढमभोजि तद्गृहे तुषारधारा मृदितेवशर्करा।

Naisadha XVI.93

111. Sukraniti IV.3.143.
112. ता केर उण कंसारतालपुड्ड संजुयविसमोयगं गोसे
उवणेमिणएयाणम्। *Samaraicca, p.187*
सुसंमिऔ------------कासारो Ibid., 189
कसारं सुसारं सुहाली मणुज्जा *Bhavisayatta XII.3*
गोधूमचर्णादिद्धृत्य शूर्पेणाभ्याहतान् कणान्। 86।
दुग्धाक्तान घृतपक्वांश्च सितया च विमिमिश्रतान्।

एलामरिचचूर्णेन युक्तान् कासारसंज्ञितान्।

Manasollasa III.1386-87

113. गोलकेन समावेष्ट्य तैलनोदुम्बरान् पचेत्।

Manasollasa III.1388

114. गुडमरिचैलामिश्रो गोधूमस्थूलचूर्णविकारः मुमुरः

Commentary Brahm Pu.

115 शोधितायां सितायां तु क्षीरं संमिश्रयेत् समम्। 15।
खरपाकावधिर्यावत् तल्क्वाथयेत् पुनः।
उत्तार्य नागरं तीक्ष्णमेलाकर्पूरकसैरः। 16।
निक्षिप्य गोलकाः कार्या नाम्ना वर्षोलकास्तु ते।

Manasollasa III.1415-17

अवर्षिवर्षोपलगोलकावली *Naisadha XVI.103*

एलाकर्पूरशर्करालवडगतण्डुलपिष्टरचितानां गोलकानामतिवृतानांलड्डुक विशेषाणाम्।

Commentry on the above.

116. Naisadha XV.104.

117. घेउरापिवचहुत्तरिय खंडयाचाउजाय।
सुहपाय मडियसोय्वट्टि फिणौओमंडिया।

Vitasavati. Kathakosa Prakarana-Salibhadra, p. 58

भोयणभुंजाविउसुहचारिहिं छडरसलड्डुअखंडपयारिहिं

Bhavisayatta V.II

Naisadha XVI.103

118. पायसं शालिमुद्गाढ्यं मोदकादींश्च भक्तितः।
पूरिकाश्च रसालाश्च गोक्षीरञ्च नियोजयेत्।

Brahma Puranam

119. दुग्धमुत्क्वाध्य तन्मध्ये तक्रमम्लं विनिक्षिपेत्। 8।
हित्वा तोयं घनीभूतं वस्त्रबद्धं पृथक्कृतम्।
शालितण्डुलपिष्टेन मिश्रितम् परिपेषितम्। 9।
नानाकारैः सुघटितं सर्पिषा परिपाचितम्।
पक्वशर्करया सिक्तमेलाचूर्णेन वासितम्।
क्षीरप्रकारनामेदं भक्ष्यं मृष्यं मनोहरम्।

Manasollasa III.1408-1411

120. Agni Purana Ch.164.
121. Y.T. 28.11-17.
122. Y.T. 28.3.7.
123. Y.T. 16.143-147.
124. Y.T. 16.149.
125. Y.T. 16.150-152.
126. निस्तुषां भाषा डाली कां द्विस्त्रिः तु पेषयेत्।
शिलायां पिष्टिकामेतां नवनौतेन संयुताम्।
गाठ वस्त्र मयः पोतच्छिद्रिता पूरित स्तथा।
ध्रामयेच्च घृते तप्ते तं निष्पौड्य तु वर्तलाम्।
सिद्धां निष्कास्य सितया सतां मर्दयेत् करे।

Y.T. 16.153-157

127. शमिता मष्टमशिन सर्पिषा मोदिता पुनः।
मर्दितामम्वसा पश्चाद्विर्तियां काण्ठ पट्टेक। 159।
नतिस्थूल कृशान्सेवां स्तलितान् पाकिस्तान्पुनः।
खण्ड पाकेन तान् पम्चाद् वध्गीयात् पिण्डवद् बुक्षः। 160।

Y.T. 16.159-60

128. Y.T. 16.161-64.
129. Y.T. 16.165-66.
130. Y.T. 16.173-74.
131. Y.T. 16.180-84.
132. Y.T. 16.196-98.
133. Y.T. 16.2033.
134. Y.T. 16.199.
135. Y.T. 16.212.
136. Y.T. 16.227-28.
137. शमितां सर्पिषा भृष्टां सिसैलादि समन्विताम्।
क्षिप्तवान्य शमिता लम्ब यूटे संग्रथितानने। 210।
घृते पचेयतः खण्डे रसौ भूतेन पाक्येत्।
गुहाकः वृंह्णे वृष्यो हृद्यः पितानिलापहः। 211।

Y.T. 210-11

138. Y.T. 16.220-22.
139. द्वि प्रस्था शुद्ध समिता चतुभोधूम गालिता।
विमर्ध पयसा स्थाप्य या वकवलत्व भाजेयात्।

सिद्धद्धे नाअिकेलस्थ पात्रतत्पकमाहरेत्।
परिभ्राम्य धृते तप्ते पचंन्तन्मन्द वहिनना।
सुपक्वां कंकणाकारां सिता लेहे विनिक्षिपेत्।
सातु कुण्डलिका नान्ना च्वाचिज जलबाल्लका।

Y.T. 16.216-19

140. Y.T. 16.68-69.
141. Y.T. 18.187-88.
142. Y.T. 189-93.
143. Y.T. 16.189-93.
144. Y.T. 16.184-85.
145. Y.T. 16.185-86.
146. Y.T. 16.194-95.
147. Y.T. 126-28.
148. Y.T. 129-30.
149. Y.T. 16.156-57.
150. Y.T. 16.223-26.
151. Poet Jayasi mentioned about the feast of Barat Party of Ratansen Padmawati.

पहिलें भात परोसै आने। जनहू कपूर सूबास बसाने।। 1।
झालर माड आए धिउ पोए। उजर देखिँ पाप गए धोए।। 2 ।।
लचुई पूरि सोहारौं परीं। एक ताती और सुठि कोंवरीं।। 3 ।।
पुनि बाबन परकार जो आए। ना अस देखे नं कबहुं खाए।। 4।।
खँडरा खूँडि खँडोई खंडी । परी एकोतर सै कठहंडी।। 5 ।।
पुनि सधान आए बहु साधे। दूध दही के मोरडा बांधे।। 6 ।।
पुनि जाउरि पछियाउरि आई। दूध दही का कहौं मिठाई।। 7।।
जवन अधिक सबासिक मुख मह परत बिलाई।
सहस सवाद सौ पावै एक कवर जौं खाई।।

Jayasi, 2012 : 271

4

Cultural Significance of Indian Sweetmeats

Sweets are closely associated with our culture. From time immemorial, they have been required during several occasions and liked by people of all age groups and all castes. Not only that, even some particular sweets are the favourite offerings of God. Sweets are also used as *prasad, sargahi*[1] and *phalahari*[2] during fastings and festivals. In some rituals/ *samaskaras* sweets are one of the essential things. Nowadays it is observed that sweets have become essentials in almost all the *samaskaras.* It is also a symbol of good omen on several occasions. People distribute sweets after getting success in examinations, competitions, and services, after finalization of marriage, birth of a baby and the like. In olden days when people visited their relatives or friends houses, they were welcomed by washing feet and giving a piece of jaggery and water. In modern times this custom seems to have been replaced by only serving a cup of tea or coffee.

Sweets as Favourite Offerings to Gods

For thousands of years, the Hindus have sought to please the gods and goddesses by showing their devotion through the offerings of sweet-dishes. It is necessary as part of the rituals connected with the worship of a particular deity to offer some kind of food. This offering is usually called as *Bhoga,* mainly of sweetmeats or any other sweet items. After the symbolic feeding to the deity, the priest and the devout take the food offered as *Prasad* (consecrated food). The Devi Bhagata Purana (IV) describes Brahman in the form of Devi the Goddess. When she is discerned in the Manipura Lotus, or the naval centre of the body, it says that she takes the form of *Lakini* who is fond of sweetmeats and does good to all. Hence the scriptures assure the devotee that sweet food is a welcome offering at all times. Puja, the private daily act of worship, is central to Hindu life. Along with incense, flowers and fruits, sweets are an important part of the offerings to the god, goddess or chosen idol of the worshipper. 'Indeed, the worshipper's idea of the sacred is said to reside in the centre of a sea of nectar, the thousand-petalled lotus where the *atman* (individual self) and the cosmic self (Brahman) are seen as one. This union is frequently compared to the taste of honey or *amrita* (some divine nectar) (Maria, 1980).

The *amrita* gives its name to the special offering and libation made by the priests. It is used to bathe an image or object during the Puja. Such an *amrita* is usually made from five ingredients such as honey, milk, *ghee,* sugar and water and is known as *panchāmrita.* Some times the feet of holy persons are washed in the *panchāmrita* as a form of worship.

Although most sweets are made all the year round, some holidays require that a special dish shall be made for that day and some have become, in the course of time, associated with certain gods or goddesses. They like these particular dishes served on their special days. For example, *Agrayanam* or *Navannapornima* is the full moon day on which the new harvest food was to be tasted. On this day the family deities are offered special worship at which the Goddess Lakshmi always presides. Rice is boiled with milk and sugar to make *payas* or *kheer* which is then offered to Lakshmi and the family deities. Then it will be eaten as the special dainty of the day. 'Jaggery, *payasam, ghee, appam, modakam,* curds, dal, all these are to be offered as food to the gods (*naivadiyam*)' (Lord Krishna in Skanda XI, Bhagavata Purana). Some couplets which are chanted at the time of offering *naivadiyam* run as follows:

Ganesh

शर्कराघृत संयुक्तं मधुरं स्वादुयोत्तमम्।

उपहारं समायुक्तं नैवेद्यं प्रतिगृह्यताम्।

(*Naivedya* made of sugar and clarified butter, which is sweet and tasteful, be taken as presents.)

Vishnu (Lakshmi Narayan)

घृते पक्वं हव्यियान्नं पायसं च सशर्करम्।

नानाविधं च नैवेद्यं विष्णो में प्रतिगृह्यताम्।

(O! Vishnu, please accept the *kheer* made from *ghee* and various kinds of *naivedya* made from milk and sugar.)

Durga

अन्नं चतुविधं स्वादु रसः षडभिः समन्वितम।

नैवेद्यं गृह्यतां देवि भक्ति में ह्यचला कुरू।।

(O Goddess! Please accept the food having fourfold taste and containing six types of juice as *naivedya* and make my devotion fruitful.)

It is customary to offer *modaka* to Goddess Durga. The couplet given below, is chanted at the time of offering *modaka*:

मोदकं स्वादुसंयुकं शर्करादिविनिम्भितम्।

मा नवेदितं भवत्या गृहाणाी परमेश्वरि।।

(O Goddess! I am ardently offering tasteful *laddu* made of *shakkar* (sugar) please accept it.)

It is found that some gods are associated with particular sweetmeats and people always offer the same such as *mukdal* for Bajrangbali, *Motichur Laddu* for Ganesh.

About one hundred years ago, people offered only those *naivedya* which were prepared at their own homes. People prepared the *bhoga* with full devotion and faith. The utensils used were made of brass and clean, and not used for daily purpose.

Halder (1391 B.S.: pp. 52-53) mentioned the name of sweetmeats, prepared specially for *bhoga*.

Takti (Thawa Gaja) : The shape is in the form of square. The thickness is about one inch. It was prepared by *maida* and fried in *ghee*. These fried ingredients were poured in *chasni* (hot sugar juice) and after some time left in air for drying.

Peraki : It is semilunar in shape and chips of coconut cooked in syrup of sugar are filled in and fried in *ghee*.

Magdha Ka Laddu : Sujji is cooked in ghee (not a little quantity of water is mixed). Sugar and almond colour is mixed in hot state. After that Laddu is prepared. In hot state sugar serves as gum and in cooler state it becomes hard. That is why the *laddu* is not broken and it lasts for several days.

Jhumko Gaja : Thin and long pieces of kneaded *maida* is prepared and folded three or four times, then fried in *ghee*. After that it is cooked in sugar syrup.

Kotkate : Kneaded *maidā* is rolled into flat bread shape but about 1/2 inch in thickness. *Moyam* (mixing of clarified butter with flour before kneading to make it more soft) is mixed in small quantity. Then cutting it into small rectangular shape it is fried in *ghee*. Finally it is boiled in sugar juice. It is hard as the Moyam is mixed in small quantity. For eating it is grinded by teeth.

Mahabir and *Mahadeva* are propitiated with sweets (*laddu*), fried gram (*ghunghuri*) and sweet cakes in the month of *Sawan*. *Sitala Mata* is worshipped with an offering of sweets (*batasha*) besides other things.

A french author Bhattacharya (1983), while working on the article on 'The dishes and the cooking in the *Candi Mangala*' gave an idea about the meals desired by different deities. Besides other things, list of sweets are also mentioned there. The sweets such as *khanda* (molasses or brown sugar), *khiri* (also said *rabadi*) with thickened milk and *amrta manda* (round sweetmeats), *Khirapuli* (of thickened milk), *Khirakhanda* (round sweetmeats with thickened milk), *chenā nadu* (also called *chanā*) round sweetmeats with casein, *padmachena* (sweetmeat with sweetened casein) are desired by deities Siva and Vishnu respectively.

The Goddess Annapurna feeds her husband and her sons with *palanna* 'a dish of rice, sugar, clarified butter, aromatic spices and fish or meat' which are cooked together for a long time by steam.

Moreover, the variety of sweetmeats, mentioned in the case of the God of Puri even if they are always prepared with milk, contrast with the unique characteristic of the dessert of Siva.

In villages of north Bihar people offered *Rota* (made of wheat flour made by quern and jaggery) to their *Gramdevata* (family deities) on several occasions such as *mundan, yagopawit,* marriage and the like.

Sweets and Festivals

Festivals, whether religious, social or seasonal, have played an important part in the life of the Indian people. Hindus celebrate hundreds of sacred occasions with festive observances. Religious festivals in honour of various deities have been mentioned in ancient Indian literature and epigraphs.[3] Religious and secular literature and inscriptions provide a mine of information about the innumerable socio-religious festivals which were held throughout the year in honour of various gods and goddesses, Nature Gods connected with trees, mountains, rivers, *nagas, bhutas, pishachas, chaityas,* stupas, etc.

On festival days, prayers were offered and sacrifices were

made to please the deities. Similarly in *Yajanas,* milk food, clarified butter, flesh and *somarasa* (a kind of drink) were offered to appease the gods.

Hindus use the moon-calendar where months are calculated according to the phase of the moon and are therefore moveable. Apart from the regular festivals which are celebrated according to the moon calendar, there is no calendar regulating the festivals or forms of worship for the village deities. In villages where there is a permanent shrine, offerings of rice, fruit, sweets and flowers, with incense and camphor, are made every day by the villagers.

The important festivals in which sweets are required are given below according to moon-calendar.

Chaitra-Purnamasi or Pajuno-Puno

The *Chaitra-Purnamasi* festival is mainly observed in the month of *Chaitra*(April-May) on *Sukla Paksha Purnima* (full-moon day of fortnight of the waxing moon). This festival is celebrated only on the houses with sons. In these festivals, after painting the five or seven small pitchers with lime or gypsum oil, sweetmeats or victuals which are fried in clarified butter are filled in the pitchers. Among these pitchers, one is treated as *karwa* and others are simple. The characteristics of *karwa* pitcher is that on that pitcher, the picture of Pajun Kumar and both his mothers are sketched. It is the custom to put only *laddus* on *Karwa* pitcher. After ending the rituals, the son brings out *laḍḍus* from *Karwā* pitcher and offers his mother. Afterwards the mother first gives the *laddu* to her son and then distributes them among other members of the family. At the time of distribution, following lines are chanted:

"पजनं के लडुआ पजनै खायँ। दौरि दौरि वहि कोठरी में जायँ।"

Vata-savitri

The Vata-savitri festival is celebrated in the month of *Jaistha* (May-June) *Amavasya* (last of the dark half of the month).[4] It is celebrated only by the married Hindu women for the sake of the longivity of their husbands. On the festival day they worship the *Veta* (Banyan) tree. They also observe fast till the *Puja* is over. The women take some articles of the worship for breaking their fast and happily return to their respective homes. Sweets are distributed to all the family members and neighbours.

Naga Panchami

The festival of *Naga Panchami* is celebrated in the month of *Shravana* (July-August) on *Shukla Panchami* (fifth day of the fortnight of the waxing moon).

शेषदीनां फणीशानां पञ्चभ्या पूजनं भवेत

(Sharma, 1978).

Rajgir in Bihar was a great centre of Naga worship in ancient times. On this day, people observe fast and worship Nagas (Cobras). The devotees offer milk, *kheer* (puddings), *panchamrita* (a mixture consisting of milk, curd, sugar, honey and clarified butter) and lotus flower to cobra. The Nagas were worshipped with perfumes, lamps sweets and flowers.

Rakshabandhan

The *Rakshabandhan* festival is celebrated specially in northern India in the month of *Shravana* (July-August) *Purnima*. Girls and married women tie a *rakhi* (wrist band) made of a few twisted golden or simple yellow threads, on the wrist of the right hand of their brothers, for their welfare and also for protection from any evil influence. Before tying the *rakhi* the sisters put *tilak* (a mark made on the forehead) to their brothers and after tying the rakhi, they give sweets to brothers and in return receive cash and gifts. This strengthens the bond of love between brothers and sisters.

Teej

The festival of *teej* is celebrated in the month of *Bhado* (August-September) on the third day of *Sukla Paksha*. This festival is also known as *haritalika*. It is purely a festival for girls and women in the honour of Goddess Parvati, the divine consort of Lord Siva. After doing the worship of the deities of Siva-Parvati the women give alms such as sweets, cloth, goods of prosperity and *Dakshina* to a priest in a small basket made of bamboo. The Narada Purana states that on this occasion, a married woman should observe fast and offer food and other presents to a Brahman; as by doing so she would attain great religious merit (Sharma, 1978).

Ganesa Chaturthi

This festival also known as *Vinayaka Chaturthi* is celebrated on the fourth day of *Sukla Paksha* in the month of *Bhadra* (August-September) in the honour of Lord Ganesa, one of the five major deities of Hinduism. On *Ganesa Chaturthi* day, people wake up early in the morning and after bath they collect various articles for the worship of Vinayaka. Then at midday, they worship the image of God made of clay with various offerings including sweet-balls. In Ganesa Puja there is a provision of twenty-one *laddus*. Among the twenty-one, five are offered to the deity, five given to the priest and the rest are distributed among the family members (Shastri, 1966). Later the beautifully decorated images are taken out in processions to the accompaniment of religious songs and music. These images are worshipped regularly for several days for gaining the blessings of the God and later they are immersed in the river. *Modakas* (sweet-balls) are distributed as *prasada* (food offered to an idol) on the occasion of the worship.

On the fourth day of *Bhadrapad* (August-September), *Ganesh Chaturthi*, the festival of Ganesh is celebrated. The elephant-headed God of knowledge and success is worshipped with great splendour, especially in the Mumbai. *Laddus* and sweets made of gram flour, are offered to the image of the God of plenty, in memory of the story of his creation (Maria, 1980).

Rishi Panchmi

It is celebrated in the month of *Bhadon* on *Shukla Panchmi*. Generally it is celebrated by the women but if in any circumstances the woman does not observe, it can be observed by her husband. After doing the worship of seven rishis[5] the sweets and puddings are given to Brahmins as alms and fast is observed with a diet of fruits.

Ananta Chaturdashi

This festival is observed in the month of *Bhadon* (August-September) on *Chaturdashi* (the fourteenth day of a lunar month) of *Sukla Paksh*.It is celebrated in honour of Lord Vishnu who as *seshasayin* rests on the great serpent *seshanaga* in the milky ocean with his consort Lakshmi massaging his feet. People observe fast on the festival day and offer fruits and sweets to the image of the God, while women sing religious songs. After the worship is over, the fast is broken and *prasada* is distributed to all. Generally people take their food at only one time. The food is without salt and vermicelli is specially eaten that day. (Konhyaju, 1945).

Kojagar Vrata

This festival is observed in the month of *Asvina* (September-October) on *Sukla Purnima* in the honour of Goddess Mahalakshmi and Devraj Indra. After doing the worship, devotees give food, i.e. *rasawar* (rice cooked in the juice of sugar cane or *Shakkar*) to worthy Brahmins.

Sharat Purnima

On *Sharat Purnima* night, people put the *kheer* (which is made of milk, rice and *guda*) in the courtyard and offer to moon and eat this offering on the next day morning. It is believed that by taking this *kheer* people will get free from diseases.

Karwachoth

The *Karwachoth* festival is observed in all Hindu families exclusively by married women on *Krishna Chaturthi* in the month of *Kartika* (October-November). On this day, people give alms to Brahmins. The alms containing ten small earthen pots full of *laddus* and the mouth of each pot is covered by *apupa* (sweet cake) and other sweetmeats. 'On this festive occasion, the mother blesses her married daughter and presents her ornaments, garments and sweetmeats' (Sharma, 1978). 'On this occasion after doing the worship of Siva and Parvati she offers thirteen *laddus,* one *Lota* and cloth to the parents of her husband' (Shastri, 1966).

Narak Chaturdasi

It is celebrated in the month of *Kartika* on the day of *Krishna Chaturdashi* on the festival day, the *Ramayana* and *Hanuman Chalisa* are recited in homes and people observe strict celebacy and fast. People offer *apupa,* banana, *laddu,* guava, etc., to deity *Hanuman.*

Diwali

Diwali, a distortion of the Sanskrit word *Dipawali,* literally means a row of lights, is performed in the Hindi month of *Kartika.* The festival of lights is observed annually in honour of Goddess Lakshmi. It is not only observed by Hindus but on this occasion Muslims and Christians too often exchange greetings and sweets.

Patashas (sugar puffs of sorts) made from sugar and *kheer* (rice cooked in milk and sugar) are used to decorate the *hatris,* or these are placed in *thalis.* The *patashas* symbolize the coming harvest of sugar cane, the puffed rice the paddy crop. Animals, gods and goddesses made from sugar (often elegant white and edible sculptures) are sold in the market for children.

For the women, it is a busy week when sweets have to be prepared, decorations made, the house cleaned, extra special food made. Diwali climaxes in the fireworks after the *puja* and after the distribution of sweets and dinner.

On this night, when the people of rest of India worship Lakshmi, the Bengalis worship Kali, spectacular images of Kali are installed, adorned and worshipped. In West Bengal, there is a spontaneous display of sweets in heaps on all sides, preparations for which are begun long time in advance.

For the Jains, Diwali is equally auspicious. The Jains

celecrate on this day the *Nirvana* of Lord Mahavir, their 24th Tirthankar (guru). Pavapuri, 60 kilometres from Patna where Lord Mahavir attained *Nirvana* at the age of 72 years, attracts pilgrims from all parts of the country, who come to pay homage to him and offer him *laddus* (sweets made of gram flour).

The devotees from West Bengal, Gujarat, Karnataka, Maharashtra and other places, far and near, also assemble in Pavapuri, to pay their homage with offerings of *laddus* and flowers at the lotus feet of their Great Master, enshrined in the temple.

Both Digambaras and Svetambaras reach there in the later half of the night carrying bowls of *laddus* and stay there till the early dawn of the next day. Several *maunds* (about 37 kg = 1 *maund*) of sweets are thus offered to the footprints of Mahavira,which are later on distributed as *prasāda* to all the devotees assembled there.

Annakut

This festival is celebrated on the second day of Diwali, i.e., on *Kartik Sukla Pratipada.* People make Govardhan mountains by cow dung. Cows are also decorated on this day. They offer sweets. All possible offerings are made on this day. The shape of the offerings look like a mountain as signified by the name itself.

Bhaiya Duja

This festival is observed on the third day after Diwali (i.e. second day of *Kartik Sukla).* This festival is known by different names in different States such as in Maharashtra it is known as *Bhau Beej*, in Gujarat *Bhai Beej*, in West Bengal *Bhai Photā* and in north India *Bhartridvitiya*. On this day, a sister anoints her brother's forehead with turmeric and prays to God for his good health and welfare and feed their brothers specially various kinds of sweetmeats, who in their turn present ornaments and clothes to them. Jimutavahana in his *Kavyaviveka* also describes this festival, when sisters fed their brothers, who gave jewellery and garments to their sisters. In *Bhai phota* which is a festival observed by the sisters for the longivity of their brothers, sweets constitute the main item offered.

Chhaṭha Festival

The *Chhatha* festival is celebrated twice a year, in the month of *Kartika* and *Chait* (March-April). The *Chhaṭha* festival is very popular for the worship of Surya (Sun God). In Bihar celebrations at the sun temple situated in village Surajpur Baragaon, adjacent to the famous Nalanda ruins are famous. The offerings containing many sweet items such as *thekua* or *khabauni* (made of wheat-flour and jaggery or sugar), *khāzā* are offered to God in a *sup* (winnowing basket made of bamboo), water mixed with *Ganga-Jal* (The Ganges water) or, milk with flowers is offered to the sun God, by the worshippers, while facing the east.

Devuthan Ekadashi

Devuthan Ekadashi is observed in the month of *Kartika* (October-November) on *Sukla Ekadashi* (the eleventh day in the fortnight of a lunar month or fortnight of the waxing moon), when women specially fast and burn ten cow-dung cakes in the evening. When this fire gets extinguished by itself, the fast is broken by taking of sumptuous food. Some new products of the season like potatoes, sugar cane, sweets and *singhara* are also put at the place of worship. The festival is specially celebrated with great joy in the villages, because on this day, the farmers and peasants enjoy the produce of their fields and particularly sugar cane for the first time in the season.

Sakata Chautha

The festival of *Sakata Chautha* is observed in the month of *Magha* (January-February) on the fourth day of *Krishna Paksha* in the honour of Lord Ganesh. The women observe a fast and offer Him fruits, flowers and sweets. *Laddus* are must in the offering as Ganeshji likes them. At some places mixture of *tila* (the seeds of sesamum plant) and *guda* are also offered to God.

Makara Sankranti

The *Makara Sankranti* is celebrated with great religious fervour on the full moon day in the month of *Magha* (January-February). *Sankranti* means a planet's passage from one sign of zodiac to another. When sun reaches Capricorn from *dhanu* (the ninth sign of the zodiac), it becomes *makar-sankranti.* It is the time when the sun enters the monsoon of capricornus. Bathing at the Ganges and giving alms has a great importance on this day. People give alms of *til ka laddu* and *khichari* (a dish prepared from rice and pulse boiled together). In north Bihar, people eat beaten rice, curd, *tilwa* (a kind of sweetmeat which is prepared from fried sesamum seeds and sugar), *tilkut* (a sweet cake prepared from sesamum seeds) in the day-time and *khichari* in the night.

Holi

This festival is celebrated in the month of *Phalguna* (February-March). This festival is greatly enjoyed by all without any distinction of caste and sex. People exchange sweetmeats (specially *apupa*) and the friends embrace each other and apply dry colour (*gulal*) or wet colour to each other all old and young wish a good luck to each other. In West Bengal this festival is known as *Dolyatra.*

Sunday Fasting

Besides the festivals described above, there are certain rituals performed by the individuals where we find the references of sweet-dishes and sweetmeats. Most of the people observe fast on week days. Among them, Sunday, Monday, Tuesday and Saturday are more popular. The Sunday festival is observed from the health point of view specially skin diseases. The name of the Sun God is different for every month and the *Ardhya,* offerings and *Prashan* are also different, only those months are given in Table 4.1 in which any kind of sweets are mentioned.

Table 4.1
Month, Name and Offerings to Sun God

Month	*Name of the Sun*	*Ardhya*	*Offering*	*Prashan*
Chaitra	Bhanu	Pomegranate	*Malpua*	Milk (three *chhatak*)[6]
Ashwin	Hiranayareta	Pomegranate	*Guda*	Three handful *guda*
Kartika	Diwakar	Banana	*Kheer*	Three handful *kheer*

Purushotam Mas

It is celebrated in the month in which *Sanskriti* is not held. This festival is also known as *Adhimas* and *Malsmas. Purushotam Mas* festival is observed for the whole month. In the end of this festival, people give alms in a brass pot containing thirty *apupas* and other sweets.

Nava Varsha Festival

The *Nava Varsha* is the New Year's day festival of West Bengal, which is celebrated every year with great rejoicing in the month of *Vaisakha* (April 14). Colourfully dressed people come out from all walks of life in a joyous mood and greet each other and distribute sweetmeats.

Sweets Used During Samskaras

The *samskaras* express beliefs, sentiments and knowledge of the ancient Hindus about the nature of human life and the universe and their relation with the superhuman powers that were supposed to guide or control the destiny of mankind. There is a mixture of religious and secular factors in the *samskaras,* though they have all assumed a religious garb in course of time.

Here only those *samskaras* are mentioned in which sweet-dishes or sweetmeat are essential for completing the performances.

Jatakarma

Immediately after birth and before the cut of the umbilical cord a ceremony called Jatakarma (the ceremonies for the new born child) is performed. During this ceremony, the child is made to taste honey, clarified butter and gold, all the while the sacred texts are being chanted.

प्राड्नाभिवर्डवनात् पुंसो जातकर्म्म विधीयते।
मन्त्रवत् प्राशनश्चस्य हिरण्यमधुसर्पिषाम्।।29।।

Goswami and Ray, 1910:83.

(The *Jatakarma* should be done before cutting of the umbilical cord. The *Annaprashan* should be performed by sanctifying the mixture of jaggery, honey and clarified butter with *mantras.*)

In *Manavagrhyasutra* it is mentioned that on this day having (poured out) sour milk, honey and water in the remainder of the *ghee,* he (father) makes the boy eat (from it) thrice, after having taken out (three portions) by means of a piece of gold.[7]

According to Hindu polity (The Ordinances of Manu), before cutting the umbilical cord of a male (child), the birth rite is ordained (to be performed), and he (must) eat honey and *ghee* in a gold spoon to the accompaniment of mantras (Hopkins, 1972).

During ancient times (2008 BC to AD 700) the expectant mother was persuaded to take some special precautions including abstaining from eating dishes which were too hot or too cold, too sweet or too bitter. At the onset of the fifth month of pregnancy, the future father offered his wife the 'five ambrosias' to eat, a mixture of sugar, honey, milk, *ghee* and curds that was the traditional offering to guests. Meanwhile a mixture of *ghee,* honey, water and curds was being hastily prepared so that the lips of the new-born baby might be moistened with it. When the child appeared, and before the umbilical cord was cut, the father bent over him and breathed on him three times while invoking the Vedas. Then in the presence of those assisting at birth, he touched him and offered him, in a golden spoon, the honey mixture which had been specially prepared wishing his son wisdom(Veda), prosperity, long life, intelligence, physical power and the protection of the gods (Auboyer, 1965).

Namakarana (The giving of a name)

Manavagrhyasutra referred that 'He (the father) should eat neither honey nor flesh until the *Pasubandhu*. KGS XXXVI.13 has: mamsam tu nasnitah; Dev says that this precept is valid for a year. c.f. VGS III.7 *Samvatsaram matatpitarau na mamsam asniyatam.* (Dresden, 1941).

Annaprasana

Feeding the child with solid food is the next important stage in the life of the child. *Annaprasana* was connected with the satisfaction of the physical needs of the child. This fact is endorsed by Susruta who prescribes the weaning of a child in the sixth month and describes the types of food[8] to be given.

षण्मासं चैनमन्नं प्राशयेल्लघुहितं च।

Sugruta Sarirasthana Ch. 10.64

(One should feed the child in the sixth month with light and suitable food.)

According to *Manavagrhyasutra* having cooked a mess of rice in milk in the fifth or sixth month (after the birth of the child), having washed and adorned (the boy) and having dressed (him) in a new garment and having made an oblation with the verse.[9]

Karnavedha

The *Karnavedha* ceremony described in *Katyayana-Sutra* is very simple. On an auspicious day, the ceremony was performed. The child was seated facing towards east and given some sweetmeats. The ceremony closed with the feasting of Brahmans (Paraskara- *Grhyasutra,* Brigista *karna-vedha sutras* 1, 2).

Diksas Observances

At the time of this *Samskara* he (the father) should cause Brahmins to partake of cakes (a kind of sweet delicate bread) smeared with *ghee* (Ibid).

Agrahayanni karma :

The rite (to be performed) on the days of full moon in the month of *Agrahayana* (November-December).

After having cooked on the day of full moon in milk, he makes (four) oblations therefrom, while pronouncing the four verses (Ibid).

Nabhyani (The Nabhya Sacrifices)

There are three Nabhya sacrifices, i.e., on the days of full moon in the month of *Phalguna* (February-March), in the month of *Asadha* (June-July) and in the month of *Kartika* (October-November). On these days a mess of rice is cooked in milk and offered.

The rite performed on the day of full moon in the month of *Phalguna* is called as *Phalgunikarma.* On this day he (who is performing the sacrifice) should first sacrifice two cakes to Bhaga and Aryaman. A parallel for this rite is to be found in KGS LXX; in which text (LXX.1) one read:

atha phalgunyam tailapu pasya juhoti and in (LXX.2) *aryama devata.*

Sweets Used on Social Occasions

There are several social occasions when people are bound to distribute sweets, on demands of their relatives, neighbours, friends and colleagues. Important among them are such as after passing the examination, getting a job, on finalization of marriage, death of an old person, success of any type and the likes. There is a common saying connected with demanding the sweets, i.e., कब मुँह मीठा कराओगे in Hindu society and मुख मिष्टी कोरओ in Bengali society.

Besides this there are many occasions when people bring

sweets. At the time of *Chhatti* the kins of the newly born baby bring presentation, whatever the presentation is, it must be given along with sweetmeats. At the time of *mundan,* marriage and the like, the *nayothari* (invitee) have to bring *nayota,* in which there is sweetmeats besides other necessary things. On going to in-law's house people generally take sweetmeats. *Barat* party brings *petari* (basket) full of sweetmeats. After marriage of a girl, her parents send *puchhāri* to groom's house to call their daughter first time. That *Puchhari* contains clothes for the groom's relatives and some *petari* (a small basket made up of bamboo) full of sweetmeats (generally *khaza*). Similarly when groom comes to take his wife, from her parent's house, he also comes with *puchhari.* Sweetmeats are also distributed among neighbours as a *bainā* (sweetmeats, etc., sent to friends and relatives on marriage and other occasions). Generally when an elder person goes to the home of a younger person he also takes sweetmeats.

On the occasion of *Teej, Chhatha* and the likes, people send sweet-dishes or sweetmeats as a *Prasad* to their neighbours. In Bihar, it is known as *bainā*. On the occasion of Diwali (after finishing the *Lakshmi Puja* at night) the shopkeepers/businessmen distribute packets of sweetmeats to their favourite customers and colleagues. The quality and quantity of sweetmeats also signify the status of the owner of that shop.

In a feast or party, according to food habits, two types of people come viz.,vegetarian and non-vegetarian. Generally the menu contains sweet-dishes or sweetmeats besides other things. Sometimes the menu varies according to the food habits of the people. At that time non-vegetarian people take non-vegetarian meal, wheras the vegetarian people take sweet-dishes or sweetmeats in substitute of meat or fish.

The people whose economic condition is good, take sweet-dishes or sweetmeats regularly before or after every meal. It is also a prestige symbol. The importance and gravity of every festivity is to be measured by the quantity of sweets consumed, and that the wealth of the aristocracy is gauged by the length of days for which *Bhiyan* (having the sweets prepared at home by paid confectioners on ceremonial occasions) is continued without break.

For an inevitable journey, the following things should be eaten depending on the day [10] to neutralize the bad effect of the journey in a particular direction, e.g., a sweet-dish, jaggery is prescribed on Tuesday.

Generally it is observed that when a person goes to the officer's residence for personal interest or work, he goes with sweetmeats.

It is believed that, when a pregnant woman likes sweet-dishes, it is presumed that she will be the mother of a male child.

If a child has profuse secretions of saliva, they say, that the saliva of the child mixed with a sweetmeat should be administered to the mother to stop it.

In Bengali's families when the relatives of groom come to see the girl and finalize the marriage, the bride's party give them sweetmeats to eat. If they take it then it is understood that the marriage is finalized. The groom party also gives sweetmeats to the girl as a blessing (*ashirvad*). The same thing happens when the bride's party goes to see the groom.

On the occasion of Vijaya Dashmi, every family prepares *Naru* (a type of sweetmeat made of coconut and molasses) and distributes it among the neighbours. On January 14, of every year they prepare *pitha*. Honey is given as a symbol of good omen. When a newborn baby first comes home, from outside (in case delivery held at hospital). Bengali people distribute sweets on the first day of the year, i.e., *Pahala Baisakh*. On the occasion of *Bipati Tarini Durga* (which will be held every year, on either Monday or Saturday) (which comes first in between the starting and returning the *Rath yatra* in the month of *Asadha* (June-July) people make *apupa* and *kheer* and also distribute it among neighbours as a *prasad*. At the time of marriage, groom's party sends the materials of *gayeda haldi*, which contains the fish made of *khoa* and other sweets besides clothes and other necessary articles to the bride's home. When bride first goes to *sasural,* she must be accompanied with a *haria* (an earthen pot) full of *rassogollas.* Before sitting on the marriage *mandap,* the groom eats sweetmeats. After the occasion of *mala badal* (similar to *jaimal* in Hindu society) bride and groom both feed sweetmeats, to each other. On the occasion of *babu bhata,* the parent of bride send the sweetmeats particularly the fish made of *khoa* and *sandesh* on which some words like *sukhe thako* (be happy) are written, to groom's house. In villages, when any person comes from outside to his relatives, at first the host gives *murhi* (fried rice) and *guda* to guests. Now such type of traditions are on the verge of extinction.

In West Bengal when one visits to see the ill person, on that occasion they carry *sandesh* for them, because it is believed to be highly nutritious and easily digestible.

References

1. On the day of fasting, people eat some sweets or sweet-dishes in the early morning as a *sargahi.* It is accustomed that hereafter nothing can be taken till the end of fastings.
2. After the end of fasting people eat fruits and sweets (only *phalahari)* as first food.
3. According to Vatsyayana, besides the customary holidays people availed themselves of certain other occasions of festivity. These were *samaja, gosti, apanaka, udijanaka* and *Samsya Krida* (Gokhale, 1959:131).
4. Some people celebrate it on the *Dwadasi* or *Trayodasi* of *Krishna Paksha* (Fortnight of the waning moon). Generally in Northern India it is celebrated from *Trayodasi* to *Amavasya* in *Jaistha Krishna Paksha* and in South India, from *Trayodasi* to *Purnima* (the full moon day) of *Jaistha Sukla Paksha* but most of the people celebrate it on *Amavasya* or *Purnima.*
5. The seven rishis are Gautam, Bhardwaj, Vishwamitra, Jamdagni, Vasistha, Kashyap and Aatri.
6. *Chhatāk*-one sixteenth of seer or five tolas.
7. This Sutra contains the so called Prasana-ceremony, which takes place before the suckling by the mother. c.f. Hillebrandt, p. 45. Kath and Vav. give a somewhat different order of events: KGS XXXIV. 4 Sqq runs:

......hutva Sahiranyakamsye Sampatan avanayed ..... (4)...... hiranyena madhyam Krtva panina mukham aabhi Samsprsya praksalya stanav anumantrayate (5) hiranyena sampatan sam nighrsya madhu cety eke tanmukhe krtva prapayayaty .....; VGS 11.8. runs:

Kamsye camase vahutisampatam avaniya
tasmin suvarnam samnighrsya vyartibhih
Kumaram catuh prasayet (Man: Prasa Payati ?)
atyantam eke suvarna prasanam udake
nighrsya dvadasavarsatayah. cf. SGS 1.24.3 and
other texts. (Dresden 1941:81).

8. The types of food were also determined by the scriptures. The simple prescription was that food of all kinds and of different sorts of flavours should be mixed together and given to the child to eat (Paroskara-Grhyasutra 19.4).

Some prescribe a mixture of curd, honey and *ghee*. The father fed the child with the flesh of the bird Bharadvaja if he wished to the child fluency of speech, with flesh of *Kapinjala* and *ghee*, if abundance of nourishment, with fish if swiftness, with the flesh of the bird Krkasa or rice mixed with honey for long life, with the flesh of bird *Ati* and partridge if he desired holy lusture, with *ghee* and rice for brilliance, with curd and rice for strong senses, and with all, if he desired every thing for the child (Ibid. Sankhyana Grhyasutra; i, 27; Apastamba Grhyasutra i, 16.1; Asvalayana Grhyasutra, i.10; Hiranyakesi Grhyasutra ii.5).

The Markandeya Puranam मध्वाज्य कनकोपेतं प्राशयेत्पापयसं तु तम्।

quoted in the Vira-mitrodaya-Samskara Prakasa Vol. -L p. 275) recommends a mess of milk and rice with honey and *ghee*. The popular practice that at last became current was of giving milk and rice.

9. Lord of food, give us food which is painless and strengthening, make (me) grow, the giver, bestow vigour on us, on (our) two and four footed ones (Ms 11.10.1:132.5-6) he causes him (the boy) to eat (from the mess) in a golden (plate), while pronouncing the verse:

The sap from food, from parisrut he drank through Brahman (?) (as) power (which is) the true force by Rta, the pure drink from (soma) juice, this power of Indra, this juice (which is) immortal and sweet (M.S.III.11.6.: 149.1-2).

According to the unanimous testimony of the texts (see Hillebrandt, i.e.) included BhGs 1.27 It runs:

(athainam sasthe monyannam prasayati

tasya sa eva prasana kalpo yo medhajanana
etavan nana bhur ity agre prasayati bhuva
iti dertiyam suvar iti trtiyam),
KGS XXXIX. 1 It runs:
(sasthe mase annaprasanam dantesu va

Jatesu, etc.) the time for this ceremony is the sixth month; VGS III.12 does not mention any month at all. It runs as below:

Agnidha nvantari putravati chagamesabhyam
istva dirghanam vyahrtibhih kumaram
catuh prasayet, etc.; probably the words
putrasya jatadante (III.9) are still valid for
the *annaprasana.*

10. *Ravi tambula soma ke darpana*
Bhaumvara gura dhaniya charabana
Sukra Kabai mohi dahi suhai
Sanno baubhirangi bhavai
Indranjiti putra ghara avai

(One should start his journey by eating betel leaf on Sunday, by looking face in mirror on Monday, by chewing jaggery and coriander seeds on Tuesday, sweetmeats on Wednesday, red mustard on Thursday, curd on Friday and *Bhaubhirangi* (clarified butter) on Saturday. If one follows this he must return by winning even the Indra).

5

The Varieties of Sweetmeats in India

Due to industrialization, urbanization and the development of commercial centres, communication systems and the availability of opportunities for various means of diffusion nowadays, almost all varieties of sweetmeats (with few exceptions) are found in almost all the states. Of course the quality varies from place to place because, besides other factors, culinary practices vary from one place to another, even from house to house. However, there are some sweetmeats which are famous for a particular place or some sweet dishes which are associated with the culture of a particular society. Some data from a number of states/zones is enumerated in this chapter. However, a complete description of all the data would be beyond the scope of the book.

Until now the sweetmeats of two states, i.e., Bihar and West Bengal are discussed in detail. Here, the idea of sweetmeats of other states are given due to two reasons. Firstly, it caters to the need of other researchers who will be interested in doing similar types of research and, secondly, after going through the earlier chapters one should be eager to know about the sweetmeats of other states or zones. Though, due to paucity of space, it is not possible to give all the aspects of sweetmeats of each and every state as discussed in later chapters, however, the name of some famous sweetmeats of other zones are given here.

India may be divided into six zones. The name of the zones and their states/ union territories are as follows:

Zone	*States*
1. Southern Zone	Andaman & Nicobar Islands, Andhra Pradesh, Karnataka, Kerala, Lakshadweep (UT), Pondicherry (UT), Tamil Nadu.
2. Northern Zone	Chandigarh (UT), Delhi (UT), Haryana, Himachal Pradesh, Jammu & Kashmir, Punjab, Rajasthan.
3. Central Zone	Madhya Pradesh, Uttar Pradesh.
4. Western Zone	Dadar and Nagar Haveli, (UT) Daman and Diu (UT), Goa, Gujarat, Maharashtra.
5. Eastern Zone	Bihar, Orissa, West Bengal.
6. North-Eastern Zone	Arunachal Pradesh, Assam, Manipur, Meghalaya, Mizoram, Nagaland, Sikkim, Tripura.

The some sweetmeats of these zones are described below.

PART-I

Sweetmeats of Southern Zone

Some authors like Achaya (1994) have managed to reconstruct the regional cuisine of various places by looking at archaeological as well as literacy evidences from India. In central and western India archaeological evidence became the mainstay. In the South Kannada and Telugu came up in the 6th century and Bengali, Gujarati and Marathi at about the 10th century AD Some writings were also available in Sanskrit from earlier periods.

In South India, there are extensive writings on food in Karnataka where various food items and their evolution can be noted over the years.

> "*Mandige* or *mandage* was a delicate baked product; when baked on a heated tile (Kenchu) it was called white-*mandige*, and when over-heated but still very soft it was *ushnavarta-mandige*, which when exposed to air became *vayuputa-mandige*. The stuffing could be varied. Sugar and *ghee* yielded *khanda-mandige;* use of multi-layered fillings of cooked *chana*, coconut shreds, dates and raisins yielded a *mandige* variation called *perane-hurige*. Today the *mandige or mande* of Belgaum is a very large and fine *parata* stuffed with finely-ground sugar containing cardamom powder, baked on an upturned clay pot, and folded into a moderately stiff rectangle." (Achaya, 1994: 118)

Baking is also done in a seal of dough (called *kanika*). This is used to prepare *bhojenadhika-roti (mandige* broken up into small pieces mixed with milk, cream, coconut milk, mango juice and sugar, and pressed into a ball). It is baked under seal on a hot tile and the vessel is turned frequently. The crust is then sliced off and *ghee* and sugar poured in before eating.

Steamed whole wheat flour in milk with spices, fried coconut grating and jaggery is then cooked in water with added cooked banana flowers, mustard seeds, and then steam-cooked. This gives *godhuma-ramba-kusuma* (Ibid).

> "Wheat dough made with sweetened milk or even cream, rolled into circles and then deep-fried, yielded the *yeriappa* and the *babara*. Balls of dough made with wheat flour, curds and sweetened cream were deep-fried to produce *pavuda*. A less viscous wheat batter prepared with sweetened milk was forced through a hole made at the base of a coconut shell cup directly into hot *ghee* to give the rope-like *chilumuri*." (Achaya,

1994:118, 120)

Many other items are also seen. There is sweet boiled rice, rice *payasam* in milk (including *panramana*), rice-derived vermicelli *payasam*, mixed rice-wheat *payasams*, rice *kadubu* with sweet fillings, *athirasa* (fried rice flour and jaggery), etc. *Rava grits, shali-anna, kesari-bath* (with saffron), *ghrtapura* (fried ball), *Kajjaya* (*Payasam*), and *ladduge* are all wheat preparations as are wheat vermicelli (Pheni) eaten with sugared milk, *purige, hurige-holige, obattu* or suiali-holige (sweet wheat *rotis* stuffed with a mash of boiled *chana*, jaggery and coconut). *Phenis* and *chirottis* were made by rolling pieces of dough, frying them in various forms and then dust therewith caster sugar. *Madhunala* was a similar small tube of dough of wheat, rice, *chana* and mashed bananas, filled with sugar, sealed at both ends and then deep-fried (Achaya; 1994: 120-121).

> "*Karji-Kayi* was a half-moon puff with a sweet stuffing; if only sugar constituted the stuffing, the result was *sakkar-burude.* Pulse flours of *chana* and black gram were also used to make sweetmeats, *Boondi* grains made using them were shaped with sugar syrup into *ladduge, pinda, moti-chur* and *manohara-unde.* The *jilabi* was made of *chana* flour; it was first mentioned by this name in AD 1600, and as *jilebi* later. Milk was the major ingredient for sweet *payasa,* as also for hal-unde (balls of sweetened *khoa*) and *halaugu halubai). Shikharinu* consisted of curd solids lightly spiced and sweetened, the modern term *shrikhand* first being used for the dish in Kannada in AD 1700. (Achaya, 1994: 121)

Other food include sugared milk, *payasa, bajja, Kajjaya* (sweet-stuffed *pakodas*), kinds of flavoured milk, *sannige* (*sago-payasa*), *semiya payasa* (of vermicelli) flavoured with sandal-wood, milk of rare quality and butter (Achaya; 1994: 121-122).

The Kodavas, a tribe of the southern Karnataka perched on the highlands, prepare a breakfast dish "of a sweetish thick steamed batter of broken rice (*thari*) liberally sprinkled with fresh coconut called *paputtu*, which is often eaten with *ghee* and the honey so plentifully found in *Kodagu*." (Achaya; 1994:123)

In Hyderabad, the very sweet, *ghee*-rich, fried bread pudding laced with almonds is called *shahi-tukda* or *double -ka-meeta*. There is also prepared *badam-ki-jali* (latticed sweets of ground almonds) and *andon-ki-peosi* (baked mix of eggs, *khoa*, *kesar* and sugar).

In Karnataka "agricultural products like rice, sugar cane, etc., are worshipped and distributed amongst the poor. Clad in colourful clothes men, women and children visit friends and relatives and exchange gifts of sugar cane, fried gingelly seeds, gur, dried coconut, groundnuts and gram" (Ghulati; 1992: 54).

In Kerala, the *acch-appam* is a deep fried rose-cookie of rice dipped in batter, drained and immersed in hot-oil. The *nai-appam* (*athirasam* in Tamil Nadu) is a deep fried, chewy, dark doughnut made from toddy-fermented rice and jaggery. The *idi-appam* (cooked rice noodles) may be eaten with sweetened coconut milk. Rice-coconut moulded into a ball (*unda*) uses fried rice and sugar syrup, *churutta (*cigar) is rice-based with crisp, translucent outer case, filled with rice grits and sweet, thickened palmyra juice (called *pani*). *Unni-appam*, is a mash of ripe jackfruit, roasted rice flour and jaggery; folded in a triangle in a *vazhana* leaf and steamed. *Chakka-Varattiyathu* is jackfruit cooked with jaggery and some cardamom (Achaya; 1994:124).

For marriages, three to four types of *pradhaman* are served along with some sweets like *boli*. The sweets among the Christians includes *avalose, neyyappam, achappam, churuttu, kuzhalappam, Mavu unda* and *cheepappam* (Kashy; 1992: 102-103)

Thayeram-pazham pani is used in marriages, consisting of sweet palmyra juice is thickened by boiling down and poured on ripe bananas, mashed together and eaten with curd. *Kozhikode* has a special sweet *halwa* made of bananas. *Payasams* use rice and milk, but *prathamans* have fruit or *dhal* or with paper thin shreds of rice roll, cooked separately and added to sweetened milk to give *palada-prathaman*. *Chatha pulisseri* is a *shraddha* speciality, a sour buttermilk preparation with pepper, salt, coconut paste, thickened boiling down. The appam batter is, fermented over night using toddy and baked in a clay pan to yields a thick soft, spongy centre with lacy crisp brown edge. Steaming in a banana leaf packet, with jaggery, grated coconut and jackfruit pulp added to the rice batter, yields *yelle-appam* (Achaya: 1994: 125, 127).

In Andhra savouries are preferred to sweets. *Ghee* and words from an important part if the meal. (Hussain; 1992 : 138).

Some types of arrangement of dishes in shown here from Achaya (1994:121)

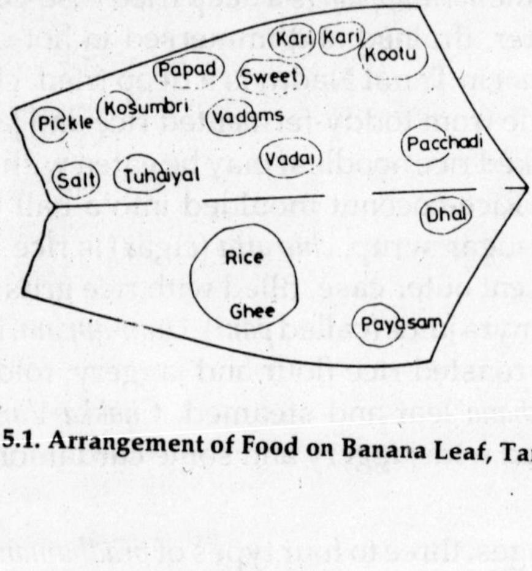

Fig. 5.1. Arrangement of Food on Banana Leaf, Tamil Nadu.

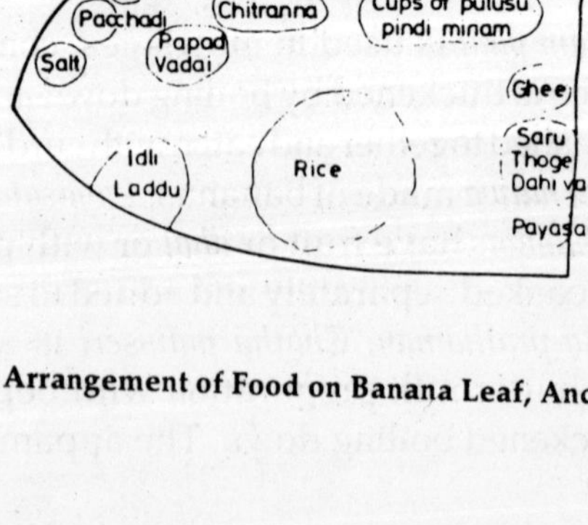

Fig. 5.2. Arrangement of Food on Banana Leaf, Andhra Pradesh.

Sweetmeats of Northern Zone

In North India, from Kashmir, *naans* may be coated with a sweet mash of dates cooked in jaggery. Among the Rajputs are Dogras who have a saying that "a man can never fail in his missions if he takes radish on Tuesdays, sweets on Wednesdays, curd on Thursdays, *rai* on Fridays, uses oil on Saturdays, chews betel on Sundays, and looks into a mirror on Mondays" (Achaya; 1994: 139).

Milk and curds, rarely used except for making tea, are now being increasingly used by the Kashmiris (Hussain, 1992: 100).

In Haryana, *rabri* (made from bajra or gram flour mixed or leavened with butter-milk) was popular. Recently, tea has replaced this among the younger generation (Malik; 1992: 62). In Gohanna, in Sonepat district, it was found by the author and his friends while conducting fieldwork in October 1999 that very large *jilebis* were sold as a very popular item at one shop. These *jilebis* were about 1-1 inches in diameter and weighed from 250-400 gms. 1/2 in weight and costing Rs. 10 each.

In Delhi *halwa, khir,* etc. are prepared only for festive occasions. Villagers may use *gur* in place of sugar in tea. It has now become a gourmet's delight. In the past *nihau, Quala gand/ calakand* from Ghantewala, *Kheer* from Hauz Kazi, *jalebis* from *Bhangi ka katra* were well known. *Halwa, sohan, pista ki long, kesarpak, rabri* and *balai, amriti* and *jalebis* are famous. A whole range of Bengali sweets are also available. Cakes and swiss pastries are of top quality (Chopra; 1992: 98-99). At present international cuisine, though costly, is also very popular.

In Rajasthan pulse-based sweets like *besan-barfi, sheera* of *mung-dal* and *churma-laddus* are available (Achaya; 1994: 140).

Sweetmeats of Central Zone

In the Central part of India, special importance goes to Uttar Pradesh. Many sweets from here overlap with those found in Bihar and of its surrounding states. Since the sweetmeats of Bihar have already been described in detail, here the sweets of U.P. take precedence.

Lapsi (a *halwa* of wheat flour), *Kirora* (rice-flour *laddu*) and *Kesara* (Kesari-bath of rava) are very prominent sweets. *Lapsi* was the flour of any grain boiled in milk and sugar.

Sweetmeats of Western Zones

In Western India, Sweets like *Vedhami, khaja, laddu, sukhadi* (from rava), *kheer* and *talwat* (fried molasses) are found from Gujarat. This was mentioned in the *Bimalprabhandha* of Lawanyasamay in 1200 A.D. The rice sweet *Aaktu*(sathvo) is also found here. Wheat items include *mandaka* or *Mande, pahalika or khaja* or *pheni, phenaka* or *sutor-pheni, murmura* or *mumra, udumbara* or *puran-puri, sohali* or *suhali* (Wheat breads coated in castor sugar), and *ghrtapura* (ghebar or ghevanra) of Surat . Milk items included *shikarini* (*shirkhand*) and *sarkara* (*dudhpeda*). Other sweets from sesame seeds were *shaskuli* or *sankli* (jaggery *chikki*). Wheat-based sweets like gujiyas, *Karanji* or *sanyavao* may also be sweet stuffed (Achaya 1994:134)

Other sweets from the 16th century from texts such as the V*aranaka-Samuchaya* in 1520 AD are *laddu* made *urad Chana,* a *dallia, moida, mung,* fine *bhoodi, bejia, sathi, suinamas.* Other wheat-based items include *mandaka, gari, ghebar, gole-papadi, gugir, mahisupa,* thin *pheni, magaz, shiro, Shakarpatna, etc.* Other sweets include *doodhpak, kheer, ghari-puri* sweet stuffed, (made of *maida*), *thandi* (nut based milk drink), *gunder-pak* (aromatic resin gaund), *sheera* (of rava, corn or *dhal*) and *mohanthal* (a *halva* of *besan* (Achaya; 1994: 135). Most Gujarati preprations include some sugar.

In Goa, the *Dos de Grao* in *besan*, grated coconut and sugar are baked together, giving a thick, firm crust and a chewy centre. Baked yams are coated with melted jaggery. *Mangada* is a soft, chenay mango cheese. Party is docorated with tender coconut stips dipped in melted sugar (Achaya; 1994:136)

Sweetmeats of Eastern Zone

In Eastern India, Chaitanya (1486-1533) is described as having eaten sweet rice-milk *payesh,* thickened milk, small sweet bananas (*chapal*), *dahi* and *sandesh. Laddu* was eaten in a work on Krishna by Krishnadas written in about 1525 AD. One of the favourite sweet items is *mishti-doi* (sweet curds), as well as milk-based sweets such as *manda, khandu* and *nadu*. The latter three were representative of the globe, being round, as the reign of Lord Vishnu. (Achaya; 1994: 129-132).

In 1406 AD the Chinese Mahuan refers to granulated sugars and candied fruits. The *Chandimangala* mentions *kheer*, and *rabdi* (thickened, sweetened milk)also. The *Chandidas Padavali*, Sri Krishna's father distributed sweets and *mistha, mittai, chini* (Sugar). Other works mention *chhanabora, khaja, jilebi, pishtak, modak, malpo, sitamishri* and *sandesh*. All are based on milk, milk solids (*khoa*) or partly thickened milk (Achaya; 1994: 132).

It is presumed that the earlier *khoa* based sweets gave way to *chhana* based sweets. The former included the *labanga-latika*, a leaf-shaped sweet glazed in sugar syrup. The simplest *sandesh* or sweetened *chhana* prepared by curdling milk (perhaps begun by the Portuguse in the latter 17th century) is called *Kanchagolla*. *Sandesh* may also be cast in moulds to resemble flowers, fruit and shells, coloured, sweetened with palm jaggery, sugar cane jaggery or sugar, sugar-coated to yield *manohara*, flavoured with orange peel, jackfruit or rose essence. Two ways were used to curdle milk. Using whey gave a soft, prishable product. Lime-juice gave a harder, longer-lasting product. *Sandesh* was made from both (Achaya, 1994: 132).

In 1868, Nobin Chandra Das of Sitanuti, aged 22 years, created the spongy *rasogolla* cooked in sugar syrup. Fifty years later his son, Krishna Chandra Das invented the *rasamalai, flattened Chhana* patties in thickened milk. In 1930 he went into mechanized production and canning milk sweets with the name K.C. Das. *Khirmohan* was made of patties dipped in thickened milk and sprinkled *khoa*. *Cham cham* was the same product in a different shape, soft, oozy and with grated *khoa*. *Mouchak* was also the same product shaped like a bee-line. *Sitabhog* used *chhana* with rice powder and looked like rice grains *Lal-mohan, Kalo-Jam* (*gulab-jamunu*), *totapuri* (like a long mango) are prepared by mixing with wheat flour, frying and immersing in sugar syrup. *Ledikeni* is a similar sweet prepared by Bhim Chandra Nag to honour Lady Canning, Vicereine of India, for a visit. Similar sweets includes *pantwa*, *Chhanar-Jilipi* and *Chitrakoot*. *Nadu* is made of coconut and thickened milk. Sweets were supplied to wealthy land lords on a large scale. Nobin Chand for instance, received patronage from the *Nawab* of Gaud and Rani Swarnamoyee. Other sweets include *payesh* and *pithe* (thickened milk, sugar, jaggery, molasses along with rice, coconut and *rava*) (Achaya; 1994: 132-133). A guideline of food placement on a plate is given in the diagram below from Achaya (1994)

The main body of the book contain much more details and description of sweetmeats from West Bengal. The small description given above is basically a guideline.

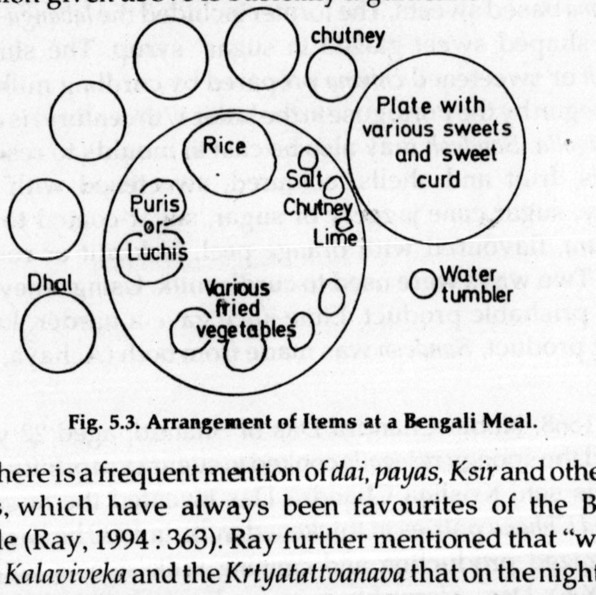

Fig. 5.3. Arrangement of Items at a Bengali Meal.

There is a frequent mention of *dai*, *payas*, *Ksir* and other milk foods, which have always been favourites of the Bengali people (Ray, 1994 : 363). Ray further mentioned that "we read in the *Kalaviveka* and the *Krtyatattvanava* that on the night of the full moon in the month of *Asvin*, friends and relatives, replete with numerous kinds of sweets prepared from flattened rice and coconut, abandoned sleep to pass the entire night in dice-play" (*ibid.*)

In Assam *payasa* and other sweets were made from milk,

curds and *ghee*. *Madhumada* had a honey base (Achaya; 1994:133).

In Orissa *motichur, charu* (rice preparation filled with milk and *ghee* offered to the gods), *sandesh* and *laddu* were the main sweets (Achaya, 1994).

Other sweets from Orissa include milk preparations like *Rasagulla, Rasamalai, Chhenapoda, Rajbhoga, Rabidee, Jilabee, Rasabali* and *Kalakand*. *Khiri* is prepared from rice. *Suji* or semiya with milk and sugar, being served as a dessert on festive occasions. Cakes called *pithas* are also served, including *manda, kakara, Chhunchipatra, arisa* and *chakiyipitha* (all being domestic preparations). Finally sugar cane juice is a well-loved beverage (Kaimal, 1992: 66).

A list of these sweets from various regions of Orissa are given below, adapted from Kaimal (1992):

Delicacy	*Place*	*District*
1. *Mahaprasad* (food offered to Shri Jagannath)	Puri (only)	Puri
2. *Kora and Khai*	Bhubaneswar (only)	Puri
3. *Chhenapodapitha* (Baked cheese cake)	Puri, Pipli, Nimapara	Puri
4. *Rasamalai*	Berhampur	Ganjam
	Balasore	Balasore
	Baripoda	Mayurbhanj
5. *Rasagolla*	Pahala	Puri
	Salepur	Cuttack
6. *Rasabali*	Kondrapara	Cuttack
7. *Chhenajilebi*	Nimapara	Puri
8. *Kalakanda*	Sambalpur	Sambalpur
9. *Rabidi*	Sambalpur	Sambalpur
	Puri	Puri
10. *Muan*	Banpur	Puri
11. *Basadahi* (Sweet curd)	Manikapatna	Puri

In Bihar, the major sweets include the flavours of *mahua* mixed with molasses and parched grain, called *latta*. Gulab *jamun, jilebi* and *rasogolla* ('Bengal delicacy'). *Laddus* like fine-grained *motichur* and sesame seed Tilkut were also found. Sweet, crisp-fried bread *khaja*, *balushahi* glazed with sugar, date-shaped *khajur* or *khurma, pua* with molasses, *pheni* ('frothy sweetmeat') were also available as were *halva / Kanchi* (made from wheat flour, dried fruits and *ghee*, the muslims adding eggs), *mohan-bhog* (a superior *halwa*), *petha* (candied ground) and *kheer* from rice, milk and sugar (*bakir* or *rasiya*) were also eaten with relish (Achaya (1994: 140-141).

Sweetmeats of North-Eastern Zone

In the North Eastern part of India, Meghalaya has its special *pu Khlein* (powdered rice with a little water mixed with molasses and fried) (Brah; 1992: 67). It may be noted that tribal foods include very little milk and milk products. Hence, in the North-East, a majority being tribal, very few sweets are found to be available.

In Manipur, milk and milk products are cousumed mainly by the Meitei farmers (Hussain; 1992: 57)

PART-II

Sweetmeats of Bengal

Banerji (1993 : 9-10) mentioned that milk and milk products became an important part of Bengali food and culture from very early times. Apart from being drunk by itself, milk was often served at the end of a simple meal, when it was mixed with a little cooked rice and white sugar or date palm sugar. When the new bride arrives at her husband's house, her first step over the threshold is timed alongside the boiling over of a pot of milk in the kitchen.

Yoghurt, too, has been an important part of daily food, especially in the summer when it is thought to aid the digestion. Aryan culture attributed auspiciousness to it and Bengali

Hindus continue to believe in that. A *tika* or dot is made on the forehead with yoghurt by well-wishing mothers or sisters whenever a child or sibling is setting out on an important undertaking.

The most sophisticated transmutation of milk in Bengal has been in the form of infinitely varied sweets, some made at home and some professionally. Certainly, no other region in India has shown such passionate absorption in sweets and appreciation of subtlety or variety in their preparation. The plump Bengali with his sweet tooth takes seriously the ancient Sanskrit recommendation, *madhurena samapayet,* a meal should be finished with something sweet, to the heights of finicky epicureanism. The Aryan tradition of central India gave us rice pudding and *kheer* or evaporated milk. To this the Bengali added his repertoire of sweet *pithas,* made with rice or wheat flour, coconut , milk, even pasted *dal.* and sweetened with sugar or *gur* from the date-palm tree; he was content with this for many centuries (*ibid*)

Literary evidence from before the tenth century reflects the wide disparity between the diets of the rich and the poor. The feast served at the wedding of the princess Damayanti, as described in the *Naishadhacharita* (probably written around the tenth century), included so many dishes. Besides other dishes, for sweet dishes there were many kinds of *pithas* and the inevitable sweet yoghurt.

As discussed earlier the long period of Muslim rule from the eleventh century to the demise of the Mughal empire and the take-over by the British in the mid-eighteenth century, firmly established Islam as the second most important religion of Bengal. Due to this, "culinarily, the impact of Muslim cooking was at first mostly to be seen among the leisured and affluent classes, especially the *Nawabs* who represented the Mughal empire in Bengal. But, however restricted initially, it led to the development of a Bengali Muslim cuisine which is distinctly different from the Mughal cuisine of northern India and the Nizami cuisine of Hyderabad. It is less rich and more subtle than both of them, tending to substitute yoghurt and lemon juice for the cream and solid *kheer* of other Muslim cooking" (Banerji, 1993:12)

"The innovative genius of the Bengali cook, both Hindu and Muslim, has found expression in modern times in an amazing array of sweets, most of them based on milk. The concept of *pithas* being synonymous with sweets is now an archaic one. Instead there are the *sandesh*, the rosogolla, the *pantua*, the *chamcham*, or the *rosomalai* to be enjoyed. All of these are made, fully or partly, with *chhana*, the solid part of curdled milk. These *chhana* sweets are Bengal's contribution to the Indian universe of sweets. In other parts of India, sweets are either of the *halva* category or based on *kheer* thick enough to be solidified. This is probably because for a long time people there believed that 'cutting' the milk with acid to make *chhana* is a sin. Krishna, whose idyllic pastoral childhood among the cowherds of Brindaban has been the subject of such a large body of poetry in central and northern India, is depicted as a mischievous boy stealing butter and cream, but never *chhana*.

"This passion for *chhana* and its offspring is something very recent in the history of Bengali eating. Even into the mid-nineteenth century there is no mention of *sandesh* or *rosogolla*, the twin pillars of Bengal's sweet repute. The eminent Bangladeshi historian, Professor Abdul Razzaque, is convinced that there was no domestic midwifery in the birth of these sweets. They were probably devised by the professional sweet-makers in the markets during the latter half of the nineteenth century. This is probably the reason for the sweets still continuing to be mostly made in shops rather than at home. Over the last fifty years, famous sweet shops have risen and fallen in the cities of Dhaka and Calcutta, and each in its hey day has been famous for one or two particular products. The *sandesh* from Bhim Chandra Nag, the *rosogolla* from K.C. Das (whose father Nabin Chandra Das is supposed to be its creator), the *mishti doi* from Jalajoga, are all indications of the importance of the *moira*, professional sweet-maker, in Bengali society.

"Tradition pictures the *moira* as a huge, immobile mountain of flesh, sitting in front of his stove or in front of a huge platter of white *chhana* which he manipulates with the ease of long practice. He is utterly oblivious to all else in the world and so satiated with his own products that he never touches them any more. Of course not all *moiras* are embalmed in stupor. The great Bhim Chandra Nag was once challenged by Lady Canning , the then Vicereine of India, to create a new sweet for her birthday. In response, the master craftsman invented something which is neither the *pantua* (akin to the *golapjamun* served in Indian restaurants everywhere), nor the *langcha*, a similar, bolster-shaped creation. This new product, large, spherical, succulent and fragrant, became known as the *ladikanee* after its patron, Lady Canning. While many shops make them today, the Bhim Nag *Ladikanee* is still considered special" (Banerji, 1993: 14-15).[1]

At the time when the refrigerator was an unknown, milk had to be boiled several times to keep form spoiling. If there was a large amount of unused milk for some reason, one would stirring the milk over a low flame until it became almost solid. This *Kheer* or *ghano dudh*–literally thickened milk–was sweetened with sugar and served as dessert with dinner.

Regarding the culture of Bengalis Banerji (ibid. 42) mentioned that no visitor could leave the house without the ritual of *mishtimukh*, or sweetening the mouth.

Baisakh is a great time for Hindu weddings. In the early forties, in wealthy houses and in wedding feasts, besides other menus, last but not least, came the sweet yoghurt, *mishti doi*, with a variety of sweets and, in last the sweet-spiced *paan* is served. The Bangladesh wedding feast is quite another matter. The Muslim elite's foundness for meat has set the standards for the middle class too, and the wedding menu probably has remained constant for the last half-century. However, a yoghurt and cucumber *raita* and a dessert of *firni* completed the meal.

The last and most terrible month of summer, *Jaishtha*, mid-May to mid June, is a boon for fruit lovers. In this season one can find the sweet dishes made up of fruits. Banerji (ibid; 65) mentioned about the rich delight of mango pulp mixed into *kheer* thick rich evaporated milk. To most Bengalis *Rajshahi* (not in Dhaka, but in the town of Rajshahi, in the northern Bangladesh district of the same name) is famous for two things: the best *langra* mangoes outside the Benares and the wonderful kanchagolla, a kind of milk-based sweet, made in Natore on the outskirts of the city.

The first day of *Barsha* is generally honoured with the eating of a special meal, made more enjoyable by the drastic drop in temperature created by the rains and cloud covered sky. In this season people relish with *pithas* made up of *Atap*[2] rice

For the devout Hindu, particularly the *Vaishnavs*, *Janmashtomi* is a day of total fasting. In the old days affluent households would organize non-stop singing of devotional songs for eight or twenty-four hours. As if to compensate for the rigours of such a day, custom decrees that one of the most glorious offerings of nature, the ripe palm or *taal*, should be eaten after *Janmashtomi*. The ripe *taal* cannot be eaten directly because of its fibrous content and the bitter element in its pulp. Once peeled, therefore, the fibrous sections of the fruit are rubbed against a woven surface to extract the thick saffron pulp and juice. It has a very strong, almost intoxicating aroma which fills the house and alerts the neighbours as well as the flies. The extract is then loosely tied up in a cloth and left hanging for as long as five or six hours, until the bitter juices have dribbled out.

The pulp is too cloyingly rich to eat by itself, so Bengalis have devised two methods to deal with it. One is to cook it slowly with milk and grated coconut to make a creamy *kheer*, one of the classics of East Bengal. The other, familiar to me from my own West Bengal childhood, is to mix it with both rice flour and wheat flour, as well as a bit of grated coconut, and fry it in the form of little round *boras*. There are no near equivalents for the extraordinary taste and flavour of *taal* pulp. Its full-bodied fruitiness resembles that of the mango, but has an extra honeyed quality which can make it oppressive if you absorb it for too long. But those lovely crunchy *boras*, brown on the outside and saffron inside, did not linger long enough to oppress anyone. I could well understand why a popular Vaishnav song visualized Nanda, the dairy farmer and Krishna's adoptive father, dancing gleefully as he consumed his tall boras". (Banerjee: 1993).

At the time of *Ashtami* (the eighth day of Durga puja) dinner, there was usually the simplest of desserts, *Kheer*. This was simply milk, evaporated slowly over a low flame. Though it must originally have started as a measure to preserve and utilize excess milk in the days before refrigeration, *kheer* remains a great favourite an Bengali households. When made as a chosen dessert, 1 litre (1 3/4 pints) of milk, reduced to about 600 ml (1 pint), was considered to be of the right consistency. Once that was done, sugar, the amount varying according to the cook's preference, would be added and the pan removed from the stove and left to cool. Sometimes tangerines from the rare first crop, an expensive treat, would be peeled and the inner pulp from the segments stirred into the cool *kheer* (ibid.).

"On the evening of Bijoya Dashami, the images in the community *pandals* are loaded on to trucks and taken to the nearest river, the Hooghly in Calcutta, for the final rite of *bhashan,* throwing them into the water. It is then, in the wake of the departed goddess, that the most beautiful aspect of Bijoya Dashami comes - the discarding of all ill-feelings of hostility, anger and envy. Within the family, younger people touch their elders' feet in *pronam* and receive their blessings, while contemporaries embrace each other with good wishes. As the evening deepens, relatives, friends and neighbours drop in to convey their Bijoya greetings. They must be offered sweets, which cannot be refused - even diabetics put fragments into their mouths to honour the custom. And so the visits go on until the day of the full moon, the visitors bringing along more sweets to add to the household stock. The commonest sweet is the *sandesh,* because it is dry and easy to carry. But there is nothing to stop you from bringing an earthen pot of *rosogollas* swimming in syrup, or even variations like *rajbhog* or *pantua*. None of these are made at home, for most people do not wish to rival the *moira*, the professional sweet-maker." (Banerji; 1993)

"It is on the autumn full moon that Lakshmi is worshipped with special rites and ceremony. One popular song eulogizes the state of grace the world has achieved because of her blessings: the rivers are full of gently burbling waters that reflect the stars in the sky, the fields are full of golden grain and each household has one or more of the plump brown cows whose copious flow of milk is like a tidal wave of white flowers. Perhaps it is this association of milk with plenitude that makes *payesh,* or Bengali rice pudding, one of the most important offerings for Lakshmi in Bengali homes." (Banerji; 1993)

"*Payesh,* made in Lakshmi's honour is always distributed among neighbours or relatives. It is usually cooked outside the kitchen in specially sanctified surroundings. Usually a portable stove and special pots and utensils are used. Our *payesh,* very different from the insipid, somewhat glutinous mess that is served in dormitory kitchens in the West, is derived from the Sanskrit word *paramanno,* which means the ultimate or best kind of rice. With time, of course, the ingenous Bengali has devised many kinds of *payesh* is something that has to be cooked in milk. And there are no short cuts to it, like using any kind of canned evaporated milk or condensed milk. For the very special taste of *payesh*, (as of *Kheer*) comes from the milk being very slowly reduced in volume over a low flame. Cream, which is such an important thing in the West, is hardly used in Bengal. Probably the tropical climate makes it difficult to skim the cream from the milk. And cold or chilled milk is never drunk, it is always boiled to kill the bacteria. However, when hot milk is left uncovered, a thick skin will form and that is often skimmed off to be heated over low temperatures and yield *ghee*. In *payesh* the sweetening agent is usually plain sugar except in the winter, when date-palm sap is available and lends its own distinctive flavour to the milk. Brown sugar from sugar cane is never used because it tends to ruin the creamy texture of evaporated milk."(Banerji, 1993)

For rural Hindu women and even their urban counterparts as late as the 1950s, *Agrahayan* was also the month for a quaint ritual in honour of the sun called Ritu or Itu Puja. By the end of the month, some, if not all, of the rice in the field had been harvested and brought home. So, on the final day of *Agrahayan,* the Sun-god would receive a final offering of rice pudding made with the new rice and sweetened with the earliest *gur.*

During *Shradhdha,* besides other things the meal ends with sweet yoghurt and *mishtis.*

Banerji (ibid; 128) mentioned that she found magnum sizes of *rosogollas* at Barisal in Bangladesh. Further she mentioned about the pleasantest surprise she had with eggs was in Bangladesh.

The pleasantest surprise I had with eggs was in Bangladesh, during my first experience of the great Muslim festival of Shab-e-Barat, night of destiny. On this night, all devout Muslims are supposed to visit the cemeteries where their family members are buried, to light incense sticks and say special prayers. These observances are important because on this night the fate of every believer is determined in heaven for the coming year. For an outsider like myself the most memorable aspect of Shab-e-Barat was the quaint custom of eating bread (mostly made with rice flour) with different kinds of *halua* on the following day. Mostly households will make huge quantities of bread (flat discs like *chapatis*) and distribute them to beggars who come in droves. This obligatory sharing of food on festive days with those who possess nothing is one of the most beautiful aspects of Islam. It was only on that occasion that I realized what infinite variety and skill goes into the making of *halua.* It could be made out of flour, arrowroot, ground yellow split peas, eggs, carrots, gourds and even meat. (Banerji; 1993)

Some parts of Bengal provide better habitats for the date-palm and the coconut tree than others. The districts of Barisal,

Faridpur and Khulna are particularly well-known and a popular adage in Bangladesh says that the district of Faridpur is noted for its thieves, swindlers and *khejur gur!* But though the trunk provides such a delightful sweetener, the actual dates from the date-palm tree are nowhere near as tasty as those from desert climates.

The date-palm sap is made into three types of *gur* liquid, grainy and the solid chunks of *patali*. The sap is heated in huge *karais* over wood or coal stoves and it is only an expert who can gauge the different degrees of cooking to achieve the right textures. The arrival of *gur* in the market is the signal for the professional sweet-makers to start preparing one of their most popular products, *sandesh* flavoured with the new *gur*. This *nalen gurer sandesh* has a browny-pink tinge and is very dear to the plump Bengali's heart. At the beginning of the season, *gur* is sold in its liquid form, *jhola gur*. This comes in earthen pots and disappears fast enough. In rural areas the fermented *gur* is made into a kind of cheap liquor which tribals and poor villagers drink. It was this same *jhola gur* which inspired committed following from exceptional Bengalis like Sukumar Ray, our version of Edward Lear or Lewis Carroll. In one of his delightful poems he spun out an absurdly contradictory list of all the good things of life, and the very best of the best was bread with *jhola gur*. The solid *patali gur* can be stored and used for quite a few months after winter is over, and refrigeration gives it even longer life. The most notable application for it is its use in *payesh*, in place of sugar. The pure nutty sweetness of the *gur* makes this winter *payesh* a Bengali gourmet's dream. (Banerji; 1993)

Shantiniketan in Birbhum district holds an annual *Poush Mela* which draws crowds from many places. In terms of food, *Poush* is the specific month for eating two things - one being *mulo,* a species of long white or pinkish white radish, the other being all kinds of rice-wheat-coconut based sweets described by the collective term, *pitha*.

Of the thirteen festivals in twelve months that have become a Bengali proverb, the last day of *Poush* is probably the only one that is purely based on the pleasures of eating. In the old days when rural and feudal life meant extended families and communal festivities, there was great scope for gifted women to show off their various *pithas*. Modern urban life is sadly divorced from that, but the art of the *pitha* lives on.One of the simplest, *rasbara,* is made from pasted *kalai dal* which is whipped till very frothy, then fried in round balls and finally soaked in syrup. Another very simple *pitha,* the *chitoi pitha*, is made from rice flour mixed with water and left in a covered, heated, greased earthen saucer around which some water is sprinkled to keep the *pitha* from being too dry. (Banerji; 1993)

The bulk of *pithas*, however, are sweet rather than savoury. The vital ingredient of *pitha* (*pulipitha*) is *khejur gur* which permeates the milk and makes this a treat one long for during the rest of the year.

Since *khejur gur* does not seem to be available outside Bengal (even Indian grocery stores do not sell it abroad), the only way to make this in the West will be to substitute white sugar for the portion of *khejur gur* in the recipe that follows. In the absence of *gur* a vital flavour of Bengal will be missed, but the *pitha* itself will provide an essential Bengali delight.

To show how Bengalis have come to terms with the universal human situations of separation, sorrow, forgiveness, reunion and rediscovery in the framework of their domestic life, Banerji (ibid) gave several examples with reference to food. Here the author of the present book gives only those examples which includes sweet-dishes or sweetmeats on their menu. On the great day of Id-ul-fiter, the people go out into the streets, visiting each other, dressed in new clothes, the ritual offer of vermicelli cooked in milk or syrup and *ghee*, the laughter, the greetings, the embraces, the touching of the feet of elders. On one of their religious festivals, Shab-e-barat, for instance, they serve many kinds of *haluas* with thin *chapatis* made with rice flour. They made *halvas* with yellow split peas, plain flour, eggs and even ground meat.

PART-III

Tribal's View on Milk and Milk Products

Tribals constitute an important segment of the population of India representing 8.08 per cent (according to 1991 census) of the total population of the country. They are distributed in three principal territorial zones, viz; North-Eastern zone, Central Zone and Southern Zone. Because of the secluded living of the groups, besides other things their food and dietary practices may sometimes be different from non-tribal populations. Food processing practices, in general, seem to differ depending on various factors like tradition, culture and individual preferences.

Almost all the tribes are carnivorous. They are voracious eaters and relish meat for which reason domesticated animals are kept for both food and sacrifices. Excepting food that is forbidden the tribals may eat almost everything.

Milk is a rare food item in tribal dietaries. However, Todas are reported to consume good amounts of butter, buttermilk, and curd though milk as such is rarely consumed, and this may be because they are buffalo herdsmen. Milk products, cheese and butter obtained from cow and yak are reported to be consumed by the Monpas of NEFA (Rajyalakshmi 1991: 12). Hussain (1992 : 67) mentioned that milk and milk products are considered as a taboo in some of the Naga tribes and it is because of this reason that *Mithuns* are not milched. Thus milk and its products are considered as impure foods. In the opinion of *Semas* "if we are going to eat the flesh of animal, why should we milk it" Butter, curd, butter-milk and cheese had never been known to some of the tribes.

Rajyalakshmi (1991:13) mentioned that sugar and molasses are reported to be rarely consumed, by the tribals. However, honey collected from woods, is reported to be a common article of food for most of the tribals.

Regional Distribution of Some Popular Indian Sweetmeats

The availability of local products has created patterns in

the evolution of Indian sweets, for example, in the wheat-growing areas of the north, there are more sweet dishes or sweetmeats made with flour and wheat products such as semolina. Climate and local custom provide further subtle influences which have given such great variety and interest to Indian sweetmeats. A sweetmeat may be quite plain and simple, though still exotic to the foreigner, or it may be exquisite in its beauty of form and presentation, its fleeting aroma and taste. But whatever form it may take, it will still be nourishing. In different parts of the country, the same basic dish may be found with almost similar ingredients but bearing a different local name and usually having its own distinct qualities. No wonder that an amazing variety of sweetmeats are found in India. Table 5.2 gives an idea about some typical Indian sweetmeats, their region[3] and principal components.

TABLE 5.2

Region-wise Distribution of Some Popular Indian Sweetmeats and their Principal Components

Sl. No.	*Name of Sweetmeats*	*Regions where Popular*	*Principal Ingredients*[4]
1.	*Bundia*	All over India	Gram flour or pea flour, colouring substance
2.	*Barfee**	"	*Khoa*
3.	*Halwa*	"	Cereals' flour
4.	*Jalebi*	"	Gram flour, colouring substance
5.	*Laddu*	"	Cereal or pulse flour, gum.
6.	*Pedhas**	"	*Khoa*
7.	*Balusahi*	Northern India	*Maida*
8.	*Darbesh*	"	Gram flour, rice flour, *Khoa*
9	*Motichur*	"	Gram flour
10.	*Rawadi*	"	Milk
11.	*Shakkarpara*	Northern India	*Maida*
12.	*Jehangir*	"	Sarustina, rice flour
13.	*Phirni*	"	*Maida*
14.	*Appam*	Southern India	Rice, jaggery, milk, coco

Sl. No.	*Name of Sweetmeats*	*Regions where Popular*	*Principal Ingredients*
			nut, pepper
15.	*Barfee**	"	*Khoa*
16.	*Mysore pak*	"	Gram flour
17.	*Payasam*	"	Jaggery, rice, sugar candy, honey
18.	*Sajjappa*	"	Jaggery, coconut, wheat, flour
19.	*Ukkorai*	"	Gram pulse, jaggery, coconut
20.	*Chandrakantas*	Eastern India	*Moong dal,* coconut
21.	*Chandrapuli*	"	Coconut, *Khoa*, camphor, sesame
22.	*Gulab Jamun*	"	*Khoa*, flour, baking powder
23.	*Rasogollas*	"	*Chhena,* arrowroot or *Maida* or *Suji*
24.	*Sandesh*	"	*Chhena*
25.	*Sitabhog*	"	Flour, *Chhena*
26.	*Anarsa*	Western India	Rice, grated jaggery, poppy seeds
27.	*Imarti*	"	Urad dal, yellow food colouring
28.	*Pinni***	"	*Rava* or *Suji, Khoa*, dry fruits
29.	*Shakurpare*	"	*Khoa, Maida*
30.	*Tilvadi*	"	Jaggery, *til*, peanuts, roasted grams
31.	*Anarsa*	Central India	Rice, grated jaggery, poppy seeds

Source : Souvenir, All India Hotels and Halwaias Federation (1978).
* In these sweetmeats frying medium is not required.
** In this dry fruits are one of the essential components.

From Table 5.2 it may be concluded that firstly sweetmeats are made of cereal flour found all over India. Secondly, sweetmeats made of milk (*chhena, khoa)* are more popular in Eastern region. Thirdly, there are some sweetmeats viz. *shakkarpara, barfee* which are popular in more than one area. Fourthly, in Southern and Western India, jaggery is frequently used in the recipes of sweetmeats and lastly, coconut is one of the basic ingredients of sweetmeats in Southern India.

Table 5.3 shows the Statewise distribution of popular sweetmeats and their principal ingredients.

TABLE 5.3

Statewise Distribution of Popular Sweetmeats and their Principal Ingredients

Sl. No.	*Name of Sweetmeats*	*Statewise Popularity*	*Principal Ingredients*
1.	*Chandrakanta*	Andhra Pradesh	*Moong dal,* coconut
2.	*Kajikai*	"	*Maida,* grams, coconut
3.	*Pakam chalividi*	"	Jaggery, rice, coconut, *til*
4.	*Barh ka lai*	Bihar	*Ramdana, khoa*
5.	*Belgrami*	"	*Chhena* or *maida*
6.	*Keshriya perha*	"	*Khoa, kesar,* sugar candy
7.	*Khaza*	"	*Maida*
8.	*Maner ka laddu*	"	*Besan* (Gram flour)
9.	*Raskadam*	"	*Khoa, chhena, posta dana*
10.	*Sohn papdi*	"	Gram flour
11.	*Tilkut*	"	*Til*
12.	*Dhol dhol*	Goa	Rice flour, coconut, milk
13.	*Gram sweet*	"	Gram pulse
14.	*Mazzipan*	"	Cashew nuts
15.	*Mava ni ghari*	Gujarat	*Maida, khoa,* baking powder
16.	*Shakkurpare*	"	*Maida, til,* baking powder
17.	*Seviyan pak*	"	*Khoa,* vermicelli
18.	*Thor*	"	Wheat flour
19.	*Til vadi*	Gujarat	*Til,* jaggery, peanuts, roasted grams
20.	*Kulfi*	Haryana & Punjab	Milk, corn flour

Sl. No.	Name of Sweetmeats	Statewise Popularity	Principal Ingredients
21.	*Pinni*	"	*Rava*, or *suji*, *khoa*, dry fruits
22.	*Shahi tukra*	"	Sliced bread, milk
23.	*Shakkurpare*	"	*Khoa, maida*
24.	*Phirni*	Jammu & Kashmir	Milk, rice, saffron strands
25.	Dry fruit desert	"	Paneer, saffron strands
26.	*Appam*	Karnataka	Rice, jaggery, milk, coconut, pepper
27.	*Khiri*	"	Rice, coconut, jaggery
28.	*Mandagabe*	"	Rice flour, gram pulse, jaggery
29.	*Mysore pak*	"	Gram flour
30.	*Payasam*	"	Gram pulse, jaggery, coconut
31.	*Shrikhand*	"	Sweetened yoghurt, saffron
32.	*Ghee payasam*	Kerala	Rice, jaggery, sugarcandy, honey
33.	*Kalk*	"	*Maida*, thick coconut milk
34.	*Sarkha puretli*	"	Jaggery, Kerala bananas
35.	*Anarsa*	Maharashtra	Rice, grated jaggery, poppy seeds
36.	*Parshad chasheera*	"	Semolina, milk, ripe banana
37.	*Shrikhand*	"	Curd, dry fruits
38.	*Til che laddu*	"	Sesame seeds, shikki, jaggery
39.	*Coconut barfee*	Orissa	Coconut, *khoa*
40.	*Gokul pithe*	Orissa	Refined flour, baking powder
41.	Gulab Jamun	"	*Khoa*
42.	Imarti	Rajasthan	*Urad dal*, yellow food colouring

Sl. No.	Name of Sweetmeats	Statewise Popularity	Principal Ingredients
43.	Mukhanwadi	”	*Maida*, cardamom
44.	Selta	”	Gram Pulse, *khoa*, milk
45.	Adirasam	Tamil Nadu	Rice, jaggery, *til*
46.	Panchakadai	”	Gram pulse, beaten rice, coconut, jaggery
47.	Ukkorai	”	Gram pulse, jaggery, coconut
48.	Banarsi pedha	Uttar Pradesh	*Khoa*, cardamom, sugar-candy, almonds pistachios.
49.	Bondiwali Gujhia	”	Refined flour, gram flour.
50.	Narial ka laddu	”	Coconut, refined flours-baking powder
51.	Petha	”	White Pumpkin, ground sugar
52.	Chandrapuli	West Bengal	*Khoa*, coconut, sesame
53.	Chhana murki	”	Paneer, sliced nuts
54.	Lady canning	”	*Chhena*, *khoa*, rice flour
55.	Rassogolla	”	*Paneer*, *rava* or semolina, arrowroot or *maida*, baking powder
56.	Sandesh	”	*Chhena*
57.	Sita bhog	”	Rice flour, *maida*, *paneer*

From Table 5.3 it may be concluded that: Firstly, in cold regions such as Jammu and Kashmir, maximum quantity of dry fruits and nutritious ingredients such as *Keshar* are used in the recipes of sweetmeats. Secondly, in Karnataka jaggery is frequently used in making sweetmeats. Thirdly, maximum number of sweetmeats made of *Chhena* and *Khoa* are found in West Bengal. Lastly, cereal's flour and other foodgrains such as *til*, *ramdana* are comparatively more used in the Bihar State.

PART-V

Nutritive Value of Indian Sweetmeats

An idea about the nutritive value per 100 gm. of Indian sweets, are given in Table 5.4. The contents of this table are divided into two categories, i.e. firstly sweets made of wheat and secondly sweets made of rice. Then each above mentioned categories are further described under five sub-headings viz., Recipes common to the whole country, Eastern region, Western region, Northern region and lastly, Southern region.

TABLE 5.4

Nutritive value per 100 gm. of Indian Sweets

Sl. No.	*Preparation*	*Calories*	*Protein (g)*	*Carbohydrate (g)*	*Fat (g)*	*Calcium (mg)*	*Iron (mg)*	*Phosphorous (mg)*
(1)	(2)	(3)	(4)	(5)	(6)	(7)	(8)	(9)
	Recipes common to the whole country							
	A.1 Sweets made of flour							
1.	Barfee	409	5.3	57.1	17.9	65	2.4	152
2.	Gulab Jamun	387	6.8	37.8	24.2	260	2.4	186
3.	Halwa (Porridge)							
	(i) Atta	263	2.6	34.1	13.0	12	1.4	72
	(ii) Khesari	136	1.7	23.7	3.8	10	1.1	53
4.	Jalebi	494	4.4	42.0	34.3	81	1.4	89
	A. 2 Sweets made of Rice							
5.	Kheer	141	4.1	21.1	4.5	80	1.0	98
6.	Kheer (without milk)	168	2.9	34.4	2.0	26	2.9	74
7.	Sweet rice	267	2.5	44.6	8.8	15	0.8	65
	Recipes in Common use in the Eastern region							
	A.1 Sweets made of flour							
8.	Choshipeetha	180	5.0	29.7	4.6	124	0.5	104
9.	Gujia	501	8.2	57.9	26.5	141	2.8	182

(1)	(2)	(3)	(4)	(5)	(6)	(7)	(8)	(9)
	A.2 Sweets made of Rice							
10.	Maalpua	278	2.3	37.4	13.1	22	0.7	78
	Recipes in common use in the Western region							
	A.1 Sweets made of flour							
11.	Shakarpara	691	3.7	37.9	58.3	12	2.2	100
	A. 2 Sweets made of Rice							
12.	Anarsa	499	3.7	63.4	25.2	26	3.4	65
13.	Modak	209	2.8	35.3	6.1	5	0.6	74
14.	Rice halwa	339	2.7	42.6	17.4	5	0.6	79
15.	Rice Laddu	502	3.6	64.3	25.3	5	0.5	55
	Recipes in Common use in the Northern region							
	A. 1 Sweets made of flour							
16.	Balushai	469	5.4	62.6	22.0	35	1.1	67
17.	Goja	499	5.9	86.7	13.9	11	0.6	50
18.	Jalebi	412	4.9	72.0	11.6	10	0.5	41
19.	Maalpua	325	4.4	44.8	14.6	14	2.6	118
20.	Panjiri	528	5.5	56.6	30.7	30	2.9	145
21.	Shakarpara	403	5.4	80.7	6.8	49	5.9	62
22.	Sohan Halwa	399	3.0	62.9	15.2	15	1.5	78
23.	Sweet Samosa	415	11.0	51.2	21.5	251	2.5	201
24.	Rice with Jaggery	244	2.0	50.7	3.7	27	3.9	60
25.	Rice Phirni	166	4.9	22.7	6.4	120	1.0	127
	Recipes in Common use in the Southern region							
26.	Barfee	503	2.6	68.6	24.3	10	8.3	33
27.	Shakarpara	583	6.2	38.2	44.7	22	3.6	165

(Pasricha, S. and L.M. Rebello : 1969)

From Table 5.4 it may be concluded that, *Gujia* of Eastern region, *Shakarpara* of Western and Southern regions and *Panjiri* of Northern region have maximum calories and among all *Shakarpara* of Western region has the maximum. Secondly,

Gujia of Eastern region and *Mitha samosa* of Western region are comparatively more proteinous sweets. Thirdly, it is interesting to note that the sweets of Northern region have maximum quantity of carbohydrates. Fourthly, *Shakarpara* of Western region has maximum quantity of fat which is followed by the same sweet of Southern region and *Panjiri* of Northern region. Lastly, *Gulab jamun* and *Mitha samosa* have maximum quantity of calcium.

References

1. Some overlapping and repetitions have occurred due to the commonality of sweets in West and East Bengal (Bangladesh). In this section some sweets of West Bengal have been also described.
2. The two primary categories of cooked rice are the *Siddha*), or parboiled rice, and the *atap* (or arwa) rice, untouched by heat. The harvested rice is paraboiled, dried in the sun and husked before marketing and storage. *Atap* rice is used for specific purposes such as the cooking of *polao, khichuri* and *payesh*, as well as being made into rice flour with which the Bengali makes a host of *Pithas*, sweet and savoury.
3. Generally, geographers and map-makers have divided India into two parts such as natural and political. But as the present investigator collected the data on sweetmeat statewise, it is not possible for him to follow the geographer's system. That is why he has divided India into six regions as given below:

   Northern India covers the states of Jammu and Kashmir, Himachal Pradesh, Uttar Pradesh and Bihar. Andhra Pradesh, Orissa and West Bengal come under Eastern India. Southern India consists of Tamil Nadu, Kerala and Karnataka. This region is situated south of 16° latitude. Punjab, Haryana, Rajasthan, Gujarat and Maharashtra come under Western India. As the Madhya Pradesh is situated in the centre, so the investigator has put it in Central India. North-East India consists of following states viz., Sikkim, Assam, Arunachal Pradesh, Meghalaya, Nagaland, Manipur, Tripura and Mizoram.
4. Sugar and frying mediums (*Ghee* or *Vanaspati*, or coconut oil and the like) are common principal components of almost all the sweetmeats. Dry fruits, essence, silver *warq* are not mentioned because these things are not essential. Generally they are used for palatable taste and make them good looking.

6

The Sweetmeat Areas of Bihar and their Traditions

The state of Bihar is in the eastern part of India. Nepal lies to the north of Bihar, whereas Orissa lies to its south. Uttar Pradesh and Madhya Pradesh are to the west of Bihar. To its east lies West Bengal. In size, Bihar is about double the size of West Bengal.

Sweetmeat Areas

A 'Sweetmeat Area' may indicate a city, town, a trading centre, *kasbā* or a village or all of them taken together or a geographical space or area within which a particular sweetmeat is popular or famous. In other words 'Sweetmeat Area' is the area which frequently prepares and feels proud of that particular sweetmeat. For example, *Shilao Kā Khāzā* is frequently prepared at Rajgir, Shilao, Bihar Sharif, Harnauth, Bakhtiyarpur, Patna, Gaya, Ranchi, Bhurkunda, Dhanbad, Jamshedpur and Chaibasa, though Shilao is famous for this particular type of sweetmeat.

Some Famous Sweetmeats of Bihar and Its Place of Origin

Every sweetmeat is popular in its own area. A 'popular sweetmeat' means, the sweetmeat has the following characteristics:

1. The people of an area in general relish the sweetmeat.
2. When we talk about the character of a place, among other things, we generally refer to the sweetmeat of that area.
3. Whenever the people of the area go outside to their relatives and friends, usually they make it a point to carry these sweetmeats.
4. When a guest comes from outside, that particular sweetmeat is served to him, or the guest may ask about it, and
5. When a tourist or visitor happens to pass through that area, he is generally keen to take with him the sweet of that area for his family members.

To illustrate, when an outsider or a tourist enquires about the famous things of Gaya, the local people will, generally, say that Gaya is a famous holy place of the Hindus and the Buddhists, but they will also never fail to add that Gaya is famous for the preparation of sweetmeats namely *Tilkut* and *Keshariya Pera*. These sweetmeats have been great attractions for all. That's why the inhabitants of Gaya, carry *Tilkut* and *Keshariya Pera* along with them as gifts when they visit their relatives outside Gaya. The people of Gaya will like to serve their guests with these sweetmeats on many occasions.

The sweetmeats *Barra* of Pakri Barawan[1] (Nawada district), *Belgrāmi* of Koath and Udwantnagar (Rohtas and Bhojpur districts respectively), *Keshariya Pera* of Gaya (Gaya district), *Khaza* of Shilao (Bihar Sharif district), *Laddu* of Maner (Patna district), *Lai* of Barh (Patna district), *Lorha mithai* of Kuru (Lohardaga district), *Pera* of Deoghar (Deoghar district), *Raskadam* of Kahalgaon and Dalsingsarai (Bhagalpur and Samastipur districts respectively), *Sohn Pāpdi* of Buxar (Bhojpur district) and *Tilkut* of Gaya (Gaya district) are the popular sweetmeats of Bihar.

Besides, there are some other sweetmeats such as *Anarsa* of Madhepur (Madhubani district); *Kala Jamun* of Vikram (Patna district); *Khaza* of Pupri (Sitamadhi district); *Laddu* of Sarsopahi (Madhubani district); *Pantoa* of Kasichak (Nawada district), *Piyao* of Ichak and Sherghati (Hazaribagh and Gaya districts respectively), *Rasmalāi* of Ghatshila (Singhbhum district), and *Rassogolla* of Barahiya (Munger district) which are also famous.

Barra

The sweetmeat *Barrā* is famous of Pakri Barawan since 19th century (about 100 years). The inventor of this sweetmeat was Ghanshyam Sah. By caste he was *Kanyakubja Vaisya Halwai.* At present, his third generation is engaged in this business. There are thirty shops which prepare *Barra,* but the *Barra* of Dulichand is famous among all. Dulichand was the son of Ghanshyam Sah. The brothers of Dulichand were not engaged in this business. The son of Surju Sah is finally settled at Rahua. All the grandsons of Dulichand are jointly engaged in this business.

According to Bado Saw, at the time of their grand-father this sweetmeat was so light and soft that if a *Adhela* (a small copper coin worth half a rupee) fell on it, the whole sweetmeat was broken into small fragments. Not only that, but it was also possible to dissolve the *Barrā* with the help of tongue and saliva. This particular quality is known as *Bhar-bha-ra-na* and the name of this sweetmeat *Barrā* has come from this quality.

In the beginning (before 1947) it was prepared in pure *ghee.* These days it is prepared in *vanaspati* and as the price of ingredients become high, the quality of *Barrā* is deteriorating day by day.

In 1978 the price of 1 kg *Barra* was Rs. 6 whereas in 1983 the price of 1 kg was Rs. 10. At present, the cost of 1 kg *Barra* varies from Rs. 40 to Rs. 45 depending upon the quality of *Barra.*

At present there are about thirty shops at Pakri Barawan who prepare *Barra,* out of which only the owner of ten shops are of Halwai caste and rest are of other castes viz., *Baniya, Kahar, Mauri* and *Teli*. The average selling of this sweetmeat of each shop varies from Rs. 300 to Rs. 400 per day while the average selling of Bado Saw's shop is Rs. 900 per day. The plain *Barra* is preserved for three months while *Barra* in syrup is preserved only for 15 days. As all the shops are situated near the bus stand, passengers purchase it frequently for their relatives and children.

Belgrami

Belgrami is a famous sweetmeat of Koath. According to Chaudhury (1966) Koath is a village in the extreme north of the Sasaram sub-division, ten miles away from Bikramganj. Here is the residence of the well-known Bilgrami family, descendants of Nawab Nurul Hussain Khan who came from the family home at Bilgram in Oudh after peace had been concluded with Shiya-ud-daula, when he received a large zamindari.

The village was the scene of Hindu-Muslim riots in 1893 and again in 1917. The village has a mixed population consisting of ex-zamindars, agriculturists, businessmen and service holders.

It is unfortunate that the Bilgrami family should now be remembered more by a particular type of sweet known as *Belgrami*. At present Koath comes under Rohtas district.

As the Muslims like the sweetmeat of *maida* so the Halwais of that time prepared this sweetmeat. This sweetmeat has been famous since about more than one hundred years. At that time, the weight of one piece of this sweetmeat varied from 200 gm. to 400 gm. Till now, the weight of one piece is not less than 100 gm. But at present the quality of this sweetmeat has deteriorated very much.

This sweetmeat was first prepared by Jagmohan Saw. By caste he was *Madhesiya Halwai*. At present his second and third generations are engaged in this business. There are about twelve sweetmeat shops. The owner of all shops except one, who is by caste Saundik, are all by caste Madhesiya Halwai.

Near about 1924, the cost of 1 kg *Belgrāmi* (prepared in pure *ghee)* was 10 annas, and in 1930 the cost was Rs. 1.50. Since the year 1960, this sweetmeat was also prepared in *vanaspati.* At that time the cost of 1 kg *Belgrāmi* prepared in pure *ghee* and *vanaspati* was Rs. 10 and Rs. 3.50 respecively. Since 1980, this sweetmeat is usually prepared in *vanaspati* though after receiving order they also prepare it in pure *ghee,* the cost being almost double. In the year 1980 the cost was Rs. 15 per kg. After 1980, the price has been raised by Rs. 2 to Rs. 3 each year. At present the cost of 1 kg *Belgrāmi* varies from Rs. 50 to Rs. 60 depending upon the quality of sweetmeat.

In these days this sweetmeat is also known as *Ṭikari.* At Babhnaul[2] there are about six sweetmeat shops who prepared *Belgrami* of *maidā* and *chhena* both. They also prepare *piyao* made of *chhena*. The owners of all shops are by caste Saundik.

The *Belgrami* made of *chhena* is famous of Udwantnagar[3] for the last ten years. There are nine shops who prepare this sweetmeat. Out of this, only one is by caste Halwai and others are Rajput, Kalwar by caste. This sweetmeat is preserved for 5 days. Local people also called it *Khurma.*

Keshariya Pera

The product *Keshariya Pera* of Gaya is famous. Like other important cities of pilgrimage in India, Gaya is one of the oldest ones. In the year 1965, the district of Gaya with Gaya as its headquarters was created (Choudhury, 1957).

Regarding the origin of name, the name Gaya according to *Bhagawat Purana* owes its origin to a demon king Gayasur who dwelt in the town in the Treta Yuga. But according to *Vayupurana,* Gaya was the name of a demon.

Gaya is one of the holiest spots for the Hindus and hardly a day passes when there is no Hindu pilgrim to offer *Pindas* in the Gaya *Kshetra* or *Dham* as it is called. Situated seven miles south of Gaya town is Bodh Gaya, the most holy place for the Buddhists. Buddhists from different countries visit the spot almost daily. It is at Bodh Gaya that Lord Buddha achieved enlightenment.

Regarding food, it is mentioned that there are various kinds of sweets and *kheer* prepared by milk. A special kind of sweet pudding is prepared with the help of milk, *ghee* and dry fruits such as *pista, kismis.* This is known as *Sakarauri.*

The inventor of the sweetmeat *Keshariyā Perā* was Baddu Saw. By caste he was *Kanyakubja Vaisya Halwai.* Originally his forefathers belonged to village Basti at Rampur in Uttar Pradesh. About three hundred years ago, Baddu Saw first came to Gaya and since then his generation is finally settled here. At present the cost of 1 kg. *Keshariya Pera* is Rs. 100 and cost of 10 grams *Keshar* is Rs. 650.

Shilao Ka Khaza

'Shilao Ka Khaza' is a famous sweetmeat of Shilao. In Bihar, two types of *Khaza* are prepared. The *Khaza* prepared at Magahi cultural linguistic zone is different from that of Mithila cultural linguistic zone. The *Khaza* prepared at Magahi cultural linguistic zone is comparatively more popular and known as *Shilao Ka Khaza.*

Shilao, is a village, 18 miles south-west of Bihar Sharif on Bihar-Rajgir-Gaya Road. This place has acquired a reputation for the excellence of its *Chura* (beaten rice) as also its *Khaza* (a sweetmeat). People have now given up cultivation of good quality of paddy perhaps because it is not economic to grow it and thus the *Churā* of Shilao may just be a ghost of its predecessor, but the fame of its *Khaza* still survives (Kumar, 1970).

That the foundation of Shilao is ascribed to Vikramaditya and the excellence of the *Khaza* and *Chura* to Halwais of consummate skill settled here by him, whose descendants now carry on the trade. This tradition is explained by the fact that 'Shilao' is contraction of Vikramashila, the name of one of the most famous of the Buddhist monasteries in India. The numerous visitors to Rajgir are ready customers for its *Khaza,* which indeed is also an economic asset to the village (*ibid*).

The inventor of this sweetmeat is not known, however, the shop of Kalishah-Sanjoy Kumar-Vinod Kumar and Kalishah-Panna Lal are the oldest shops at Shilao. According to Yogendra Prasad, his grandfather, Kalishah learned the recipe of this sweetmeat from his grandfather. After the death of Kalishah (in the year 1951 at the age of 75) their sons became separated and started their own shops at Shilao. The name of their shops also shows their traditions, e.g., Kalishah-Sanjoy Kumar-Vinod Kumar. Here Vinod Kumar is the brother's son of Sanjoy Kumar and Sanjoy Kumar is the grandson of Kalishah. This sweetmeat is sold in a particular type of pot known as *donā* (leaves of toddy tree are folded up in the form of a cup and used for holding things). There are about thirteen sweetmeat shops and all of them prepare only this sweetmeat. Some people of Rajgir purchase only *Sada Khaza* from Shilao at the rate of Rs. 45 per kg. After coating it with syrup of sugar they sell it at the rate of Rs. 60 per kg.

According to Panna Lal (55) in the year 1951-52 the price of 1 kg *Khaza* was Rs. 1. After that, according to the high price of ingredients, the cost of this sweetmeat was also raised. At the time of Janta Government the cost of 1 kg *Khaza* was Rs. 7 only. At present the costs of 1 kg. *Khaza* prepared in pure ghee and vanaspati are Rs. 100 and Rs. 60 respectively. The average sale of above-mentioned shops are 50 kg. per day. They sell maximum quantity of *Khaza* in between December 22 to January 14. The maximum sale of this sweetmeat is on 1st January. This sweetmeat may be preserved for 15 days in summer season and about 30 days in winter season.

Maner Ka Laddu

Maner Ka Laddu is also known as *Nikhuti Laddu* and is a famous sweetmeat of Maner. Maner is a large village of historical antiquities, situated in the extreme north-west of Danapur subdivision, about 25 kms. west of Patna on Patna-Arrah highway.

The district Gazetteer of Patna, mentioned that *Maner Ka*

Laddu and *Tajkhani* are not prepared due to high price of the ingredients and lack of patience in the younger generation. It is further mentioned that the local *halwais* learnt the secret of preparing these sweets from the cook of Emperor Shah Alam, who camped here (*ibid.*).

According to Suresh Prasad Gupta (at present his sweetmeat shop at Maner is the oldest and famous for *Maner ka Laddu*) the inventor of this *Laddu* was Phakir Chand Sah. After his death, Bulaki Sah who was primarily one of the main workers in his shop maintained this tradition. Shukhdeo Sah, father of Suresh Prasad has also learnt this recipe from Bulaki Sah. This sweetmeat has been famous for the last hundred years.

The peculiarity of this sweetmeat, i.e., very fine granules of *Bundia,* totally depends upon the sieves locally termed as *chanauta.* In comparison to other *chanauta* it is large in shape, heavy in weight and its pores are very fine. According to sweetmeat makers of Maner, this type of sieve is only prepared by the blacksmith Meghnath Mistri and Buddhu Bihari. Much time and hard labour is required in preparation of this *laddu.* Besides, patience also plays an important role in the recipes of this sweetmeat. Singh (1983) also mention about the *laddu* and fatness of Suresh Gupta, whose weight was 156 kg. in the year 1984.

The price of *laddu* varies from Rs. 100, Rs. 80 and Rs. 40 per kg. depending upon the quality of sweetmeat, i.e., *laddu* prepared in pure *ghee, vanaspati,* and simple respectively.

Lai

Lai is a famous sweetmeat of Barh. Barh is situated on the bank of river Ganga on Patna-Mokamah highway. It has also a station on the Eastern Railway, about 64 kms. from Patna and is a centre of considerable trade in country produce, both by rail and river. The name of the town is perhaps derived from the fact that it stands on a spot liable to the flood (*barh*) of the Ganga. The river takes a sharp turn to the north-east here (Kumar, 1970).

The inventor of this sweetmeat was not known, but the *Lai* prepared at Chondi (a place near Kutcheri) are of best quality. This *Lai* is of two types viz., *Chinni Ka Lai* and *Mawa Ka Lai*. This sweetmeat is also known as *Barh Ka Lai*. *Barh Ka Lai* has been famous since last seventy years. At Barh, *Lai* is prepared of two shapes, i.e., round and convex from both the sides. Some people were of the impression that Gaya is famous for this sweetmeat. At Gaya it is prepared in two shapes, i.e., round-disc shaped and betel leaf shaped and the people prepared it only to maintain their business and livelihood.

At Chondi, there are about twelve shops which prepared this sweetmeat, in which the *Lai* prepared by Govind Sah is of best quality and famous among all. Out of twelve shops, the owner of four shops are by caste Halwai and rest are of other castes, viz., Mauri, Dhanuk, Sonar and Teli. Generally large number of hawkers sell it at station and *kutchery*. Some of the hawkers prepare this *Lai* at their home and rest purchase it from Chondi. Most of the people, who prepare *Lai* in large quantity, purchase *Ramdana* from Mokamah.

The cost of *Lai* depends upon the size of the granules of *Ramdana*. *Lai* prepared by big size granules of *Ramdana* is costlier than that of smaller size. The cost of *Chinni Ka Lai* and *Mawa Ka Lai* are Rs. 40 and Rs. 55 per kg respectively. At Barh, it is prepared in all seasons but selling is maximum in the month of March and April. In winter season it can be preserved for 15 days whereas in summer season it can be preserved for a week.

Lorha Mithai

Lorha Mithai is a famous sweetmeat of Kuru, where according to 1981 census more than half of the population is that of tribals.[4] Kuru is a small *Kasba*. It comes under Lohardaga district (formerly Ranchi district). This district was established on May 17, 1983. It is situated on the National Highway No 51, which is 56 km. from Ranchi and 20 km. from Lohardaga.

This sweetmeat was first prepared in the year 1973 at Sagar Sweet House. The owner of this sweet house is Sagar

Sahu. According to Sagar Sahu, a person who was a drunkard, had come from Danapur to his shop and told that he was in need of a job. At first, that person prepared this sweetmeat, which was in size very much similar to *Lorha* (pestle) and weight of one piece was about 500 g. The reason being why this sweetmeat was called *Lorha Mithai.* Within six months that person left his shop and took up the same job in another shop and finally he settled at Bijupura.

In the year 1973, the cost of 1 kg. of this sweetmeat was Rs.10. Day by day, due to high price of ingredients, the cost has been increasing and simultaneously size is decreasing. At present the cost of 1 kg. sweetmeat varies from Rs. 60 to Rs. 70. In these days the length of sweetmeat is 5 inches and weight varies from 100 gm. to 150 gm. The cost of one piece is Rs. 5. This sweetmeat is also known as *Atombomb* and *Chhena Toast.*[5]

At Kuru there are about fifteen sweetmeat shops. Out of which only four shops prepare this sweetmeat. They are by caste *Halwai, Saundi* and *Ṭhaṭhera.* Every sweetmeat shop prepares 200 to 300 pieces of this sweetmeat twice a week. The average selling of this sweetmeat (per day) in each shop varies from Rs. 400 to Rs. 700. The maximum selling of this sweetmeat is on Thursday and Sunday due to weekly market days.

Beside local people, the people of Netarhat, Betla, Madhya Pradesh, Gaya, Orissa, Daltonganj and West Bengal also like this sweetmeat very much and also purchase whenever they go to Netarhat or Betla for picnic.

Pera

Pera is a well-known sweetmeat of Deoghar. Deoghar is situated about 6 km south-east of the Jasidih Railway Station, with which it is connected by a small branch line of the East Indian Railway and the railway station at Deoghar is called 'Baidyanath Dham Railway Station'. Milk and milk products are in great demand particularly by the well-to-do people. *Chhena* and *Pera* the two milk products of this district (Santhal Parganas) are well noted (Chaudhury, 1965).

This sweetmeat is prepared with the *khoā* of cow's and

buffalo's milk. At present the cost of 1 kg *pera* of cow's milk and Buffalo's milk are Rs. 50 and Rs. 60 respectively. This sweetmeat may be preserved for one week in winter season and two to three days in summer season. In the month of *Sawan,* people from outside (Mughalsarai and Ghormara) also use to come and open their temporary shops for a month. During this month there is heavy rush due to *Sāwan Melā* and this time huge quantity of *Pera* are consumed at Deoghar but the quality is comparatively low. As Deoghar is one of the important sacred centres so most of the people come here for worship from other places and purchase this sweetmeat as a *prasad* for distribution. This also helps this sweetmeat in becoming more popular.

The sweetmeat *Balvara* is the indigenous sweetmeat of this place. It is prepared by *maida* and sugar. In shape, it looks like a star. Besides, sweetmeats such as *Laddu, Tikari, Jalebi, Rassogolla*, *Sandesh, Chamcham, Rajbhoga, Orange, Sangam, Balusahi, Khurma* are also frequently prepared at Deoghar.

Raskadam

The sweetmeat *Raskadam* is famous of Kahalgaon and Dalsinghsarai. Kahalgaon town is situated on the south bank of the Ganges, 30 kms. east of Bhagalpur town. This town was formerly known as Colgong. Dalsingsarai is a town in Samastipur district. The town is a place of commercial and trade importance.

At Kahalgaon there are thirty shops, out of which eight shopkeepers are by caste Halwai and rest are of other castes viz., *Kahar, Kanu, Tamoli* and *Nai.* In comparison to Kahalgaon, at Dalsinghsarai there are sixty shops who prepare this sweetmeat. Out of sixty, ten are by caste *Kanaujiya Halwai*, eight are *Madhesiya Halwai* and rest are *Kanu, Sonar* and *Tamoli.*

Regarding price, the cost of 1 kg. *Raskadam* at Kahalgaon and Dalsinghsarai varies from Rs. 60 to Rs. 80 and Rs. 40 to Rs. 45 respectively. At Dalsinghsarai in the year 1960 the cost of 1 kg. *Raskadam* was Rs. 6. The cost was Rs. 10 and Rs. 12 in the year 1980 and 1983 respectively. The rate of this sweetmeat depends upon the quality of *Khoa* and *Chamcham* and quantity of sugar. This sweetmeat can easily be preserved for 15 days.

These days this sweetmeat is on the verge of extinction due to following reasons:

(i) People like sweetmeats made of *Chhena*.
(ii) It takes more time in preparation. i.e., atleast 12 hours, in comparison to others.
(iii) Considering the time and money, profit in this sweetmeat is comparatively less, and
(iv) Lack of patience in younger generations.

Sohn-Papdi

This sweetmeat of Buxar is famous. Buxar is an old town situated on the bank of the Ganga river. Regarding Buxar town the District Gazetteer of Shahabad mentions as follows:

It is the headquarters town of the subdivision situated on the north bank of Ganges. Buxar is said to have been the home of many of the authors of the Vedic hymns and to have been called originally *Vedagarbha,* i.e., the womb or origin of Vedas (Chaudhury, 1966).

At Buxar, there are about two hundred sweetmeat shops, out of which 70 to 75 shops are of *Madhesiya Halwai*, 50 to 60 shops are of *Kanaujiya Halwai* and rest are of other castes. Almost all shops prepare this sweetmeat. At present the *Sohn Papdi* of Shri Ram Papdi Bhandar, Arya Mishtanna Bhandar, Sopal Mishtanna Bhandar and Buxar Papdi Bhandar are famous and of best quality.

This sweetmeat has also been supplied in other states like Uttar Pradesh and West Bengal. Here it is interesting to note that about 200 families, who are by caste washermen have settled in Arab countries. When they come back to Buxar, they relish this sweetmeat very much. Not merely that, at the time of returning, they must carry this sweetmeat along with them.

Here the sweetmeats are kept in a special type of pot. At

first they arrange the sweetmeat in a brass dish and then this dish is covered with a case made of long pieces of glass.

Tilkut

Tilkut prepared at Gaya is comparatively more popular though it is prepared at several places. The *Tilkut* of Gaya is famous since more than 100 years. The inventor of this sweetmeat was not known. But the shop of Kasturi Lal Gupta at Ramna is the oldest. He claimed that his grandfather was the first man who prepared *Tilkut* at Gaya. By caste he was *Kanyakubja Vaisya Halwai* and originally he belonged to Sasaram.

According to Kasturi Lal Gupta, at that time *Dhoi Til* was not available. People had to go on the bank of river and with the help of *Shaiwal* (an aquatic plant, i.e., moss) they cleaned the black *til* and then dried it in sunlight. They fried *til* in *Handia* (a small earthen pot). As a result the product was so crisp that if one heaved the immediately prepared *Tilkut*, the whole *tilkut* was broken into small pieces. In those days, they purchased *Dhoi Til* from Daltonganj, Kanpur and Lucknow. At Ramna there are about 50 shops and except one (who is by caste *Kesharwar*) all are by caste *Halwais.*

The shop of Ram Das Kesari at Tekari road is also one of the oldest shops. By caste he is *Kesharwar.* There are about 10 shops at Tekari road. According to Ram Das Kesari there are about 60 shops at Gaya who prepare *Tilkut* permanently and presently not only *Halwais* but also other castes such as *Sonar, Tamoli, Kurmi* and the like are engaged in this business. To maintain their livelihood they prepare other sweetmeats also such as *Lai* from *Shivaratri*, i.e., *Phalgun* (February-March) to the month of *Sawan* (July-August), *Inarsa* from *Sawan* to *Diwali,* i.e., *Kartik* (October-November) and *Tilkut* from *Diwali* to the month of *Phalgun.*

There is maximum selling of *Tilkut* in the month of January and in this month, the number of shops rises to 250. According to Binod Kumar Keshari, the average selling of *Tilkut* of Ram Tilkut Bhandar in the peak season (i.e., December to February) is about 100 kg per day. Twenty-five years ago, the cost of 1 kg *Tilkut* was Rs. 1.50 and at present the cost is Rs. 80.

Traditions Connected with Sweetmeats

Diwakar (1959) in his book *Bihar Through the Ages* mentioned that both vegetarian and non-vegetarian food were eaten in Bihar. Dharmaswami refers to the wide popularity of sugar as an article of food. Cooked rice with *ghee* and curds was also considered high-class food. Dairy industries were sufficiently developed in Bihar. Curds, milk and *ghee* were not only consumed by men but also offered as ingredients of worship. Mithila was then, as now, famous for its milk and curd preparations. There is special reference to thick, perfectly congealed curd (*chap dahi*) and curd full of *ghee*. Milk was described by Abul Fazal as rich in quality and cheap. Tirhut was specially famous for its curd which was kept for a long time without becoming sour.

Kumar (1971) mentioned that the staple food of the people of Pataliputra consisted of rice, wheat, barley and gram. Milk and its products formed an important part of their menu.

Again he mentioned that by and large the people of Patna district were vegetarians. This may be attributed to the influence of Buddhism which was a positive deterrant against the slaughter of animals. With the advent of Muslim rule from the 13th century onwards, the food habits of the people began to change slightly and meat and fish came to be included in the diet of a section of people. But otherwise the vegetarian structure of food has generally been sustained. The cows of Patna-breed are milk yielding. Besides the availability of pastures in *diarā* lands and dianrs and the forest areas of Rajgir provide good fodder to cattle and thus milk supply is generally assured. She-buffaloes are also kept in large number and thus *ghee*, curd, sweets are also assured in the menu of the vegetarian diet of the people (*ibid*).

It thus transpires that sweetmeats are closely associated with Bihari culture. When persons visit their relatives specially of younger generations or in-law's house, one cannot expect them without sweetmeat. At the time of marriage, there is a ritual in which the newly wedded couple is provided with some varieties of sweets specially *Dahi* (curd) and *Bundiā* mixed together. This is consumed by the husband and wife after they mutually feed a bit of it to each other. On the occasion of *Chhati, Janeu* (sacred thread wearing ceremony), married people give either clothes or money or both as a *Neutā,* but sweetmeat is very essential along with it. One can see a big size of *Batāsā* at the time of *Tilak* and *Mundan* ceremony which has some special role on such occasions. Some people also judge the prestige of a man through the quantity of sweetmeats he serves on festive occasions.

Various Factors for the Popularity of Sweetmeats

Here it would not be out of place to discuss the reasons for the popularity of the famous sweetmeats mentioned earlier. There are various factors responsible for the popularity and each of them will be discussed one by one.

Ecology

Ecology, i.e., climate, temperature, quality of water and the like, of a particular place, play an important role to make the sweetmeat more popular. During fieldwork, the author asked several persons regarding the causes of popularity of a particular sweetmeat. Most of them replied that *Yaha Ka Aabo Hava Kuchha Aiseh hai Ki Is Taraha Ki Mithai Dusare Jagaha Nahi Banai Ja Sakati.* (Due to peculiarity in climate it is not possible to prepare such quality of sweetmeat at other places). Further due to lack of expert workers, it is also not possible to prepare same quality at other places. The author thinks that the second reason is more reliable because, in Ranchi almost same quality of *Tilkut* are prepared by expert workers though the climate is totally different from that of Gaya.

According to the sweetmeat makers of Shilao due to difference in the climate and taste of water (including the presence of some quantity of Sulphur in local water) it is not possible to prepare such quality of *Khaza* elsewhere.

Quality, Proportion and Combination of Basic Ingredients

This is another important factor due to which a particular sweetmeat becomes popular at a particular place. As the other people do not know the actual process or recipe and exact combination of ingredients, they are unable to prepare same quality.

Regarding the difference in taste of the same sweetmeat at a particular place, the price of *maida*, sugar and *vanaspati* are fluctuating very frequently. If we raise the price of *Khaza* according to variations in price of these ingredients, this will affect the business. So it is better to maintain this variation with adding more quantity of sugar and this will affect the taste of sweetmeats.

Besides the climate, other factors such as purity of ingredients, proportion and combination of ingredients are also responsible for popularity of a particular sweetmeat. The quality of ingredients also play an important role in the popularity of a particular type of sweetmeat. Regarding the popularity of *Maner Ka Laddu,* the quality of gram which are grown near around the *Diara* (an island which is formed in the bed of river after a tide) is much better and the *Besan* prepared with this gram is much light.

Fire

Intensity and medium of fire also plays an important role in making a sweetmeat more popular of a particular place. Baddo Saw of Pakri Barawan said that about 50 years ago, his forefathers prepared the sweetmeat on the fire made of wood. In that case it was easy to control the flame. There is also a little difference in the taste of the products which are prepared on the flame of wood and coal.

Lack of Patience and Expert Workers

This is also one of the important factors. Due to lack of patience in younger generations, the quality of sweetmeats are deteriorating day by day. Patience during the straining of basic ingredients is the most essential thing. In a hurry, most people fry the basic ingredients in high temperature as a result the natural fragrance of the basic ingredients is burnt and it spoils the taste.

As an example, other than Gaya, *Tilkut* is prepared at other places also but due to lack of expertise they are not in a position to prepare good quality of *Tilkut*. Generally, in winter season the *Halwais* of Gaya go to other places, viz., Bokaro, Jharia, Patna, Ranchi, Jamshedpur and the like, for preparing the *Tilkut* on daily wages. At that place, a single worker has to do all the work, i.e., frying the *Til*, preparing the *chasni*, and finally pounding of the material due to which it is not possible for them to prepare good quality of *Tilkut*. Therefore if the expert workers at a place try to prepare the good quality of sweetmeats then it may be possible to some extent.

Non-availability of Basic Ingredients and Important Tools

It is quite obvious that if the basic ingredients of a particular sweetmeat are not available in other places then it is not possible to prepare such a quality of sweetmeat elsewhere. Similar is the case with tools connected with recipe of a particular sweetmeat. For instance, skimmer and quality of *besan* by which they prepare *Maner Ka Laddu* are not available at places other than Maner, so except Maner, this sweetmeat is not prepared elsewhere. As a result this sweetmeat becomes popular at Maner only.

Personal Reputation

It is another factor due to which sweetmeat prepared by a particular person becomes more popular in comparison to others. Besides the factors mentioned above, popularity of a sweetmeat also depends upon personal reputation. It is not necessary that if two persons prepared the same sweetmeat with same ingredients in similar conditions then the result will be the same.

Place of Sweets in the Indigenous Dietary Pattern in the Cultural Linguistic Zones of Bihar

Vidyarthi et. al. (1979) in his book *Changing Dietary Patterns* and *Habits: A Socio-cultural Study of Bihar* discussed in detail about the dietary pattern and habits of the people of Bihar and indigenous dietary habits and recipes of the people of Bihar. Here, the present dietary habits of the people of Bihar and food requirement of the people, and indigenous diets of each cultural linguistic zone under separate sub-headings viz., main, supportive and subsidiary diets are discussed in detail.

In Bihar, the dietary habit reveals some of the similarities and dissimilarities among different zones. This is due to the diverse ecology, which is at the root of all food habits. They have thus developed different food traditions.

Regarding the present dietary pattern and habits of the people of Bihar it has been mentioned that the people have begun neglecting indigenous diet of less nutritive value on the grounds of the social stigma attached to the consumption of some of the dietary items and recipes. People are in the habit of taking specific food items in the morning, in the afternoon, and at night. They also vary their food during the rest period, working days, holidays. They even have demarcations for their own kinsmen, of their own community, for other castes and so also for other religions. In other words, food has a lot to do with the social relations between individuals and groups of individuals. There are seasonal variations in main food items too.

The general idea about the present dietary pattern of each region are as follows:

Magahi Region

The staple food in the Magahi region consists of rice, wheat, maize and *marua*.. The food items which are usually purchased by the people from hotels and restaurants are : tea, *nimki*, sweets, *kachauri, singhara, pakaudi, jalebi,* etc. The people who come to the market usually take sweets to their home for kids.

The morning diet which is known as *nasta,* generally includes *roti* (bread), *dara* or *Daliya* (*Hominy,* i.e., maize hulled and boiled in water or *sattu).* Some of the families (about 10 per cent) use these food items along with beverages like milk, tea, whey or *marjhor*. Besides, some persons add *bhunja* or preparation of milk viz., *Kheer* or *Sewai* or curd. The *khana* (afternoor diet) includes items like *bhat, da, roti, tarkari, sattu* or *dara*. Similar items of food are consumed by the people at dinner. There are some familes (specially the youngers) who take some types of eatables apart from the regular hours. These could be either sweets or fruit or snacks or any of the regular items taken again. Generally special dishes are prepared even among vegetarian items by the people of this region. It consists of two categories viz., *Pakki* and *Kachchi*. The *Pakki* food consists fo items like *puri, tarkari, dahi-chini, bundiya,* and other sweets. While *Kachchi* includes *bhat, dal, sag, danaur, tilauri* and *papad*. On special occasions they prepare *puri, mohanbhog, kheer, sewai, malpua, bari,* etc.

Bhojpur Region

The staple diet of the people of this region is rice. It has become the usual practice among the people of Bhojpur to support their diet through hotels, restaurants, food stalls and hawkers. The usual food articles purchased from the hotels are *tea, puri, kachauri, nimki, khurma* and othe sweets. *Jalapan* or *panipiwa* or *jalkhai* or *muha lagawan* are the local terms for morning diet in Bhojpur region. It consists of *roti, tarkari* or *bhunja* or *dara* or *satti* or even *bhat*. The lunch *(bhojan)* of this region consists of three sets or general food, i.e., (i) *bhat, dal, tarkari,* (ii) *roti, tarkari,* and (iii) *sattu*. The dinner also consists of the same except that the *sattu* eaters change to *litti* during the night meal.

Among the vegetarian diets two main sets, i.e., *Pakki khana* and *Kachchi khana* of dietary items are served. *Pakki khana* consists of *puri, tarkari, bundia* and sweet curds and some kinds of sweets. *Kachchi khana* consists of *bhat, dal, tarkari, achar, tilwari, danauri, chutney, ghee, dahi, papar,* etc. Traditionally, deities are offered special food items. Almost all the food materials are prepared in the house, but a few fruits and sweets are brought at shops. The prepared food items for deities are *puri pua, jawar,* milk, *lawa, dalpuri, gulera* and sweets, etc. On some important occasions other items like *kheer, puri, phulwari, halwa, rasiao, malpua, dalpuri, sewai* and *litti* are prepared.

Mithila Region

In this region the staple foods are mainly cereals like rice, wheat, maize, grams, jaggery, as well as milk and curd. Everybody in the family takes food in the house. Apart from this,. either for a change or due to circumstances, people take their meals in the hotel. More than half of the Hindu familes, due to their rigid caste structure donot take their food in places other than their own houses. The morning diet, i.e., *Jalkhai* consists of food stuff like *chura-dahi,* jaggery or sugar. In this hour, tea and milk as beverages and a few special food items of vegeratian varieties like *makhana* and *kheer* are common among the rich-families. Almost all families consume rice during afternoon meal. The night meal is known as *Khanai* but the food stuff is almost the same as in the case of the afternoon meal and rarely varies according to their respective economic groups. So far as the special characteristic of this area is concerned, special food items like *dahi* (curd) is most often and lavishly used. *Pakki khana* of this region consists of *puri,* vegetables, *dahi, sakrauri* and sweets. *Kachchi khana* includes *bhat, dal,* vegetables along with *dahi* and sweets. Besides, the Maithils have also a great fascination for fish. For the deities, offerings like *pua, thekua, kheer, puri, malpua, tilwa, dalpuri* and many types of sweets are both prepared and purchased.

Tribal Region

In the tribal region, the main food items are rice, wheat, maize, *marua, mahua,* lentils, different edible roots, shoots, leaves, fruits and vegetables. Among non-vegetarian food items mention may be made of fowl which is a favourite among many. For their food materials, the tribals depend on their fields or the forests and nearby weekly and bi-weekly markets. Tribals enjoy prepared food on visits to the weekly markets or regional towns. Prepared foods like *bhat, dal, tarkari, puri, kachauri, pakauri, singhara, bara, dalmot, guguni, dasuka, nimki, aluchap,* various sweets and many others are taken. Tea, *hanria* and wine available in the market are also taken by them.

Regarding food requirements of the people it was mentioned that "The daily dietary pattern among the tribals varies from tribe to tribe according to their cultural typology. There is no such common diet which shows the importance of ecology and economy of the people there. Some of the tribals go without food for days together. So the question of the breakfast, lunch and dinner are not relevant for all the cultural groups in the diverse tribal regions. On the whole, it may be said that they take food items like *bhat*, vegetables, *harnia, pitha, roti, mahua,* wild roots, fruits, leaves, shoots and few others.

Grierson (1975) mentioned that the general term for a meal is *rasoi* and also known as *bhanas* in East Tirhut. The morning meal is called *nashta.* Other names of morning meal are *panpiyae, panpiyai, jalpan, jalkhai* and *jalkhawa* other local names are *jalgheraw* in Champaran, *panpiyai* in Gaya and *dana* or *dana-duni* in Shahabad. *Panipiyai* is also used to mean the food eaten by the labourer in the intervals of work in the field. This is also called *lukum* in the west.

The mid day meal, which is the main meal of the day, is called by the people *kalewa, kaleu.* In Tirhut it is called *kaleu,* though according to dictionaries and pandits this is a light morning repast. Local names for this meal are *khay, khaiya, khaik, kalaw* in Patna, Gaya, South Munger and South Bhagalpur respectively.

An evening meal which is a light food just taken before sleeping is called *sanghana.* In south-west Shahabad it is called *bealu* and *berhatiya* in Champaran.

Lastly, sweetmeats made of *chenna* and *khoa* viz. *kalakand* and *Raskadam* are not popularly found in Bhojpur zone.

References

1. The name indicates the places of origin of the sweetmeats concerned.

2. Babhnaul village comes under Sasaram subdivision, situated at a distance of 17 km north of Bikramganj. A metalled road (Bikramganj-Dumraon) runs near the village. For Koath the people dropped by bus at this place and by *tanga* they have to go to Koath which is about 7 km far from Babhnaul.
3. Udwantnagar is situated about 8 km south of Arrah, the District Headquarters. It is under Arrah Police Station and Udwantnagar Development Block. The village is said to have been set up in the name of Shri Udwant Singh an ancestor of Babu Kunwar Singh. The Garhwar Rajputs form the bulk of population.
4. According to 1981 Census the total population of Kuru is 52, 618 and the Schedule Tribe population is 27,656 (Lal, 1982).
5. When *Lorha mithai* is divided (breadth-wise) into two equal halves and in the middle of each half (lengthwise) cream is stuffed, then it is called *Chhena Toast.*

7

The Sweetmeat Areas of West Bengal and their Traditions

West Bengal is bounded on the north by Sikkim and Bhutan; on the east by Assam and Bangladesh; on the south by Bay of Bengal and on the west by Orissa, Bihar and Nepal.

Halder (1926) in her book *Bengal Sweets* mentioned that in the wide realm of confectionery, Bengal has attained the same unique position with regard to the whole of India as Italy appears to hold in the continent of Europe. In no other part of this vast peninsula, will be found such a wide range of confectionery as are to be met with, in this sweet province flowing with 'milk and honey'. And the reason is not far to seek. For even in the National Anthem of Bengal, poignant allusion is made to the "Sweet air, sweet water, sweet corns and sweet fruits" of the motherland.

The sweet tooth of Bengal is proverbial. Indeed the great role that Bengal sweets play in the social life of the Bengali people will be judged by the fact that "it is said that no dish is complete without them even in daily courses, that; the lunch is sometime entirely composed of them that every menu is enjoined to be finished with sweets"

In Bengal, sweets have been identified with cordiality and amity to an amazing extent. The index of honour shown to invited guests is furnished by the variety and superiority of the sweets offered in their entertainment. Whenever there is a friend of the family in the house, he or she may take leave only after "sweetening the mouth". By each stratum of society in every part of Bengal, sweets have also been accepted as an emblem of hospitality. If one goes even to the remotest villages and asks for a glass of water simply, that person will surely get it but not without sweets—may they be a few pieces of sugar candy.

And thus, it is said, that in Bengal, the advent of any noteworthy event in the family or in the society is heralded by an unlimited provision of unrestricted distribution of sweets.

Famous Sweetmeats of West Bengal and their Place of Origin

The sweetmeats such as *Jal Bharā Sandesh* of Chandannagar (Hugli district), *Kachagulla* of Ranaghat (Nadia district), *Kheer Pantoa* of Raghunathganj (Murshidabad district), *Lengcha* of Shaktigarh (Barddhaman district), *Malpua* of Jiaganj (Murshidabad district), *Manohara* of Janai and Beldanga (Hugli and Murshidabad districts), *Moa* of Jaynagar (24 Pargana district), *Morabbā* of Siuri (Birbhum district), *Motichur* of Bishnupur (24 Pargana district), *Nikhuti* of Shantipur (Nadia district), *Sandesh* of Calcutta (Calcutta district), *Śarpuriya* and *Śrbhaja* of Krishnanagar (Nadia district), *Sitabhoga* and *Mihidana* of Barddhaman (Barddhaman district) and *Sponge Rassogolla* of Calcutta (Calcutta district) are famous sweetmeats of West Bengal.

Besides, there are also some famous sweetmeats such as

Adait Bhoga of Bolpur (Birbhum district), *Babarsa* of Khirpoi (Medinipur district), *Chhena Barra* of Baharampur (Murshidabad district), *Kaju Sandesh* of Kanthi (Medinipur district), *Khaza* of Indas (Bankura district), *Maicha* of Beliator (Bankura district), *Raghavasai* of Maldah (Maldah district) and *Raskadam* of Aurangabad and Maldah (Murshidabad and Maldah districts respectively).

Jal Bhara Sandesh

The sweetmeat *Jal Bhara Sandesh* of Chandannagar is famous. Chandannagar is 37 kms. from Calcutta. It is a beautiful laid out quaint little town, giving no hint that it was much more important trading centre than Calcutta at one time. This sweetmeat is only prepared at Chandannagar.

It is a unique type of sweetmeat. By name it seems that *Jal*, i.e., mixture of syrup of sugar and rose-water is stuffed (*Bhara*) inside the sweetmeat *Sandesh*. This sweetmeat is the oldest kind of *Sandesh* prepared with *Chhena* and white sugar in particular technique of sweetmeat preparation. It is prepared with the help of *Chhāchha* (mould).

This sweetmeat was first prepared by Surya Kumar Modak in the year around 1856. He was by caste *Modak*. At present his second and third generations are engaged in this profession. Their shops are situated side by side at Barasat G.T. Road, Chandannagar.

There are about 200 sweetmeat shops at Chandannagar and most of them prepare this sweetmeat. *Rasabara* is an indigenous sweetmeat of this locality. It is a syrupy sweetmeat made of *maida* and *safeda* (flour of rice). Besides, the sweetmeats such as *Danadar, Rassogolla, Bundia, Jalebi, Gaja, Lengcha, Chitrakut, Chhena Murki, Mitha Singhara, Gujia, Malpua, Motichura Laddu, Gulabkhas, Kala Jamun* and several varieties of *Sandesh* are also prepared there.

Kachagulla

This sweetmeat of Ranaghat is very famous. Ranaghat is

situated on the bank of the river Churni and covers an area of about 3 sq. miles. Very little is known about the early history of this town. It is said to have been called Ranighat originally after the Rani of Krishnachandra and Maharaja of Nadia (Majumdar, 1978).

Sanehamai Ma was the lady who first started the preparation of this sweetmeat at Ranaghat. She prepared the sweetmeats at home and her son Bishu Paul (who is one of the best players of Eastern Railway) sold it at the railway platform. In due course, popularity of her sweetmeats spread around the town. The people from Pabna, Rajsahi, Bagura, Siliguri, Murshidabad used to come for purchasing the sweetmeat to Ranaghat.

There are many factors behind the popularity of the sweetmeats of Ranaghat. Ranaghat is one of the important railway junctions of old E.B.R. and present Eastern Railway. Five branches of railway lines are mingled here[1]. Besides, bus facilities for several places are also available. So transportation facilities play an important role in the popularity of such sweetmeats. There are so many grazing grounds around the Ranaghat. Due to this facility, people of this locality domesticated large number of cows and buffaloes. So the sweetmeat makers of this locality are able to get sufficient quantity of pure milk. Ghosal (1983) mentioned that population of this town comes near around 80,000 and there are 73 licensed holders of sweetmeat shops. The famous sweetmeat shops of this town are of Haridas Paul, Jageshwar Pramanik, Sudhir Pramanik, Mahadeo Ghosh and Ravi Karmakar.

Besides the above, *Pantoa, Mouchak, Nikhuti, Chhana Ka Chamcham, Rasmalai, Kala Jamun, Kheerer Sandesh, Khirmohan, Rajbhog* and *Kalakand* of good quality are also prepared at Ranaghat.

Kheer Pantoa

The sweetmeat *Kheer Pantoā* of Raghunathganj is famous. This sweetmeat is very much similar to the *Pantoa,* but here instead of *Chhena*, *Ksira* is used as a basic ingredient. As a result this sweetmeat is very soft in nature and delicious in taste.

The shop of Badal Ghosh is one of the famous sweetmeat shops at Raghunathganj. His grandfather first prepared this sweetmeat about 150 years ago. The members of Badal Ghosh's family are fully engaged in this profession. They have opened their sweetmeat shops at Chapra, Jamalpur, Calcutta, Katua and Kanpur. To maintain the reputation still they prepared this sweetmeat with *Ksira* of cow's milk.

Besides, the sweetmeats such as *Orange, Rajbhog, Chamcham, Sandesh, Jalebi, Kachagulla, Laddu, Rasmalai* are also prepared at Raghunathganj.

Lengcha

The sweetmeat *Lengchā* of Shaktigarh is famous. There are much controversies regarding the invention of this sweetmeat. However, one of the important stories regarding the invention of this sweetmeat runs like this.

About hundred years ago there were two persons named Shashi Bhushan Dutta and Khudiram Dutta who opened their shop in the market of Shaktigarh. According to Kanhai Lal Dutta, Haradhan Dutta first came here in the year 1838 and Khudiram Dutta (his sister's son) came here in the year 1925. At that time a *karigar* of those shops was lame. Generally people called that shop as *Langra* (Lame) *Ka Dukan*. At that time Vijoy Guha was one of the famous merchants, who liked varieties of sweetmeats very much. Once he asked that lame *karigar* for preparing a new variety of sweetmeat. On the request of Vijoy Guha he prepared a new variety of sweetmeat which was bigger in size and barrel in shape. People of that locality liked this sweetmeat very much. As this sweetmeat was prepared by *the Langra Karigar* so people called this sweetmeat as *Lengcha*. At present the son of Khudiram Dutta named Kanhai Dutta is also engaged in the same profession. That shop is popularly known as 'Lengcha Mahal'. At the same time a new sweetmeat shop was opened by Hem Ghosh. His contributions also helped in making this sweetmeat more popular.

Nowadays this sweetmeat is prepared in two sizes, i.e., big and small. 1 kg *Chhena,* 100 gm *maida,* 100 gm. *safeda,* 100 gm. sugar and 100 gm *khoa* are required for preparing the 30 pieces of big size *Lengchā.* This sweetmeat may be preserved for 3 to 4 days in winter season and 2 to 3 days in summer season.

Besides *Lengcha,* the sweetmeat such as *Sandesh, Rajbhog, Rassogolla, Danadar, Chhena Gaja, Mihidana* are also prepared frequently at Shaktigarh.

Malpua

The *malpuā* is the famous sweetmeat of Jiaganj. Jiaganj is situated on the east bank of the Bhagirathi, 9 km. north of Murshidabad and opposite to Azimganj station on the Eastern Indian Railway (O'Malley, 1914).

Due to lack of authentic information nothing can be said regarding the period and invention of this sweetmeat, however, it is one of the oldest and famous sweetmeats of this area. Regarding the popularity of this sweetmeat, according to Das (1983), the place Jiaganj seems mostly populated by believers of Jainism and it is customary among them to eat *bhang* (an intoxicant substance) for becoming intoxicated. After eating the *bhang* when one is fully intoxicated they want to eat sweetmeat of *karra pāk* (hard syrup). Due to this, the sweetmeat *malpua* became popular at Jiaganj and its surrounding localities.

The basic ingredients of this sweetmeat are *chhena, sujji* and *maida.* This sweetmeat is prepared in hard syrup. The colour of this sweetmeat becomes chocolate due to boiling it in hard syrup for 2 to 4 hours. As a result, one cannot eat much of this sweetmeat at a time.

The sweetmeat shop of Devendra Nath Ray is one of the oldest shops at Jiaganj. Once the name of Jiaganj was Baluchar so people also called it as *Baluchari Malpua.*

Besides, the sweetmeats such as *Laddu, Manda, Jalebi,*

Chamcham, Rassogolla, Pantoa and *Rajbhog* are also frequently prepared at Jiaganj.

Manohara

There is a contradiction regarding the popularity of this sweetmeat. Some people say that this sweetmeat is famous of Beldanga, whereas other people say that this sweetmeat is famous of Janai (Hoogli district). After interviewing several persons the present conclusion was reached that : *Manohara* of Beldanga is popular in North Bengal region and *Manohara* of Janai in South Bengal region. Regarding its tradition, the sweetmeat of Beldanga is older than that of Janai. Here, it is surprising to note that the people of one region (North West Bengal) do not know about the *Manohara* of the other region (South West Bengal).

The basic ingredients of this sweetmeat are *chhena, khoa* and sugar. Besides, nutmeg, mace, cloves, cardamom and poppy seeds of good quality are also mixed. The peculiarity of *Manoharā* is that after giving the shape, this sweetmeat is dropped in the syrup of sugar one by one and kept on banana leaf for sometime. When the sweetmeat becomes dry, then it is arranged on a tray. As a result this sweetmeat is covered by the coating (thin layer) of sugar.

This sweetmeat is not preserved for more than one day. *Manda* is the indigenous sweetmeat of this locality. This sweetmeat is prepared only with the help of sugar.

Besides, the sweetmeats such as *Kala Jamun, Rajbhogs, Lengcha, Malpua, Aam Sandesh, Barfi, Kachagulla, Pera, Kokoa, Sagrika* and *Gaja* are also prepared frequently at Beldanga.

At Janai, Guli Moira is famous for this sweetmeat. He prepared this sweetmeat 60 years ago. *Bundia* of big size and *Jibe Gaja* are the indigenous sweetmeats of this locality. Besides, *Rassogolla, Sandesh, Nikhuti* (this sweetmeat is different from that of Shantipur for which it is famous) *Danadar, Bundia,* and *Guja* are also prepared at Janai.

Moa

The sweetmeat *Moa* of Jaynagar is famous. Jaynagar is

situated on the Adi Ganga, an old channel of the Ganges, 31 miles south of Calcutta (O' Malley, 1914).

Probably this sweetmeat was first prepared at Pal Raujo of Telipara Mohalla of Jaynagar (Biswas, 1984). This sweetmeat is prepared every year from the month of *Aghan* to *Magh* or up to the Saraswati Puja.

Besides nature and cold weather of winter season, *Payala Guṛa* of palmjuice and parched rice of *Kanakachura* paddy are two principal acquisitions of this sweetmeat. The person who prepares such type of molasses is called *Siyulivala*. The stockists purchased about 80 to 90 quintals of *Moa* during Xmas and supplied to other places. During off season of this sweetmeat, they prepared another sweetmeat, i.e., *Chandrapuli* from the month of *Asadh* to *Kartik* or up to the festival of *Bhaiya Duija* to maintain their livelihood.

The basic ingredients for preparing 10 kg. *Moa* are as follows:

Payala Gura 4 kg. Sugar 4 kg. *Kanakchura Dhan Kă Lava* 5 kg. or 10 *Paila; Ghee* 200 gm; Cardamom 10 gm; Poppy seeds 10 gm; currant 100 gm. This sweetmeat is prepared on wood flame.

This sweetmeat may be preserved for seven days. In Jaynagar, we also found other sweetmeats such as *Rassogolla, Lal Jamun Danadar, Chhenar Gaja, Khirer Chop, Sandesh* and *Chamcham* but in winter season they only prepare *Moa*.

The quality of this sweetmeat has been deteriorating day by day. In these days inferior quality of *Moa* are also found at Diamond Harbour, Baj Baj, Bag Bazar, Kalighat, Behala, Tolleygunj, Bhawanipur, Balleyganj and Bahu Bazar of Calcutta. To sell this sweetmeat at cheaper rate they used not only inferior quality of parched rice but also used *Mata* and *Gāda* instead of *Payala Gura*. *Gada* is the dregs which occurred at the time of preparing the syrup of sugar. They also used piece of coloured coconut instead of pistachio.

It is interesting to note that since last few years this sweetmeat is also becoming popular at Ranchi (Bihar). During summer season people used to frequently bring *Moa* from West Bengal and sell at Ranchi.

Morabba (Succade)

The sweetmeat *Morabba* is famous from Siuri. The word *Morabbā* has come from an Arabic word *Murabbā*. According to Bangla dictionary the meaning of this sweetmeat is 'any fruit which is boiled in the syrup of sugar'. Really, it is the gift of Muslim *karigars* (Das, 1983). Siuri is the principal town and administrative headquarters of Birbhum district situated 2 miles south of the Mor river, with a railway station on the Ondal-Sainthia branch of the Eastern Indian Railway. The name Siuri is reported to be a contraction of Sihuri (O'Malley, 1910).

Though this is a famous sweetmeat of Siuri but it was first prepared at Rajnagar which is 25 kms away from Siuri. Once Rajnagar was the capital of Birbhum. The king of Rajnagar named Bodioj Jamal (1718-52) first prepared the *Morabha* of *Bel* and *Chalkumhara* with the help of *Pathān karigar*. Few years ago people used to bring raw materials from Rajnagar and they only cooked those materials in syrup of sugar at Siuri because *karigars* of this place had a curse that if somebody boils the fruit then it would be a sin. In these days also, people used to bring some raw materials from Varanasi. Not only that, the main *karigar* named Mishri Lal of a famous sweetmeat shop which is situated near bus stand belongs to Varanasi.

In the year 1921, Devendra Chandra Bhowmick of Siuri established a factory for preparing the *Morabbā*. The name of the factory was D.C. Bhowmick & Company Birbhum Morabba. According to his eldest son, before the Second World War his father also supplied this sweetmeat abroad. This sweetmeat is available at Siuri in the following shops viz., Morabba, Deys Morabba, Dadubhai Nandagopal Jalpan and Asim Sweets. It is also available at Bolpur in two sweetmeat shops viz., Awadh Sweets and Netaji Sweets.

The various Morabbas sold are as follows: *Papita* (Papaya) *Ka Morabba, Lal Mircha Ka Morabba, Āam* (Mango) *Ka*

Morabba, Aawala (Myrobalan) *Ka Morabba, Bel* (wood apple, Aegle marmelos) *Ka Morabba, Cherry Ka Morabba, Kamranga Ka Morabba, Ananas* (Pine apple) *Ka Morabba* and *Parwal Ka Morabba*. According to D.K. Saha M/s. New Dadu Bhai Sweets they sell maximum quantity of *Bel Ka Morabba* which is followed by *Satmul Ka Morabba*. If this sweetmeat is protected cautiously, then it may last for ten months.

Few years ago *Kaviraj* (a title of physicians of West Bengal) also prescribed such sweetmeats as a medicine. For example, they prescribed *Bel Ka Morabba* for gastric problems ; *Chalkumhra Ka Morabba* for plethora, worms, and constipations; *Haritki* (Yellow myrobalan) *Ka Morabba* for piles, dysentary and anaemia; *Awala Ka Morabba* and *Satmul* (bulbous root Dioscoria fascinulato) *Kā Morabbā* for health and nutrition.

More or less, *Bhatua Ka Morabba* is prepared at several places of Bihar, West Bengal and Uttar Pradesh. This sweetmeat is also famous of Agra (UP) and popularly known as *Agra Ka Peṭha*.

But nowadays the importance of this sweetmeat is decreasing due to some reasons such as decreasing in numbers of *Kaviraj,* lack of forest, non-availability of basic ingredients and lastly, modern jam and jelly also affects its importance to some extent.

Motichura

The sweetmeat *Moṭichura* of Bishunpur is famous. Bishunpur is the headquarters of the subdivision of the same name, situated few miles south of the Dhalkisor river (O'Malley, 1908). It is 201 km. from Calcutta. Historically Bishunpur is the most interesting place in the district as it was the ancient capital of the Mall kings. Their rule continued even after the ascendance of Muslim rule in India. There are relics of the past indicating the pomp and grandeur of the place. There are three most popular sayings in which the popular things of Bishunpur are mentioned. The sweetmeat *Motichura* is one of them.

Kalipada Singh, grandson of Ram Kishore Singh, the last

king of Malraj dynasty, said that about three centuries ago, Gosai Das Nag first prepared this sweetmeat at Bishunpur with the cooperation of the people of Malraj dynasty. At that time, this sweetmeat was prepared in pure *ghee* and over saturated with *ghee* also. Whoever lakes it in mouth it gets immediately absorbed within no time. It is so light that it floats in water also. Gosai Das Nag prepared such type of sweetmeat and gave it to the king. So the king awarded him the title of Mandal. In olden periods *Besan* was prepared with *Piyala Phala* (the fruit of the tree *Chirongia sapida*). Then *chalgura* was mixed in it and small size *Bundi* prepared. After that it was saturated with syrup of sugar and given the shape. But nowadays such quality of sweetmeat is not prepared due to high price and non-availability of basic ingredients.

Nikhuti

This is a famous sweetmeat of Shantipur. Shantipur is situated on the left bank of the Hooghly. It covers an area of about 9.5 sq. miles (17.10 sq. km). The town is equidistant from Ranaghat (the sub-divisional headquarters) and Krishnanagar (the district headquarters) and is linked to both the towns by road and railway.

It is said that about 100 years ago a person named Ishwar Bipin Bihari Indra first prepared this sweetmeat. At present his third and fourth generations are engaged in this profession. In outlook this sweetmeat is very much similar with the fruit mulberry.

The basic ingredient of this sweetmeat is *chhena* and the recipe is somewhat similar with that of *Jalebi*. This sweetmeat is served after sprinkling the fine mixture of nutmeg and cardamom.

In olden periods, another sweetmeat viz., *Makhāsandesh* was also famous but due to lack of expert *karigars* and non-availability of basic ingredients it was totally extinct. This sweetmeat is made to order, but again due to high price of ingredients, not a single customer had come since last twenty years for this sweetmeat.

The sweetmeats such as *Malai Chamcham, Khirer Chop, Chhenar Murki, Rassogolla, Mouchā, Gujiā, Ladycany, Pantoa, Gaja, Mitha Singhara, Kalakand* and *Rajbhog* are also frequently prepared at Shantipur.

Here, it is interesting to note that there are some sweetmeats which are also prepared at other places by the same name but either their basic ingredients or recipe or both are totally different, e.g., *Nikhuti.* This sweetmeat is also prepared at Krishnanagar by the same name but their recipe is totally different from that of Shantipur.

Sandesh

Sandesh is one of the oldest and famous sweetmeats of West Bengal actively associated with Bengali traditions.

The basic ingredients of this sweetmeat are *Chhenā* and good quality of sugar. The quality of this sweetmeat mostly depends upon the experience of *karigars* and how they stirred raw material with *Taru* (an instrument).

The references of this sweetmeat have also come in Chaitanya-Bhagwat and Chaitanya Mangal. The book *Hutum Panchea Naksa,* written by Kali Prasad Singh has important place in Bengali literature. In this, on the occasion of *Durgastav, Saraswati Puja* and *Vivah Prasanga,* the references of this sweetmeat have also come. Similarly, in the book *Jamai Sasti* by Din Bandhu Mitra and *Hemanta* written by Ishwar Gupta references of this sweetmeat have also come (Ray, 1979).

Not only Indians but foreigners such as Fredrick Pinkat and W.S. Kein also praised this sweetmeat. After tasting the *Sandesh,* Fredrick Pinkat remarked "it is a food for the Gods and the noble race of Bengalis" (*ibid*).

According to Ray (1979), some varieties of *Sandesh* such as *Good morning, Lord Rippon* and *Bag Sandesh* are totally extinct. He further mentioned the following varieties of *Sandesh* such as *Golla, Batabi, Manohara, Khir Puli, Manoranjan, Badam Takhti, Abaka, Nayana Tara, Gulapi Pera, Bag, Tal Sans, De Do Manda, Kasturi* and the like were found till the end of the 19th century.

It is said that, taste of people is changing according to time perspective. Such changes also affect the quality and varieties of sweetmeats. In these days, following varieties of *Sandesh* such as *Pan Sandesh, Apple Sandesh, Dilkhus, Ice-cream Pranhara, Kasturi, Coco, Naler Gurer Sandesh, Parijat* and the like have replaced the old ones.

Sarpuriya and Sarbhaza

The sweetmeat *Sarpuriya* and *Sarbhaza* of Krishnanagar are famous. Krishnanagar is headquarters of the district, situated on the left bank of the Jalangi, 9 miles (14.5 km.) above its junction with the Bhagirathi. The town covers an area of 6.5 sq miles (Majumdar, 1978).

Dvijendra Lal Roy (a famous poet of West Bengal) also gave references of these sweetmeats in one of his poems which runs as follows:

Uh, Sandesh Bunde Gaja Motichura Raskara Sarapuriya
Uh, Garoche Kunidhi Dayemaye vidhi Katana budhi Kariye
Yadi dau taha Khali-ah
Madiye badane dheliye

Visvakosa (Bose (ed) 1317 B.S.:285) defines these sweetmeats as follows:

Sarpuriya : It is an Indian food and made of *Sar* (the cream of curdled milk), *Chhana, Khoa*, almond and pistachio nuts. *Sarpuriyā* of Krishnanagar is very famous and useful food.

Sarbhaza : It is also an Indian food. It is prepared by frying *Sar* in *ghee* and saturated with syrup of sugar. It is very delicious in eating.

About 100 gm. almond, 25 gm. pistachio nut, 2 gm. nutmeg, 800 gm. *Khoa*, 400 gm. sugar and two pieces of *Sar* are required for preparing 1 kg. *Sarpuriya*. These sweetmeats are prepared with hard labour, patience and time. About 35 years ago people prepared *Sar* at their home. But, nowadays they purchase it from the village hawkers because it is prepared in small *Hariya* on the flame of cow-dung. Pieces of *Sarpuriya* are also called *Rakam Barfi*.

In *Sarbhaza*, thick and round layers of *khoa* (about 250 gm.) and *Sar* are arranged one after another. In this way four pieces of *Sar* and three pieces of *Khoa* are required for this purpose. After cutting in pieces it is fried in *ghee*. After that, it is saturated in syrup. Pure and good quality of sweetmeats are found at Krishnanagar.

The sweetmeat shop of Adhar Chandra Das is famous at Krishnanagar. At present his second and third generations are fully engaged in this profession. Besides, *Kheer Peṛa, Cake Sandesh, Aam Sandesh, Kheer Chamcham, Kadam, Kalakand, Gaja, Bālusāhi, Kheerpuli, Sagrika, Kala Jamun, Rassogolla, Nikhuti* and *Bundiā* are also prepared at Krishnanagar.

According to *The Statesman* dated 22 April, 1981 the quality of the famous sweets of Krishnanagar have deteriorated because of scarcity and high prices of certain ingredients. According to sweet dealers, if the traditional quality is to be maintained, prices will have to be exorbitant. There are about 80 sweet shops in Krishnanagar town, six of which are famous for their products. *Sarpuriya Sarbhāza, Nikhuti, Barfi, Sandesh, Khirpuli* and *Rakam Barfi* are still in great demand. But sweet dealers now have to use low grade of spices because most spices are expensive. *Jafran,* which adds to the colour and taste of *Sarpuriya,* is scarce and only inferior varieties are available at high prices. The quality of casein has also deteriorated. If *Sarpuriya* is to taste as good as it once did, it will have to be sold at much higher rates.

Sitabhog and Mihidana

The sweetmeats *Sitabhoga* and *Mihidana* of Barddhaman are famous. Barddhaman is a principal town and administrative headquarters of the district situated on the Banka river and the main line of the East Indian Railway (Peterson, 1910).

Sweetmeats are very largely consumed by the higher and middle-classes, and the confectioners of Burdwan and Mankur are famous for their *Ola Khāzā* and *Kadma.* Among the peasantry, however, the only sweetmeat consumed, besides treacle in its raw unmanufactured state is *Mudki,* i.e., parched and husked paddy dipped in treacle and on high days and holidays *patali* (*ibid*).

How these sweets gained popularity? There is a history behind it. At the time of Britishers, Haridas Dey was a canteen manager of Barddhaman railway station. He had another shop in the market viz., Adarsh Mishṭanna Bhanḍar. Once a higher officer had to came for inspection at Barddhaman railway station. On hearing this news, all the staff were overcome by fear because that officer was of hot temperament. When he visited the platform, Haridas Dey served these sweets to him. On tasting the sweets, he became happy and wanted to know the names of such sweets. On seeing the smiling mood of the officer the staff was surprised. Haridas replied, the sweet which is of turmeric colour is *Mihidana* and the white one is known as *Sada Bhoga*. In these days, this sweetmeat is known as *Sita Bhoga* which is a corrupted form of a word *Sada Bhoga*. Many people were of the opinion that this sweetmeat was first prepared by Sitanath Nandi so this sweetmeat was known *Sitabhog* after his name. The role of Bhairav Chandra Nag and his grandson Nimai Nag are no less important in making these sweetmeats more popular.

At that time the basket-ball match was usually held in Arvind Stadium at Barddhaman. Once there was a match in between the Markin (British team) and Chinese team. When the game was over, these sweetmeats were served to the players of both teams. After eating, the British players said that it is a delicious sweet and Chinese players exclaimed *Hen Hou Chi* (How nice it is!).

These days, the quality of such sweetmeats have deteriorated due to following reasons: Firstly, the rise in cost of basic ingredients, secondly in olden periods the people ground the rice in *Janta* and now it is ground in flour mill as a result the actual sweetness is burnt and the softness of the sweetmeat has disappeared and thirdly, due to lack of expert *karigars*.

Besides, the sweetmeats such as *Kheer Kadam, Sandesh, Rassogolla, Danadar, Rasmalāi, Parwal Ka Miṭhāi, Moicha, Peṛa, Chitranjan, Buniyā* and moulded form of sweetmeats are frequently prepared at Barddhaman.

Sponge Rassogolla

Rassogolla, that enchanting sweet, so dear to millions in India, was born in the year 1868 a concept of the genius of Nobin Chandra Das, the famous confectioner of Bagh Bazar, Calcutta. Originally his forefathers were inhabitants of Barddhaman district. Last seven generations, lived in Hat Khola Mohalla of Calcutta. They first came to Calcutta in the year 1554 (*The Jugantara*, Bangla Newspaper, October 29, 1981). Since last seven-eight generations their forefathers lived in Bagh Bazar (The *Bartaman,* Bangla Newspaper, July 14, 1985). Their forefathers had the business of indigenous sugar and also were the exporters of quality of sugar. To meet the requirements of diabetic patients (who are barred from taking sweets) K. C. Das introduced special sandesh and Rassogollas for them by mixing sorbitol[2] instead of sugar with *chhana*.

Traditions of Sweetmeats

Regarding various types of sweets in ancient Bengal, Chakravarty (1959) mentioned that, no ancient writer of Bengal seems, however, to have taken the trouble to write and leave for the knowledge of posterity an exhaustive account of *Paka Pranali* or of the process and methods commonly adopted and the ingredients generally used by the people in ancient Bengal for preparing different kinds of cooked food and drink. In the absence of any definite evidence in the matter, it is better to conclude that the householders in ancient Bengal most probably entertained their invited guests even on special occasions like marriage, funeral ceremony, etc., not by making offers to them of different kinds of fried cakes made of flour along with some cooked vegetables, fish, meat, sweets, etc., for their feast as we find at present, but by giving them for their meal, simple boiled rice (*anna*), *pāyasa* or *paramanna,* that is to say, rice boiled in milk, mixed with sugar, along with, in all probability cooked vegetables, fish, meat, etc. (*ibid.*).

The existence in early days and the prevalence down to present day in Hindu society in Bengal of words like *Pisṭaka,*

Modaka or *moya, laḍḍuka,* etc., leave no doubt that there were confectioners in early days in Bengal. *Pisṭaka* or many types of boiled and fried cakes popularly known in Bengal as *pitha,* which we find in Bengal today and sweets or sweet cakes of round shape or *Ladduka* which are commonly known as *laru* were probably not unknown in Hindu society in ancient Bengal. There is no kind of positive evidence, however, to show that modern varieties of sweets called *Sandesa* and sweet juice balls of round shape called *Rassogollā,* and *Pantua* were prepared by the confectioners and consumed at large by the people in ancient Bengal as we find at present (*ibid*).

There are references in some early works of Hindu canon of the Bengal school like *Kalaviveka* and *Krtya-tattvar nava* to the custom of partaking flattened rice or *cipitaka* along with sweets containing the kernel of the coconut fruit on the night of the full moon (*Kojagari-Purnima*) in the month of *Asvina,* (i.e., roughly the period in between the middle of September and the middle of Octorber (*ibid*).

A verse of the *Prakrta-paingala* also gives us a similar idea of the scarcity of essential articles used for preparing palatable and expensive sweets in a poor man's home. A poor man is described here as proclaiming in an emphatic way that he would certainly be in a position to prepare twenty round fried sweetcakes or sweets everyday if he could get a quantity of clarified butter (*ghitta*) weighing atleast one seer (*sera ekka*). However poor a man might be, he might think himself prosperous and fortunate enough like a king if he had in his possession some quantity of rock-salt, however small its quantity might be. The verse of the *Prakrta-Paingala* is quoted below:

"*Sera ekka jai pāvai ghitta*
Mandā bisa pakaila nitta.
Tanku ekku jai Sindhava pava,
jo hau ranka so hau raa."

(*ibid*).

The kernel of both green and ripe coconut fruit seems also

to have been used as solid food by people in ancient Bengal. Various kinds of sweets are prepared nowadays in West Bengal from the kernel of ripe coconut with the help of molasses or sugar. It appears from a study of the *Kalaviveka* and the *Kityatallavarnava* that such simple sweets were in all probability used as food by common people in Hindu society in ancient Bengal, more especially on the night of the *Kojagari-Purnima,* that is to say, on the night of the full-moon in the month of *Asvina* shortly after the annual worship of the Goddess Durga (*ibid*).

It appears from a careful study of the ancient literature and the early inscriptions of Bengal, that natural cow's milk, goat's milk, etc., *Payasa* or a preparation of sugar and rice boiled in milk, condensed boiled milk (*ksira*), the cream of boiled milk (*navanita*), and the by-products of milk like curd, whey, casein, butter and clarified butter, etc., were used as food or drink by the people in ancient Bengal (*ibid*).

The word *maṇḍa* has been used in a verse of the *Prakrtapaingala* to denote a round cake or a sweetmeat of a round shape. The word *modaka* seems in all probability to have been used in Hindu society in ancient Bengal to denote sweetmeats or any kind of sweet confectionery. The word *Ladduka* seems also to have been used in Hindu society in ancient Bengal to denote all kinds of cooked or specially prepared cakes. It may be noted in this connection that an image of the God Vinayaka is very interesting on account of the fact that it is depicted as tasting sweets (*ibid*).

According to the current traditional ideal in Hindu society in Bengal, a full fledged banquet requires a perfect and a balanced menu. There should thus be in an ideal full-course dinner some edible objects which are essentially pungent (*katu*) in taste, some edible objects which are essentially bitter (*tikta*) in taste, some edible objects having an essentially sour (*amla*) taste, some objects which are essentially of an astringent (*kasaya*), some edible substances having a saline (*lavana*) taste and lastly some edible foods which have an essentially sweet (*madhura*) taste (*ibid*).

Bengali culture pursuits received zest when Calcutta became the capital of India in 1833. The Bengali cuisine also reacted to the situation. Nobin's *Rassogolla* acquired an international stature and Dwarik's sweets like *Sandesh* and *Pantua* and sweet curd together with other varieties acquired the distinction of Bengali delicacy and sophistication (Banerjee, 1979).

Showing the tradition of sweetmeats in Calcutta, Sinha (1977) also referred the name of Nawin Modak, Bhim Nag and Dwarika Ghosh. The content runs as follows:

Raja Chaitanya Singh of Bishunpur had pawned the deity of Madan Mohan of Bishunpur to Gokul Mitra, a rich man of Calcutta. Gokul Mitra, installed the deity in a temple built by him. Then he brought down the priest and other *Saivites* (temple servant) from Bishunpur in order to carry on the services of the deity as before. According to the evidence of Banksi Bādan a descendant of the priest's family, the services of Madan Mohan have not been modified after the transfer of the deity to Calcutta. The services are carried on account of the prescriptions in the *Govind Lilamitra* by Krishna Kaviraj. The confectionery concerns of Nawin Modak and Bhim Nag in Calcutta were set up in order to supply sweetmeats for Madan Mohan in Gokul Mitra's temple. Similarly the concern of Dwarika Ghosh was founded for supplying *Dadhi, Chhena* and *Makhan* for the services of Madan Mohan in Calcutta.

The author thinks that the sweetmeat industry had developed in Brindawan and then in Bishunpur and finally in Calcutta for the worship of Radha and Krishna.

Akbar, M.J. (ed.) (1984) mentioned that sweets have been part of the Bengal diet for a few centuries at least and the art of sweetmeat making has flourished in prosperous times. Many trace the wide variety of Bengali sweetmeats to the 19th century when the port of Calcutta and English education and trade made Calcutta the rich centre for British colonial trade. Sweetmeat stuffings present a great variety—coconut, spices, syrup, thickened milk, *Chhana* and pulses. Sweetmeats are usually fried, deep fried or steamed. A very special sweet of

Bengal is *Mishtidoi.* Found hardly anywhere else it is sweetened yoghurt made of milk that has thickened slightly over a slow flame and then allowed to set after the addition of arrowroot to give it body. Served cold it can make a meal memorable.

Another set of sweets that are rarely found in shops is *Payesh.* Any auspicious occasion in the Bengali home is celebrated with *Payesh,* usually made of rice although *Payesh* can be made of semolina, beaten rice, spaghetti, noodles and even bread. Another set of sweets are *Piṭhas.* There are many varieties of *Pithas* though the most common one is the sweet potato *Piṭha* even on *Makar Sankranti* in January. Other varieties include coconut *Pitha, ashkeypitha.*

Haldar (1926) mentioned that especially the Bengali ladies are so solicitous of sweet relations that they will not hand over anything but sweet substances—scrupulously eschewing sour and bitter things—directly to anyone for fear of estrangement. In welcoming the new bride in her husband's home, the mother-in-law offers her a bit of jaggery so that no cross words might pass between themselves in future house-keeping. Similarly in entertaining the new son-in-law, no salt is to be served to him for, it might embitter the relationship.

Though sweetmeat is actively associated with Bengali culture, but along with this, fish is also an important item for them. On some occasions, where no vegetarian food is restricted for Bihari people on such circumstances that food is one of the essential items for Bengalis. For example, in marriage ceremony Bihari people (with few exceptions) do not serve non-vegetarian food whereas non-vegetarian food is a must for Bengalis. Here, the term non-vegetarian food is exclusively meant for fish.

Various Factors for the Popularity ot Sweetmeats

Now the question arises why a particular sweetmeat of a particular place becomes popular and the same sweetmeat of the other places are not? The various factors which effect the taste and popularity of the sweetmeats are discussed as follows:

Basic Ingredients

Basic ingredients play an important role in the quality of sweetmeat. These consist of: (a) process of preparing the basic ingredients, (b) quality of basic ingredients, and (c) purity, proportion and combination of basic ingredients.

(a) In olden periods, people prepared basic ingredients such as *Chhena, Khoa* and *Besan* at their homes. But now they purchase such things from the market and this affects the quality of sweetmeat. For example, *Besan* prepared by quern has natural sweetness which is burnt in the flour mill. Due to this the sweetmeat *Motichura* of Bishnupur is deteriorating day by day and one can say that it is on the verge of extinction. (Besides, non-availability of basic ingredients also plays an important role in the extinction of some particular sweetmeats). Similarly *Chhena* and *Khoa* prepared by indigenous method are more tasty and nutritious in comparison to the *Chhena* and *Khoa* which are nowadays frequently available in markets.

(b) The quality of sweetmeat depends upon the quality of basic ingredients. Due to high price of basic ingredients, the sweetmeat makers used either lower quality of basic ingredients or the substitute of the basic ones. As mentioned earlier, in and around Calcutta people prepare the sweetmeat *Moa* not from *Payara gura* but they used simply lower quality of jaggery. But at Jayanagar they continue to prepare *Moā* from *Payara guṛa* which is why this sweetmeat is famous of Jayanagar. Climate is also one of the important factors. Even though one may get good quality of *Payara gura* (though it is impossible) but it is impossible to prepare same quality of *Moa* at other places.

(c) According to Jibantara Haldar purity, proportion and combination of basic ingredients are the real factors for making a sweetmeat more popular. Here, purity means how the sweetmeat maker finished the preparation of sweetmeats. In this, frying, temperature of cooking medium and stirring are the main things. According to Haradhan Nag frying and stirring of basic ingredients are a very difficult task for sweetmeat makers. It is such a crucial point that, if one fries it little more or less, then the actual taste of sweetmeat changes. This depends upon the experience of *karigars.* Regarding proportion and combination, Jag Bandhu Das said that several persons of Krishnanagar prepare this sweetmeat but they do not know the actual proportion and combination of basic ingredients, as a result, the sweetmeat *Sarpuriya* and *Sarbhaza* prepared by them are not famous. He adds that if a person knows the actual proportion and combination of basic ingredients, then anyone can prepare good quality of sweetmeats anywhere.

Ecology

Ecology is one of the important factors due to which a particular sweetmeat of a particular place becomes more popular in comparison to other places. Besides, climate and temperature, the quality of sweetmeats also depends on the environment of that locality.

As referred earlier, the quality of by-products of milk depends on the quality of milk, i.e., whether the milk is of cow or buffalo? Not only that, the milk of village or hilly areas is much sweeter and contains more fat than that of urban areas. So if at any place there are sufficient number of grazing fields, naturally the sweetmeat prepared in that locality is more palatable than other places where there is scarcity of grazing fields. Nowadays in urban areas, people milk the animals (cow/buffalo) with the help of pitutrin injection. Regular use of this injection also affects the quality of milk.

Experience and Patience

This is another factor upon which the popularity of sweetmeat also depends to some extent. Regarding the sweetmeat *Sandesh,* Haradhan Nag said that more or less people know about the basic ingredients of a particular sweetmeat and its recipes but without experience and patience it is impossible for anybody to prepare good quality of sweetmeats. In preparation of sweetmeats there are many stages and each and every stage has its own crucial point. If one deviates from that point, the quality of sweetmeat differs. On being asked about the secrecy of his sweetmeats, he simply replied that it was nothing except the experience and patience of *karigars.* Proportion and combination of basic ingredients also depends upon the experience of *karigars.* Practically, it is impossible for *karigars* to weigh the basic ingredients at every stage and at that the experience of *karigar* works. When the milk is on the stage of curdling it totally depends upon the experience to save the milk from this stage by mixing *khabar soda.* The thickness and intensity of syrup for a particular sweetmeat also depends upon the experience of *karigars.* So in some sweetmeats such as *Sandesh, Jal Bhara Sandesh, Mihidana* and *Sitabhog* this factor plays an important role in making such sweetmeats more popular.

Fire and Cooking Medium

The quality of sweetmeat also depends upon the flame of fire, i.e., whether it is of wood or coal? The sweetmeat prepared on the fire of wood is more palatable than the fire of coal.

For example, the sweetmeats such as *Kachagolla* and *Pantoa* of Ranaghat are mostly prepared on the fire of wood and also by the milk of rural cows/buffaloes. These sweetmeats are also prepared at several places but the taste of such sweetmeats are not alike with that of Ranaghat. At Ranaghat there are sufficient number of grazing fields. As a result, the people of that locality get sufficient quantity of milk. Similar is the case with Raghunathganj. Ghoshal (1983) collected the information from Haringhata Milk Dairy and mentioned that at Ranaghat they prepare about 676 kg. *Chhena* in a day and collect 6152 kg. of milk from that dairy.

Regarding the popularity of sweetmeats such as *Lengcha* and *Nikhuti,* Kanhai Lal Dutta of Shaktigarh and Golak Indra of Shantipur have said that besides the quality of basic ingredients, cooking medium and fire made of coal or wood also affects the quality. Kanhai Lal has said that the sweetmeat *Lengcha* is famous from his shop because he prepared this sweetmeat on fire made of wood. As the price of clarified butter is very dear so they use *vanaspati* but the taste of sweetmeats also depends upon the quality of *vanaspati.* Golak Indra has said that besides fire of wood and cooking medium, goodwill and fame are also responsible for the popularity of his sweetmeat.

Preparation through Scientific Way

According to N.N. Das of Messrs K.C. Das Private Limited, Calcutta, *Sponge Rassogolla* of his shop is widely known because of its sponginess and this has been possible only because of the scientific way by which this sweetmeat is prepared. In the whole process only the round shape to *chhena* is made manually and the rest, i.e., boiling, curdling, bathing, grinding, packing process are done through machines. So, N.N. Das is of the opinion that during the course of preparation of sweetmeats, if it is frequently handled with naked hands, then there is great chance of impurity. The purity of basic ingredients on the one hand and the scientific way on the other hand are keys to his success.

But the author thinks that the scientific way is not the key to popularity of all kinds of sweetmeats. If whole process is done by machines then there will not be natural sweetness, for example, *Motichur* of Bishunpur. In olden days *besan* was prepared with the help of quern but nowadays it is prepared through flour mills. So actual sweetness is not found in present *Motichur* for which it is famous.

Personal Reputation

Besides the factors mentioned above there is one other factor, i.e., personal reputation which has nothing to do with the recipes or basic ingredients. But in spite of that, it plays an important role due to which a particular sweetmeat becomes popular of a particular place. Regarding this factor, N.N. Das says that in these days, due to several reasons, the quality of sweetmeats is deteriorating day-by-day and most of the sweetmeats are prepared everywhere. But goodwill or personal reputation or fame of a particular confectioner of a particular place plays an important role in making the sweetmeat more popular. He further says that he has prepared good quality of

Sitabhog and *Mihidana* for last ten years in comparison to Barddhaman but in spite of that, people's version lays emphasis on the sweetmeats prepared at Barddhaman.

P.K. Saha when asked about the secret of popularity of the sweetmeat *Morabba* also lays emphasis on *Jashs* or goodwill. Nowadays this sweetmeat is prepared at several places but the quality of sweetmeat which is prepared by his brother is of superior quality. Here it is interesting to note that P.K. Saha himself prepares this sweetmeat by using the same process and with same basic ingredients, yet the quality has diferred from that of his brother's.

Similarly the sweetmeat *Manohara* is prepared by several persons at Beldanga. Nowadays Bablu Saha's sweetmeat is famous. Mahadeo Chandra Saha of Beldanga has said that few years ago the most sincere and expert *karigar* of Bablu Saha's shop joined his shop. After getting that *karigar* this fellow was confident that his sweetmeat would compete in the market. But unfortunately he could not compete. So he is also of the opinion that besides other things, fame is one of the important factors due to which a particular sweetmeat becomes popular of a particular place or shop and against, 'Fame' and 'Goodwill' or personal reputation nothing can be done.

References

1. It connects Calcutta with Gede on the Bangladesh border, with Lalgola and with Shantipur. Another branch line leads via Bongaon to the Bangladesh border. Ranaghat carries a large river traffic and is one of the principal seats of commerce in the district.
2. See Appendix-1 for Sorbitol-A Natural Sugar.

8

Communities Associated with Sweetmeats and their Professional Associations

It is well known that Aryans of the Vedic period were divided into four *Varnas,* having considerable social mobility. In course of time, intermarriage between the people of different *Varnas,* either *Anuloma* or *Pratiloma* led to the emergence of a number of castes.

Simple cases of *Anulomaja* sons were those born of *Brahmina* father and *Kshatriya* mother, Kshatriya father and Vaisya mother, and Vaisya father and Sudra mother who assumed the castes of their fathers but tainted by the blemish in their mothers, they would be called *anulomaja* or *apasada*, Brahmanas, *Kshatriyas* and *Vaisyas.* Sons of mothers two degrees below (*Dvyantaritajatah*) were the following:

Brahmin father + *Vaisya* mother = *Ambastha*

Brahmin father + *Sudra* mother = *Nishada* or *Parasava*
Kshatriya father + *Sudra* mother = *Ugra.*

(Agrawala, 1970)

Halwai and *Moyra* castes come under *Ugra.* The Halwai equivalent to the Bengali *Maira*, are sellers of sweetmeats. They and Kandus provide the only food the orthodox Hindu can eat with unwashen hands. But according to W.W. Hunter, "*Halwais* are the confectioners of India. They are not very strict Hindus as they join in the worship of the Musalman Saint, Ghazi, Miyan" (Hunter, 1976).

Northern India

In Northern India *Bharbhunja*, *Halwai* and *Kandu* castes are close kin, though the precise nature of their kinship is uncertain. All three claim to be *Madesiya Vaisyas* and certainly all three have *Madesiya* sub-castes. Sherring (Blunt, 1969) calls *Kandu* a sub-caste of *Bharbhunja*. Risley treats the two names as synonyms in Bihar and Bengal. In Gorakhpur, the Bharbhunja caste, and in Azamgarh, a *Halwai* sub-caste are regarded as offshoots from the *Kandu* caste, whilst in Kanpur the *Kanaujiya Bharbhunja*, so long as he follows the Halwai's occupation is said to intermarry with the *Halwai* caste. In all probability, the *Kandu* is the oldest of three, and has given branches to both the *Bharbhunja* and the *Halwai* at all events in the east of the United Provinces (*ibid*).

Origin

The occupational caste of confectioners, numbered about 3000 persons in the erstwhile Central Provinces and Berar (Bihar) in 1911. The caste gives no account of its origin in Northern India, but it is clearly a functional group composed of members of respectable middle-class castes who adopted the profession of sweetmeat-making. The Halwais are also called *Mithaihas* or preparers of sweets and in the Uriya country are known as *Guria* from *Gur* (molasses) or unrefined sugar. The caste has several subdivisions and territorial names, generally derived from places in Northern India as *Kanaujia* from Kanauj, and *Jaunpuria* from Jaunpur; others are Kandu, a grain parcher, and *Dobisya,* meaning two score, one of the *Guria* subdivisions is named *Haldia* from *Haldi* (turmeric) and members of this sub-caste are employed to prepare the *Mahaprasad* or cooked rice which is served at the temple of Jagannath and which is eaten by all castes together without scruple. The *Gurias* have exogamous divisions or *Bargas,* the names of which are generally functional, as *Darban* (door keeper); *Saraf* (treasurer); *Bhitarya* (one who looks after household affairs) and others.

Status

The social standing of the *Halwai* is respectable. According to Nesfield, His art, implies rather an advanced state of culture, and hence his rank in the social scale is a higher one. There is no caste in India which considers itself too pure to eat what a confectioner has made. In marriage banquets it is he who supplies a large part of the feast, and at all times and seasons the sweetmeat is a favourite food to a Hindu requiring a temporary refreshment. There is a kind of bread called *Puri,* consisting of wheat dough fried in melted butter, which is taken as a substitute for the *Chapati* or wheat pancake by travellers and others who happen to be unable to have their bread cooked at their own fire, and is made by the *Halwais.* (Russell, 1916).

The real reason why the *Halwai* occupies a good position perhaps simply results from the need of other castes to take sweetmeat from him. Among the higher castes, food cooked with water should not be eaten except at the hearth after this has been specially cleansed and spread with cowdung, and those who are to eat have bathed and otherwise purified themselves. But as the need continuously arises for travellers and others to take a meal abroad where they cannot cook for themselves, sweetmeats and cake made without water are permitted to be eaten in this way, and the *Halwai*, as the purveyor of these, has been given the position of a pure caste from whose hands a Brahmin can take water.

The Halwai community of the north-western India is actively engaged in confectionery. They are often confounded with the Kandu, who is properly a grain parcher, though he also deals in sweetmeats. These two castes are however, totally distinct, and do not inter marry.

This community enjoys a character for personal purity. Brahmins will take water from their hands, and all Hindus except the *Sarwariya Brahmins*, will eat *Puris* (bread of wheaten dough fried by them in melted butter). They eat the flesh of goats and sheep, but more particularly that of animals which have been offered in sacrifice. They eat food cooked with butter (*pakki*) cooked by Brahmins, *Kshatriyas* and all respectable *Vaisyas* excepting *Kalwars.* They will eat food cooked in water *kachchi* only when prepared by members of their own caste or by their priests. Only *chamars* and other menial castes will eat their leavings. The *Acharwala* or (preparer of pickles, jams, etc.,) is generally an independent Muslim trader, not a Muslim *Halwai*, as seems to be the case in Bengal. In the eastern parts of the province, the Hindu *Halwai* often makes jams and condiments (*chatni*) (Crooke, 1974).

Making sweets is the special business of this caste, but some have taken to agriculture and a good many to moneylending and other mercantile business like *Baniyas.* Their women, who often manage their shops, have in some places an equivocal reputation.

Marriage

There are a number of endogamous sub-castes, some of which are of territorial origin and others which are possibly recruited from Hindu tribes who have taken to the occupation of making sweetmeats. The last census gives the *Kanaujiya* as their only important sub-caste. According to the complete lists, the *Halwai* are peculiar for the very large number of sections derived from local towns and places.

The age for marriage runs from five to twelve, and the better off members of the caste marry their daughters in infancy. One of the clansmen acts as *Agua* (negotiator). It is forbidden to marry again during the lifetime of the first wife without leave of tribal council. The levirate is permitted and prevails generally, but it is not enforced on the widow and her right to select a second partner is recognized. Marriage is as usual of three forms:

(i) *Shadi or Charhauwa,* the respectable ritual; (ii) *dola* used by poor people, and (iii) *Sagai* for widows. In the first *pairpuja* (the worshipping of the bridegroom's feet) by the father of the bride and *sendurdan* (the smearing of vermilion) on the parting of the bride's hair are regarded as the binding part of the ceremony, which goes through the usual states of *barrekhi* (betrothal) and *lagan* (fixing of the marriage day). Then comes a special ceremony called *anaj chhuna* (the touching of the grain); at a lucky time fixed by the *Pandit* they send for some *urdi* pulse and grain, and the women begin to grind it. During this ceremony, no widow or woman married by *Sagai* is allowed to be present. Then follows the *Gitgauna* (singing), when the women commence the marriage songs, and next comes the *matamangara,* when some earth is collected and brought into the marriage shed, when all the women get some sweets and oil for their hair. Then follows the anointing (*tel haldi*) and on the day before the procession starts the clansmen are fed (*Bhatwan*), while the father and mother of the bridegroom do the *matri* or *matri puja,* which is an emblematical remarriage. Their clothes are tied together by the Brahman, their feet stained with dye (*mahawar*), and they worship an image of the *Naugraha* (nine planets) made of cow dung. At the bride's door the *dwar puja* is done in the usual way. The clansmen are then fed, and some food is sent from the bride's house for the bridegroom, while he eats it, the barber rubs his father's feet with a mixture of barley flour and turmeric known as *Chikas,* and the clansmen are given *mirchwan* (a mixture of sugar and pepper dissolved in water) to drink. On the day after the marriage (*barhar),* the boy is solemnly fed on rice and pulse *(Khichari)* when the bride arrives at her husband's house, the deities of Gangaji, Sati and Mahadeva are worshipped and on the fourth day (*chauthi*) the bride's father sends a present of rice, sweetmeats, butter, clothes, etc., out of which a part is set aside as an offering to the *Deotā* (Godlings). This is known as *bujhwat*.

Childbirth and Initiation

When a woman is in the eighth month of pregnancy, the *athwansa* ceremony is performed. Husband and wife are dressed in new clothes and five kinds of butter cakes and five varieties of fruits in season are placed in her lap. The other ceremonies are the ordinary type. When a boy is five or six years old, the ceremonial shaving (*mundan*) and ear piercing (*kanchhedan*) are done at some shrine, such as that of the Vindhyabasini Devi at Bindhyachal. This marks the boy's initiation into caste privileges and from that time he is bound to conform to the tribal rules regarding food.

They have both a Hindu and a Muslim branch. Hindu *Halwais* are rarely initiated into any of the recognized sects, but are by preference *Vaishnavas*. Their clan deity are *Mahadeva, Hardiya,* or *Hardaur* and the *Panchonpir,* among whom *Ghazi Miyan* is most regarded. He is worshipped on the ninth of Kuar with cakes (*bara), urad* pulse, boiled rice, bread, and a goat is sacrificed. These offerings are placed on seven stones near the family shrine. Mahabir and Mahadeva are propitiated with sweets (*Laddu*), fried gram (*ghunghuri*) and sweet cakes in the month of *Sawan*. When a child is attacked with smallpox a pice is waved round its head and put behind its pillow, a pit is dug in the ground and *sharbat* prepared of five different fruits is poured into it, and Sitala Mata worshipped with an offering of sweets (*batasha*), fried gram (*ghunghuri*) and garlands of flowers. Their priests used to be of the special class of Brahmins known a Kinnara Misra, but these have now taken to music as their profession, and have fallen into disrepute. Their place has been taken by ordinary *Sarwariya Brahmins*.

Their are two classes of *Halwais*: (1) The confectioner proper who makes sweetmeats and vends them at his shop either wholesale or retail, and (2) The *Khwancha-farosh* (tray man) who buys from the confectioner and sells as he walks the streets or squatting at a booth (Hoey, 1880).

Titles and Sub-Castes

The titles of the Halwai castes in Bihar are Chaudri, Das, Modi, Sahu. It has eight sub-castes viz., Kanaujia, Magahiya, Bantiria or Balamtiria, Pacchainya, Madesia, Purbiya Bhojpuria, Koranch and Maltaria. Pachhainiya Madesia and Purbiya Madesia are also known as Tinmutia Madesia and Chhaumulia Madesia respectively. Section of the few important sub-caste are as follows:

Sections of the Kanaujia Sub-caste

There are five sections in this sub-caste viz., Kachua, Kusmaulia, Laskoria, Lukathia and Santop Palwar.

Sections of the Bhojpuria Sub-caste

There are twenty sections in this sub-caste viz., Akhandhari, Amghat, Basaria, Basdebpur, Bharsahar, Bijaibanaras, Dhakais, Dharkia, Gauli, Gauthaha, Jabalia, Kandwar, Karo, Kosta, Naorakhia, Narauni, Pachattar, Pachopat, Pator and Sakarwar.

Section of the Korench Sub-caste

Pindwal is the single section of this sub-caste.

Sections of the Purbiya Madesia Sub-caste

The sections of this sub-caste are as follows: Anjer, Akhanberi, Ami, Anar, Anokonwar, Anrua, Asarmatta, Sadabasti, Bijai, Baksar, Bakutari, Banebanaras, Baniapathar, Bansahar, Bator, Chanwar, Chausa, Chilhar, Padukli, Daharak, Dariapar, Dehadbanaras, Deoghat, Dhakais, Dhakait, Dhanej, Dhema, Doem, Den, Gahunagaona, Gangopali, Hatser, Indri, Jewel, Jirebasti, Kada, Kalasdih, Kandar, Kangkol, Kara, Karar, Karkado, Karni, Kasiaon, Katari, Kathej, Kesaur, Khonta, Kotsa or Kora, Kurisar, Kusar-Pakri, Lakhansaria, Larauni, Lolutra, Mahepura, Mail, Manimanaras, Marar, Marua, Mohar, Nageswar, Nagneswar, Naknesa, Ninghiam, Pachauta, Pachottar, Paiharwara, Phuli, Raksise, Sahuri, Sakarwar, Sakin, Sakrol, Sarauli, Sidhpur, Sikia, Sinhagarh, Sinharas, Sisotar, Sonhar, Tari, Ubhar and Ughar.

Sections of the Pachhainya Madesia Sub-caste

The sections of this sub-caste are as follows: Akhanbari, Basaria, Bharauli, Bijaibanaras, Chauberia, Dhakais, Dhanauta, Dhaneswar, Dighwara, Dumri, Gangautia, Gauangahunar, Gureni, Hanriaot, Jawalia, Kachwar, Kahinwar, Kandel, Kanpakar, Karadhanauta, Karariha, Karu, Kausar, Khirkatora, Khopriha, Maruaha, Narauni, Pachottar and Panthpakar.

Halwai Castes of Bihar

Halwai are food preparing castes, corresponding to the Bengali Modak, who are also makers and sellers of sweetmeats. They form a very important element in Hindu society, as together with the following caste, they provide the only food that the orthodox Hindu can eat with unwashed hands. According to Hunter (1975) the *Halwais* in Patna are divided into the four classes, viz., *Madhesia, Kanaujia, Kuranesh* and *Gaur*, and their number in Patna was 9,176.

Position of Halwai in the Regional Hierarchy of Caste in Bihar

Gait (1902) has divided the castes of Bihar in seven groups, viz., (1) Brahmins, (2) Other castes of twice born, (3) Clean Sudras, (4) Clean castes with degraded Brahmins, (5) Castes lower than the above whose water is not usually taken, (6) Low castes who abstain from beef, pork and fowls, and (7) Unclean Sudras.

Clean Sudra comprises castes from whom water may be taken and who have good Brahmins as their priests. For hierarchial position or to show the relative rank of the different castes he divided the caste in two sub-castes, i.e., Sub-group (a) and Sub-group (b). Gait has put *Halwai* in Sub-group (a). The castes in Sub-group (a) may be said to enjoy a higher social status than those in Sub-group (b).

Halwai Caste and its Ethnographic Background

Halwais (*Mithiya*), the confectioner caste of Bihar, often confounded with the Kandu, who are properly a grain parcher, though they also deal in sweetmeats. The two castes however, are entirely distinct, and do not inter marry with each other. The name *Halwai* is derived from *Halwā* a sweetmeat made of flour, clarified butter and sugar, coloured with saffron and flavoured with almonds, raisins and pistachio nuts (Risley, 1891).

In Sanskrit the term *Halwai* is equivalent to *Modaka*. Regarding the origin of *Modaka*, Sanskrit dictionary mentioned that it originated by *Kshatriya* father and *Sudra* mother (Varma, 1967).

Social Status

The social status of the *Halwais* is respectable and Brahmins will take water from their hands. "Their art", says Nesfield, implies rather an advanced stage of culture and hence their rank in the social scale is a high one. There is no caste in India which is too pure to eat what a confectioner has made. In marriage banquets, they supply a large part of the feast, and during this the sweetmeat is a favourite food to a Hindu requiring temporary refreshment all times and seasons. There is a kind of bread called *Puri*, which contains no sugary element, but yet it is specially prepared by men of the confectioner caste. It consists of wheaten dough fried in melted butter, and is taken as a substitute for the *Chapāti* or wheaten pancake by travellers and others who happen to be unable to have their bread cooked at their own fire. With the exception of Brahmins, there is no class of men in India which declines to eat a buttered pancake prepared by the *Halwai*; and considering the immense amount of fuse (involving even forfeiture of caste) which is attached to the domestic fire place, this says much for the respect in which the *Halwai* are held. As in the case of the Bari, the caste which makes leaf-plates for all classes of the community, considerations of general convenience have no doubt contributed something to the social respectability of the confectioner caste. The rules of the caste regarding their own diet are much the same as those followed by other Hindus of about the same status. None of them will eat the leavings of the higher castes, even of the Brahmins who serve them as priests; and members of the *Madhesia* sub-caste profess to abstain from wine.

Occupation

Only a small proportion of the caste have taken to agriculture, and those are mostly occupancy *raiyats.* Men of the *Magahis* and *Bantiria* sub-castes are often servants or petty shopkeepers, and many *Magahia Halwais* combine grain-parching with the characteristic business of their caste. The Muslim *Halwais* found in most districts of West Bengal are an entirely distinct class and there is no reason to suppose that they are recruited by conversion from among the ranks of the Hindu confectioners. According to Wise (Risley, 1981) the art of preserving fruits in sugar or vinegar is unknown to the Hindus, and all the preserves procurable in the bazars of the East are made by the Muslim *Halwai*, who, however, destroys by too many spices and by excess of sugar, the natural flavour of the fruit. The *Halwai* prepares jams of mango, coconut, ginger, and *bel* and candies of oranges, citrons, and *bel* fruit. The pickles (*achar*) consumed in large quantities by all Muslims are of three kinds, i.e., prepared with vinegar, mustard oil or salt. The *Halwai* likewise makes his own vinegar with molasses, sugar, and water and with it preserves vegetables and fruits of all kinds. Mangoes and limes are, however, also added. *Jaraka,* or fruit in brine is highly recommended as an aid to digestion when eaten as dessert. Arab pedlars bring the best to Bengal, but in Dacca the aromatic lime, known as Kaghasi from the fineness of its rind, is usually preserved in this way (Ibid).

Marriage

The sub-castes and sections of *Halwais* give no clue to the origin of caste which is clearly a functional group composed of members of respectable middle-class castes who adopted the profession of sweetmeat-making. The sections, which are very numerous, seem to be of the territorial type, and bear no traces of either totemism or eponymy. The rule of exogamy is carefully observed. A man may not marry a woman of his own section, or of the sections to which his mother and his paternal grandmother belong. These sections moreover, are taken into account on both sides; so that if the proposed bride's mother belonged to the same section as the bridegroom's paternal grandmother, no marriage can take place; although the parties themselves belong to different sections. Prohibited degrees are reckoned by the standard formula calculated to seven generations in the descending lines.

As a rule *Halwais* marry their daughters as infants, but they do not take an extreme view of the necessity of doing so, and no slur attaches to a man who from poverty or any other reason is unable to get his daughter married before she attains the age of puberty. In fact, some *Halwais* of the *Kanaujia* sub-caste do not think it right to get their daughters married before they are eleven or twelve years of age. The marriage ceremony in vogue does not differ materially from that used by other Bihar castes of about the same social status. *Sindurdān* (the smearing of vermilion on the bride's forehead) and the parting of her hair is deemed to be the binding portion of the ritual. Polygamy is permitted when the first wife is barren, but in no case may a man have more than two wives. A widow may marry again (*Sagai*). A very singular custom is observed when a bachelor marries a widow. The ceremony takes place, as is the usual practice, in the widow's house, but before going there, the bridegroom is formally married in his own house to a sword or a piece of iron, to which he applies vermilion as if it were his bride. With this may be compared the usage common among the Kandu caste of marrying to a sword a daughter who by reason of some physical defect is not considered likely to find a husband. The theory seems to be that the full marriage ceremony is a sort of sacrament, which must be partaken of by everyone at least once in life. On the question of divorce there is some difference of practice among the sub-caste. The *Kanaujia* and *Pachimi Madhesia* do not recognize the authority of the *Panchayat* (Caste Council) as between husband and wife, and if a woman proves faithless they turn her out of the house without further ceremony. In the *Magahiya* and *Purbiya Madhesia* sub-castes a charge of unchastity on the part of the wife or of persistent ill-treatment on the part of the husband is laid before the *Panchayat*, who after taking evidence and hearing what both parties have to say, may dissolve the marriage, either partly, thus being at liberty to marry again.

Religion

The majority of the castes are *Vaishnavas*, and comparatively few adherents of other sects are found among them. For religious and ceremonial purposes they employ *Maithil Brahmins*, who are received on equal terms by all other members of the sacred order, except by those who regard it as unworthy of a Brahmin to serve any man as priest. The minor God Ghaninath is worshipped on Saturdays with offerings of rice, fruit, and sweetmeats, which are afterwards eaten by the members of the household. At marriages a fee is paid by the bride, and (just double) by the bridegroom for the worship of this deity. The members of the caste also hold in honour Bandi, Goraiya, and other minor Gods of Bihar, and many of them are adherents of the Panch Piriya sect. *Halwais* burn their dead and perform the ceremony of *Mayra* on the thirty-first day after death.

Halwai Castes of West Bengal

Halwai, equivalent to Bengali *Mayra* or *Modak* (sometimes known as Madhu Napit), are the sellers of sweetmeats. In the southern part of the province there is a division called Kuri, often mispronounced as *Guriya.* They are a very important element in Hindu society as they with the Kandu provide the only food that the orthodox Hindu can eat with unwashed hand. Kandu also known as *Bharbhunjah* (called in the older books *Bhujari* quaintly translated 'frymen') are the men who prepare parched rice, known variously as *Chira* or *Murhi* and still more commonly as *Chira-murki.* The sub-divisions enumerated are *Ganrar* (Bengali) and its *Behar* equivalent *Gonr Madhesiya* and *Karaunch*. A caste in Bengal called Rarhi following the same profession are fabled to have been originally boatmen, and to have abandoned that calling. Hence there may possibly be some connection between Gonr and Gonrhi besides mere similarity of names which is why they are often confused. The Karaunch is remarkable for the fact that the name is also common to a subdivision of the Bhaskars (or

Sangturash) the stone mason caste, coupling this with the fact that one of the occupations of Kandu is the building of mud walls and another that of brick—laying. Beverley was half inclined to believe that the Bhaskars may be an offshoot of them. The Kandu also make gunny cloth into bags and are sometimes found as diggers and *gharamis* or thatchers. The class is very numerous, and anyone who has been compelled to travel rapidly will easily comprehend its value in the Hindu social scale, though the preparation of food they sell, is far from palatable to the European stomach (Beverley, 1872).

According to Thompson (1923) the *Mayra* (the sweetmeat maker caste) is most numerous in Western Bengal and adjoining districts of Central Bengal, but there is also a large colony, nearly 30,000 in Rangpur, though no other Northern Bengal districts has as many as 700. The *Mayras* returned at 121,534, 3.8 per cent less than in 1911 and 5.1 per cent less than 20 years ago. The decrease may be put down to the fact that the *Mayras* are most numerous in the Western Bengal district which have lost population during the last decade but it is also possible that some of the caste changed to the *Kayasthas,* for they claim the name of *Kayastha Kuri.*

O' Malley (1913) mentioned that according to census 1872 and 1981, changes in them more especially among the lower castes, tend to bring about the formation of separate caste, e.g., the *Madhunapit* are barbers who became confectioner.

Titles and Sub-castes

The *Mayras* of Bengal are known by a number of titles such as Ash, Chandra, Datta, Barat, De, Dan, Gui, Indi, Loha, Nag, Nandi, Rakhit and Raj. There are four sub-castes in Central Bengal and two in Dacca viz., Raoh-asram, Mayur-asram, Aja-asram, Dharm-asram or Dharm-sut and Ekpatia, Dopatia respectively.

In all there are twelve sections viz., A 'lamyan, Bharadwaja, Chandrarishi, Debrishi, Madhurishi, Kasyapa, Gautam, Majurrishi, Ganesrishi, Nagrishi, Sandilya and Somrishi.

Hierarchial Position of Castes in Bengal

Gait (1902) had divided the castes of Bengal in seven groups, such groups are similar to those of Bihar. The group of functional castes, formerly, nine but now seventeen known as the *Nabsakhas* is the type of this group, but it includes also several other castes whose rank is on a par with that of *Nabasakhas*. They are arranged in alphabetical order as follows.

Those marked with a capital (N) are among the nine, castes who according to the *Parasara Samhita* originally formed the *Nabasakha* group:

Bauri (N)	Mayra (Madak) (N)
Gandhabanik	Napit (N)
Kalita	
Kamar (N)	Patial
Kansari	Raju
	Sadgop (N)
Kashta	Sankhari
Kumhar (N)	Sudra
Kuri	Tamli
Madhu Napit	Tanti (N)
Malakar (N)	Teli and
	Tili (N)

Nabasakha is usually taken to mean the nine branches or arrows, but some say that it means the "new branches" as indicating recent recruits from Buddhism (Gait, 1902).

Distribution of Mayra Castes and Variations Since 1872

In Rangpur Mayra includes 25,000 persons who returned as Kuri but it is doubtful how many of them belong to the true confectioner caste. The occupation shown on the slips for these persons was usually, 'cultivator' or 'field labourer' and seldom the characteristic employment of the Mayras. There is a local caste known as Mech Kuri who are cultivators and live like the Meches in scattered hamlets, and closely resemble that tribe in dress, appearance and social customs. Possibly many of the persons who returned as Kuri belonged to this community. In Kuch Bihar there are some people called Kuri Sajjan who are said to be half Mech, half Koch many possibly being the same as the *Mech Kuri* of Rangpur. Further south, on the bank of the Meghna, there is a small community known as *Lohait-Kuri.* They claim to have descended from a Kaibartta boy who was bought by a man of the confectioner caste during a season of famine. The tradition, however, like many others, has probably arisen from the similarity of name and the probability seem to be that the *Lohait-Kuris*, like the *Mech Kuris* and *Kuri Sajjans* are an offshoot from some non-Aryan tribe. They are fishermen by occupation and angle with a rod from a boat drifting with the current. Kuri may either be an old tribal name like Mech or Paliya or it may be a corruption of the word 'coolie' which was applied to these people, in the same way as Central Bengal where 'Buna' is used, with reference to tribes from the Chottanagpur plateau (Ibid).

Mayra Caste and its Ethnographic Background

Modak, Maira and *Kuri* are the confectioner caste of Bengal proper. They being a heterogeneous functional group should be distinguished from the *Madhunapit*, on whom popular usage sometimes confers the titles *Modak* and *Kuri*. Some, indeed, regard the *Madhunapit* as a sub-caste of *Mayra*, but it will be seen from the article on *Madhunapit* that there are grounds for believing that group to be a distinct homogeneous caste owing its origin to a schism among the Napits. In Central Bengal the *Mayra* caste is divided into four sub-castes, i.e., *Rarh-asram, Mayur-asram, Aja-asram* and *Dharm-asram* or *Dharm sut*. In Dacca, where there are comparatively few *Mayras* and the occupation of sweetmeat making is almost wholly in the hands of the *Madhunapit*, the former group has only two sub-castes, i.e., *Ekpatia* and *Dopatia*. The distinction between these include: the former in their marriage ceremony simply carry the bride seven times round the bridegroom, while the latter carry both round in concentric circles, the bridegroom following the inner and smaller circle of the two.

Occupation : *Mayras* believe the making of sweetmeat to be their original occupation, but many of them at present day have entered government service or taken occupancy of *Raiyats*. They will, however, on no account cultivate sugar cane themselves or take any part in the preparation of molasses. In a country where sweetmeats form a staple article of diet, and are often the only food that an orthodox Hindu can partake of on a journey, when they have no time to cook food. It is essential that there should be no doubt about the social status and ceremonial purity of the caste which supplies the community with sweetmeats. *Mayras*, therefore, rank among the *Navasakha*, and Brahmins will take water from their hands. Their own rules regarding diet are those of most respectable Hindus. They will eat cooked food only with Brahmins, and will take water or sweetmeats from members of the *Navasakha* group (Risley, 1891).

Internal Structure : The various sections of the *Mayra* caste show a singular mixture of elements derived from the Brahminical *gotras* and survivals from the earlier which we find among the non-Aryan castes. It is impossible to determine, what tribes may have contributed to form the Mayra caste as we now find it, but the fact that distinct traces of totemism may be discerned, will perhaps be held to justify the conjecture that the group is not wholly of Aryan extraction. As a rule, marriage within the section is strictly prohibited, but in some parts of the country, the law of exogamy is disregarded, and marriage is regulated solely by calculation of prohibited degrees. *Mayras* have not yet developed a full-blown system of hypergamy, but they appear to be on the road towards doing so, for the families who bear the title Ash, Barat, Das and Nandi are called Kulins. At present, however, the distinction is meaningless so far as marriage is concerned. Men belonging to Maulik families may marry Kulin women, and the only privilege attached to Kulinism is the right to receive presents of cloth, etc., at marriages and other domestic festivals.

In *Vishwa Kosh* it is mentioned that Mayra caste is the offspring of *Kshatriya* father and *Sudra* mother (Bose, 1311 B.S.: Vol. 15, 451).

Marriage : Mayras profess to marry their daughters as infants, but they are not as particular in this matter as the higher castes, and instances of girls marrying after puberty, though rare are said to occur occasionally without entailing any serious loss of reputation for the family concerned. The marriage ceremony is performed in accordance with orthodox usages; *Sampradan* or the giving and receiving of the bride, being the essential portion of the rite. A price, varying according to the social status of the parties, is paid for bride. Polygamy is permitted, no limit being placed, in theory atleast, on the number of wives a man may have. A woman involved in adultery is turned out of the caste.

Religion: The castes profess to be orthodox Hindus, belonging for the most part to the *Vaishnava* sect. They regard *Ganesh* as their special deity and makes images in his honour. The special season for his worship is towards the end of the cold weather, before the sugar cane crop has been cut, and freshly prepared molasses cannot be used in the manufacture of sweetmeats until the God has been duly propitiated. Brahmins officiate as their priests, and are not looked down upon by other members of the sacred order. In Manbhum, the deities like Mohan Giri, Sahib Mia Sashthi and Bhadu are among their minor Gods, whom the members of each household worship with sacrifices of goats and offering of rice, fruit and sweetmeats. In this domestic worship Brahmins take no part. The dead are burnt and the ashes thrown into the Ganga or any other river that may be conveniently situated for the purpose. *Sradh* is performed on the thirty-first day after death.

Entry of Non-Sweetmeat Making Castes in this Profession

There have been a considerable change in the pattern of life of the *Halwais* and Mayra communities. The change in their occupational structure is easily perceptible. People no longer stick firmly to their traditional occupations. *Halwais* or Mayras whose income from traditional caste occupations have been alternative meagre have adopted alternate professions like running a fair price shop, agriculture, government contractor, service, etc. Some of them have involved themselves into new professions. This was because their traditional professions have ceased to be profitable, while other jobs are lucrative and offer them better opportunity to earn more. The change of occupation has led to temporary or permanent migration to other places.

In a caste, the profession is determined by birth and a child born in a particular caste has to follow the occupational calling practised by that caste. He finds his occupation reserved by virtue of his caste. This notion is almost gone with the modern attitude and outlook of the people.

In ancient period the profession, sweetmeat making was exclusively meant for traditional castes, i.e., *Halwai* in Bihar and Mayra in West Bengal. But from the Table 8.1 we find that nowadays about 60 per cent of other castes are engaged in this profession. Now the question arises what are its reasons and what are the forces or factors responsible for such changes? All the factors or avenues responsible for the changes may be grouped under headings like education, economic factors (money, market and employment), adoption of scientific and machine technologies and economic backwardness.

Educational Factors

The spread of education through the establishment of different educational institutions at different level of education was one of the factors. The increasing numbers of educational institutions like primary, middle and higher secondary schools, colleges and universities have opened a new dimension in the spread of education. These institutions help to remove the abuse of illiteracy to wrest out their inner qualities and to help in their mental make-up. These education centres perform good service to the people. The students after completing the courses of primary, middle and higher secondary schools, enter colleges and universities as per their interest of higher education. An educated mind can easily understand the futility of different social prejudices and the casteism. These educationally enlightened masses with new ideas and outlook, invoke a great change by eliminating the orthodox thinking and activities in the life and culture of the people in question.

TABLE 8.1

Shops owned by Halwais and Other Castes

Sl. No.		*Name of Places*	*Approximate Number of Sweetmeat Shops*	*Number of Shops owned by Halwais*	*Number of Shops Owned by other castes*
1.	BIHAR	Arrah	200	100	100
2.		Barh	40	10	30
3.		Bhaktiyarpur	10	6	4
4.		Bihar Sharif	450	250	200
5.		Buxar	200	120	80
6.		Deoghar	250	75	175
7.		Ghatshila	100	25	75
8.		Kuru	8	2	6
9.		Udwantnagar	9	1	8
10.	WEST BENGAL	Barddhaman	50	10	40
11.		Beldanga	40	20	20
12.		Chandannagar	200	40	160
13.		Janai	15	3	12
14.		Jaynagar	30	20	10
15.		Raghunathganj	150	30	120
16.		Shaktigarh	7	1	6
17.		Shantipur	35	12	23
18.		Siuri	20	1	19
	Total		1814	726 (40.02%)	1088 (59.98%)

Economic Factors

Economic factors like money, market and employment have made a great change among the people of this community. Barter system, with all its difficulties has almost vanished from the rural areas, and money has taken the place of barter system, as these days people living both in rural and urban areas become dependent on cash, and their exchange begins with cash.

Money Market and Employment

Market is another economic factor which has brought about changes in the life of this community. Market is the place of exchange of goods. Here the people come in contact with the various sections of people with their different lifestyles, dress, food habits and customs which help to some extent influencing the life of the people.

To seek employment is another economic factor due to which these traditional castes have left their traditional profession. The people go for employment in the different places, within and outside the area.

In this connection the present investigator had the opportunity to talk to two *Halwais* of West Bengal and the views given by them are as follows:

Economic Backwardness

Shanker Lal Chowrasia is of the opinion that as most of the people of this caste are poor so they are not in a position to establish their separate shops. So due to economic backwardness they are compelled to work as a *karigar* at sweetmeat shops.

Adoption of Scientific and Machine Technologies

The adoption of scientific and machine technologies specially in the preparation of basic ingredients of sweetmeats also play an important role in this connection. As such apparatus are costly so the people of this community who belong to low income groups never think of purchasing this apparatus. So one can see that many capitalists employed *Halwais* as *karigars* in their firms and from their hard labour they earned lots of money.

Gora Chand Ghosh in this connection said that the *Halwais*

purchase milk (one of the important basic ingredients of sweets) from *Goalas* and prepare different varieties of sweetmeats. By this way, they earn more money. So *Goala* castes think that if they prepare the sweetmeats they will benefit more in comparison to *Halwais.* So in these days most of the *Goalas* possess this profession.

The All India Hotel and Halwai's Federation

The necessity for organizing the Indian styled hotels and sweetmeat shops was felt by the state units of the hoteliers and *Halwais* which met at Ahmedabad on 10th January, 1956, on the occasion of the Fifth Annual Session of the Bombay State Hotels Federation which was held on a grand scale. At that time Sri Fulchand Jain and Sri Motilal Badkul of Jabalpur took the initiative along with the leaders of the Bombay State Hoteliers and an ad hoc committee was formed. In September 1957, an All India body met at Bhagwan Kala-Wadi at Bhubaneshwar, and Bombay, and decided to form an All India body and adopted the Constitution. The next session was held at Jaipur on 14th and 15th September 1963. The Mahamandal organised a silent procession in July 1962 at New Delhi for the application of the provisions of the Employees Provident Fund Act to the Hotel trade.

The federation strongly represented its case before the Joint Select Committee and it was on account of this representation and for technical offences, light penalties were prescribed by the Joint Select Committee, which has now taken the shape of law.

In December 1967, the Federation launched its agitation in New Delhi, against the partial decontrol policy of the Government of India regarding sugar, as a result of which 116 hoteliers and *Halwais* coming from different States (Gujarat, Maharashtra, UP, MP, Bihar and Orissa) participated and courted arrest. This agitation was withdrawn on the assurance of late Sri Jagjivan Ram, the then Honourable Union Minister for Food.

The Federation vigorously carried on its agitation against

the partial decontrol policy of sugar and were engaged in vigorous campaign for the exemption of eatables, sweets and beverages from the sales tax, and the modification of the strict provisions of the Prevention of Food Adulteration Act.

Definition

The name of this association is *Akhil Bharatiya Khadya Peya Mishthanna Vikreta Mahamandal* (ABKPMVM). The term *Akhil Bharatiya* means All India, and *Khadya-Peya-Mishthanna Vikreta* means 'dealers in eatable, drinks and sweetmeat articles', and include hotels (residential) boarding and lodging houses, guesthouses, lodging houses, boarding houses, restaurants, cafes, canteens, tea shops, coffee-houses, refreshment rooms on railway stations, railway restaurants and dining cars, sweetmeat shops, halwais milk and *lassi* shops, cold drink houses, aerated water manufacturers, and dealers of bakeries, dairies and such shops which are generally known as and fall under general term 'Catering Establishments' and shall include all dealers of *Khadya* (Eatables) and *Mishthanna* (Sweetmeat) articles of any description '*Khadya-Peya Mishthanna Vikreta*' will be termed as hoteliers and *halwais*. Mahamandal means '*Akhil Bhartiya Khadya Peya Mishthanna Vikreta Mahamandal* (All India Hotels and Halwais Federation)'.

Sweetmeat-Makers Association of Bihar

The name of the Sweetmeat Association of Bihar is *Bihar Rajya Mishtan Bhojan Vikreta Sangh* (BRMBVS) established in 1954. There were many reasons behind the establishment of this institution as given below.

Before the establishment of this institution there was lack of unity among the *Halwais* and hoteliers. At that time, they had to face a lot of problems and due to lack of unity, nobody would bother about it.

Everybody knows the utility and importance of the business of sweetmeat makers. The people engaged in this business always do the service of people. Besides this, Bihar Government had no sympathy for these people and always introduced new rules and regulations which many times went against the interest of the *Halwais.* This attitude of the government combined with the lack of unity among themselves, lead to the emergence of such an association.

Day by day their problems became complex. In the mean time our country became independent. But their problems remained as usual. At last, Surya Prasad Singh, Shisa Maharaj of Ranchi, Ram Naresh Singh of Jamshedpur and many persons left their business and went to several places of Bihar. They consulted hoteliers and *Halwais* and discussed about their burning problems. Later some more people took interest and gave their support. The role of P.K. Ghosh, the owner of New Pintu, Patna was significant as he bore the whole initial expenses in forming the association.

On 25th and 26th December, 1954 a general meeting was held at Patna under the Presidentship of Nithai Chandra Ghosh at his residence. The function was inaugurated by the then Minister Dr Anugrah Narayan Singh. On that occasion this Association was established. Ram Naresh Singh of Jamshedpur and Surya Prasad Singh of Ranchi were elected as first President and Secretary of this Association respectively. At present, there are more than 105 branches of this association in Bihar.

Sweetmeat-Makers Association of West Bengal

The name of this Association in the West Bengal is *Paschim Banga Mistanna Babasayee Samity* (PMBS). Due to the imposition of government restriction on production of sweets in 1965, the sweetmeat industry felt the need of a 'Joint Front' to represent their cases before the government. So in 1967, *Paschim Banga Moffusil Mistanna Babasayee Samiti* was set up. And in 1979, the *Calcutta Mistanna Babasayee Samiti* was merged with this *Samiti* and a new association, *Paschim Banga Mistanna Babasayee Samiti* was set up. The registered office of the association is in Bankura. The registered office of the Calcutta unit of the Association is Jayasree located at, Bow Bazar with Paresh Chandra Sen of Sen Mahasay and Tapas Hazara of

Jayasree as President and Secretary respectively.

Problems Faced by Sweetmeat Dealers

Now, it would be relevant to discuss the problems faced by sweetmeat dealers which came up in course of the study.

Tradition Bound Market Undergoing Change

Surprisingly, sugar is not the biggest problem of the traditional Indian sweetmeat market of Calcutta. Nor is it price fluctuation of basic ingredients which makes a sweetmeat maker to constantly adjust the quality and size of the sweetmeat to keep his customers from going to a competitor. The problem is one of the subtle changes, a shift towards cosmopolitanization in a market very much traditional. It is a change which has made even the most traditional shops rely more and more on innovation and even diversification and less on public taste, brand, loyalty and goodwill.

Imitation is a typical problem of the sweetmeat market today, which is polarized between the extreme conservation of Bhimnag and Jadab Chandra Das and the adaptability and pragmatism of Gupta Bros. and Mithai. Traditionally, the trade has almost entirely relied on word-of-mouth for propagating its taste and name. The traditional shops have never thought of planned promotion let alone marketing. These traditional shops have been a great believer of the celebrity testimonial. A major problem with the traditionalists is learning to communicate with the public as an individual and not as a connoisseur. For instance, the trade has made no attempts to patent brand names. As a result every shop has a *Abar Khabo* or *Raso Raaj* which can be very confusing for the new consumers.

Another problem for the traditional ''name'' shops has been extreme family fragmentation. Sweet making in West Bengal for centuries has been essentially a family business, a secret passed down from generation to generation. Today, with each member in their respective shops of the famous families of Girish Chandra De, Dwarikanath Ghosh and Bhim

Chandra Nag claiming knowledge of the original taste, it is very difficult for the public to distinguish between the real and the imitators.

Mushroom Growth of Sweetmeat Shops

It is surprising that the mushroom growth of sweetmeat shops in Calcutta, the bulk consumption of fluid milk made by them and the huge profit amassed by their owners at the cost of the people and the State everyday have not engaged the serious attention of the government and the Income Tax authorities.

According to official sources, the number of sweetmeat shops recorded in the Licence Register of the Milk Directorate has already reached a fantastic total figure of above 10,000 as against about 6,000 in 1968. The Milk Directorate, which issues licences to these shops has not been able to deal with this menacing growth in the number of such shops thus resulting in diversion of fluid milk from the open market to the shops, instead of government dairy, to the detriment of the interest of the people. Having very little power to control the market supply of milk or its price, the Directorate staff occasionally organizes surprise raids on such shops only to check whether they are run with proper licence. If the shop owner fails to produce a license, a case is instituted against him. In fact, the Directorate has already instituted cases against several unlicensed shops in the court. But they paid the fine promptly and went back to run their establishment.

A high profit margin, a comparatively small-capital outlay, the minimum risk involved in the business and the maximum scope provided for evasion of sales tax and income tax are believed to be the major factors which have lured a large number of budding entrepreneurs into this trade and have promoted them to invest a chunk of their surplus money.

Load Shedding

Due to load shedding small shops have to pay a heavy price. Bimal Krishna Mandal of Manasa Mishtanna Bhandar said, "Since we do not have enough capital to buy generators, our sales are affected because of frequent power cuts." However, load shedding which has struck a death blow to many an industry in West Bengal has not affected the bigger shops much. Ramjibhai Chaurasia of Ganguram's Chowringhee branch said, "Power cuts do not worry us much. Whenever there is load shedding we switch on our mini generators for the sale counters"

Labour Problems

The sweetmeat trade is also dependent on skilled workers. To retain them it has been forced to almost double wages in the past decade or so. Another issue that is worrying the industry is labour problem. Labour problem is one of the major problems which the sweetmeat owners have to face.

In the course of the study it was seen that all the shops (about five) of Jalayog were under lockouts, following strike by the employees. The strike at Jalayog started after the transfer of a manager from one branch to another. The manager, it is said, was asked by the management to go to another branch without issuing any transfer order and no rise in pay. When he refused to go, he was chargesheeted and finally his services were terminated. The employees of all the branches numbering about 100 did not approve of the management action and went on strike.

Two branches of Ganguram on Harrington Street and Beckbagan, also remained closed for quite sometime owing to labour problems.

Bhim Nag was also having labour trouble for about six months in 1981 when the family members had to run the shop. Referring to the labour problems in the shop the managing partner said, "In 1981, the employees, numbering about 45 demanded higher wages, which we thought to be too much." Following the management's refusal to pay extra wages, the workers went on strike and decided to start their own sales counter in front of the shop.

High Rate of Taxation

Nearly 2.5 million people in West Bengal are engaged in the sweetmeat industry. Indeed, it is more than an industry. These are the people who through the generations have helped to make it an art. There are about 55,000 confectioners in West Bengal. In Calcutta alone, the number will be a staggering 7000 to 8000 (*The Statesman*, April 9, 1983). But a lot of problems mostly man-made, now threaten to sour the sweetness that was there in more than one sense.

One of the major problems that the industry has to contend with is the high doses of taxation being imposed by the West Bengal Government. A sales tax on sweetmeats has been in force since the 1940s. Traders complain that it has been steadily going up over the years even though the trade has been forced to contend with steep increases in the prices of inputs and establishment expenses. The costs of sugar, milk and fuel each of them vital in the manufacture of sweets have gone up many times.

There are license fees of various types. A sweetmeat seller in Calcutta has to pay about a dozen type of taxes of license fees to the State Government, the corporation or to the police. The sweetmeat trade is bitter over a further hike from seven to eight per cent in sales tax levied on its products. It was raised to 7 per cent in 1977 from 6 per cent in 1967. In 1979 it went up to 8 per cent. But it is not possible for sweetmeat sellers to charge customers the tax, as most of the purchasers are very small.

In 1969, the State Government, through a special order brought the sweetmeat industry under the wing of cottage industry. But the industry does not get benefits and facilities normally given to the cottage industry. So long the sweetmeat sellers had been paying Rs 250 as eating house license fee. In the year 1985, the Calcutta Police was planning to impose Rs. 250 as licence fee for each individual item. For instance a shopkeeper has to pay Rs. 250 on sweets, Rs. 250 on salted items, Rs. 250 on tea and coffee and Rs. 250 on *Lassi* and other drinks.

Most of these sweetmeat shops do not pay income tax at all and it is known that there is no sales tax on sweetmeats as such. Only if any shop register a total sale of about Rs. 10,000 in a year they are required to pay sales tax. But that applies to other commodities as well. This is a point which has gone to the advantage of sweetmeat shop owners and to the disadvantage of the commercial tax directorate, which has neither any suitable machinery to assess the volume of production and sale of sweetmeats nor any method to check and cross-check their figures. One reason is that while in case of other manufacturers, the sales tax and income tax officials check the figures at the point of purchases of raw materials; here in case of sweetmeats, the raw material, milk is bought from so many unregistered and untraceable sources that any such check by officials becomes virtually an impossible task.

The pattern of sales at most sweetmeat shops, a *Rassogolla,* or two or a few pieces of *Sandeh* at a time, makes it difficult to pass the burden of the sales tax on to customers. Then again stiff competition especially among small shops situated close to each other in the same locality, makes it essential to keep the prices down and the majority of the traders end up bearing the sales tax themselves.

Restriction on Production of Sweets

Sometimes, under special circumstances, the Government has to put some restrictions on the production of some a particular sweetmeats, for the time being. They even bar some items temporarily. For instance the sweetmeat industry in West Bengal had received a severe jolt in 1965 when the P.C. Sen ministry restricted sweetmeat production under its sweetmeat control order. The reason obviously was the shortage of milk supply. As a result production came to a total halt in Calcutta. Later on the restrictions were lifted. However, restrictions on the production of '*Rabri*' still exist.

Harassment to Entrepreneurs

Sometimes the sweetmeat dealers are unnecessarily harassed by the government officials. Due to this, they have to face a lot of problems.Here the present investigator cites an example in this connection, which he has gathered during the fieldwork at Ranchi.

G.C. Ghosh, for the first time planned to set up a factory at the cost of Rs. 14 lakhs for manufacturing 100 per cent export-oriented *Sponge Rassogollā* for export at Kokar Industrial Estate in Ranchi. It would have helped the country in earning foreign exchange of about Rs 30 lakhs per year. It is unfortunate that it could not be materialized because of alleged harassment by a section of officials of the Ranchi Industrial Area Development Authority.

The entrepreneur, is reported to have secured clearance of his project report for the factory from the Small Industries Service Institute (SISI) of the Government of India. The SISI had sent the project report to RIADA for allotment of necessary land and other assistance for the cent per cent export oriented venture.

But the RIADA had allotted the entrepreneur only 9000 sq. ft. of land against the required 22000 sq. ft. assuring him of further allotment of the vacant land adjacent to his proposed factory premises after its completion. The adjoining land was required for erection of godown.

Banking on this assurance of RIADA, the entrepreneur completed his factory with his limited deposits and bank loans amounting to Rs. 14 lakhs. Later RIADA was denying him the adjoining vacant land.

The entrepreneur alleged that the vacant land in question was allotted to the brother-in-law of an influential officer of the public sector CCL. He further alleged that some officials of RIADA had hatched up a plot to ruin his factory by allotting that nearby vacant plot to other persons for setting up mobile oil chemical and poultry-feeding factories which would invariably pollute the atmosphere of his export oriented *Rassogolla* factory.

The entrepreneur called upon the RIADA to discontinue

the contracts of those factories. He claimed that his factory would be the only SISI sponsored unit in the country for manufacturing *Rassogolla* for export. He stated that besides producing one tonne of *Rassogolla* initially, his factory would produce jam, jelly and other food products for export, earning foreign exchange worth Rs. 27 lakhs per year.

Non-Availability of Raw Materials at Fair Price

Inadequate supply of sugar, coal and kerosene and rising prices of flour and some ingredients had put the sweetmeat, industry in difficulty. According to the estimate of S. Barat, General Secretary of the PMBS the industry required about 6000 quintals of sugar daily. Because of the shortage of sugar, they were prepared to carry on with about 5000 quintals. But the West Bengal Federation of Sugar Dealer's Association, which had been entrusted with the distribution of sugar had been able to supply not more than 450 quintals a day to 1,500 shops out of 6000 shops in Calcutta alone. He said no sugar had been sent to the shops in greater Calcutta and in the districts.

The procedure for distribution of sugar was so "unimaginative" that only those who purchase sugar in bulk from wholesellers would benefit. Even trade licences, milk supply permits and rent receipts were not considered valid documents for the purpose.

The steep rise in prices of sugar, flour, *vanaspati* and other basic ingredients had hit the industry badly. Sweetmeat sellers buy sugar in the open market at an exorbitant price. The industry is facing a crisis because of government indifference and apathy. The sweetmeat sellers never got essential raw materials at a fair price. The industry asks "If the bakeries can get *maida* and *vanaspati* at a price fixed by the State Governments then why the sweetmeat industry should be deprived of this facility?" In other States the Sweetmeat sellers are issued licences by which they get their raw materials at controlled prices. Moreover it is widely known that instead of buying sugar from black market for their own requirements many a shop owner diverted a part of their stock in the black market.

9

Diffusion of Sweetmeats and its Factors

Change constitutes one of the universal characteristics of human culture. No living culture is static. All the changes that take place in a culture may be because of two factors, i.e., internal and external. Evolution implies change because of internal factors while the changes that come by way of external factors may be because of diffusion.

According to *International Encyclopaedia of the Social Sciences*, diffusion implies the spread of culture from one ethnic group or area to the other (Heine-Geldern, 1972). The theory of diffusion emerged in the early years of this century. According to diffusionists various culture complexes develop at various times in different parts of the world and later on diffuse over other parts of the earth. According to them, cultural complexes or traits may be carried by migrating people into an area where they settle down temporarily and may be communicated to the local inhabitants living there. Diffusionists are of the opinion that culture has grown in course of history, not because of evolution, but because of transmission of culture due to historical happenings and mutual contacts. Such historical happenings, which led to the transmission of culture and provided a theory to the study of culture growth and culture parallels, was called 'diffusion'

Similarly, in the present context of diffusion of sweetmeats, when a new sweetmeat has been evolved in a culture, there is a tendency on its part to be passed on to other cultures or societies. This passing of a sweetmeat or the traits connected with it from its original place to other places and getting integrated in the local traditions of that place is called as diffusion of sweetmeats. For example, *Shilao Ka Khaza* originated at Shilao but nowadays it is prepared at several other places like Bihar Sharif, Gaya, Patna, Ranchi, Jamshedpur where it has gained popularity and become a part of the local traditions connected with sweetmeats. As such, we can say that *Shilao Ka Khaza* has diffused from Shilao to other places as mentioned above.

Sweetmeats play an important role in our culture as they have a great social and cultural significance and some traditions are also associated with them. As apparent from foregoing discussions, sweetmeats have a diffusionable trait. Diffusion of a trait helps in understanding the growth of culture. In view of this the present study on *Anthropology of Sweetmeats* would remain incomplete without the study of their diffusion.

The Present Angle of Analysis

The study of diffusion of the sweetmeats and its factors was made from two different angles; firstly, in a historical perspective, and secondly from the angle of 'W' formula. They will be discussed here one by one.

During the course of fieldwork the present investigator took interview of about fifty sweetmeat-makers of Bihar and West Bengal and could discover eleven factors responsible for the diffusion of sweetmeats from one place to the other. These factors help in the understanding of diffusion in historical perspective.

It was found that the diffusion of sweetmeats took place at four different levels viz., All India; Zonal (Inter-State); State; and Regional (cultural-linguistic zone within a State) levels. Besides, five case-studies of different categories of sweetmeats were taken-up which further substantiate the understanding of the diffusion of sweetmeats. Those sweetmeats were *Rassogolla, Raskadam, Shilao Ka Khaza, Belgrami* and *Maner Ka Laddu*. The sweetmeats like *Rassogolla* have diffused on all India level; *Raskadam* on Zonal level; *Shilao Ka Khaza* on State level; *Belgrami* on regional level and lastly *Maner Ka Laddu* presents a case which did not diffuse from their original place at all.

To folllow the 'W' formula[1] model forty-five sweemeat-traits based on colour, basic ingredients, shape, size, condition of syrup and the like were selected from Bihar and West Bengal during the course of fieldwork at these two places. For this purpose the investigator used a list of traits connected with sweets and checked it with different sweetmeat sellers by appliying sampling method.

In this formula : 'W' stands for $\frac{a + d}{a + d + b + c}$
where $a = + +^{-}$, $b = + -^{-}$, $c = - +^{-}$, $d = -^{-}$.

In other words, 'W' is agreement divided by total. The presence (+) or absence (-) of a trait was recorded from 32 places (16 places from Bihar and 16 places from West Bengal) based on the observation of at least five sweetmeat shops located at different places in an urban centre such as near railway station, court, bus-stand and the main market. A few famous sweetmeat shops of the town were also selected by random sampling method. For the purpose of showing the presence of sweetmeat traits, only common sweetmeats and the trait connected with it were considered.

Diffusion of Sweetmeats in Historical Perspective and their Factors

In the study several factors were found to be responsible

for the diffusion of sweetmeats and the traits connected with it. The sweetmeats diffuse on all India, zonal, State and regional levels.

Location of Shops nearing State Borders

Before 1912, Bengal, Bihar and Orissa came under a single province. It was during the Coronation Darbar at Delhi on the 12th December, 1911 these Provinces were separated with effect from the Ist April, 1912, and Bihar, Chotanagpur and Orissa were placed under a Lieutenant Governor-in-Council (Chaudhury, 1962). From Ist April 1936 Bihar was a separate Province (*Ibid*).

There are certain towns and cities located at the borders of the two States which are marginal areas. For example, the places such as Dhanbad, Ranchi, Jamshedpur, Ghatshila are located in such marginal areas where we find comparatively maximum number of Bengali population in comparison to other places of Bihar. At such places we find the sweetmeats of both the States, i.e., Bihar and West Bengal. At Ghatshila only such sweetmeats are found, which are of Bengali origin, e.g., *Raskadam, Rassogollā, Rasmalāi.* and we do not find any sweetmeat which are prepared in North Bihar. At Jamshedpur, and Ranchi also we find such sweetmeats (viz., *Sandesh* made of *Tal Gura, Chhenā-Jalebi* and *Moā*) which are not prepared in North Bihar. At some other places of Bihar also we find some Bengali sweets but mostly in those shops where either the owner or the *karigar* are Bengalis. Similarly, at Calcutta we also find some sweetmeat shops which exclusively prepare Dacca sweets such as *Kacha Gulla, Rāghavsai,* such sweetmeats are famous of East Bengal.

Migration or Immigration of a Community and Sweetmeat-Makers

There are several circumstances under which people have to migrate from one place to the other. This may be within the State, from one district to the other, or outside the State. This factor also plays an important role in the diffusion of sweetmeats and traits connected with sweetmeats.

Literally, a community is a group of people which lives within a territorial area and shares a common way of life. Thus, the members of a community exhibit similarity in language, customs, mores, traditions and many other things. When such a community migrates to another place, they interact with the local people. On such circumstances business-men are very alert and watch carefully the necessary consumption pattern of that community. After sometime they supply those goods to their new customers. For example, at the time of industrialization of Ranchi many South Indians came to this place and the local hoteliers had to cater to their favourite dishes like *Dosa, Iḍli, Barra, Utpam.* Not only that, their favourite sweetmeat *Mysore Pak* is also now prepared in many sweetmeat shops, it is another thing that most of these shops are owned or manned by South Indian people. Another interesting case refers to *Belgrami* sweet. When the Belgrami family came to Koath, at that time sweetmeat makers who accompanied them prepared a special type of sweetmeat for them. Nowadays Koath is also famous for such sweetmeat popularly known as *Belgrami.*

Migration of sweetmeat makers also plays an important role in the diffusion of sweetmeats. During fieldwork the present investigator found several cases in which the sweetmeat makers left their original shop and went to other places. At those place either they opened their own shops or joined another sweetmeat shop as a *karigar*. For example, due to migration of *karigars* from Danapur to Kuru we find a special type of sweetmeat popularly known as *Lorhā Miṭhai* which was introduced by them. Nowadays Kuru is famous for this sweetmeat.

The sweetmeat *Shilao Ka Khaza* diffused from Shilao to several other places. Through the diffusion of this sweetmeat, this investigator wanted to show as to how the migration of *karigars* (sweetmeat-makers) helped in the diffusion of sweetmeats from one place to other. It was Munimji who for the first time prepared *Shilao Ka Khaza* at Ranchi in the year 1978. Previously, he was working as a *karigar* in a sweetmeat shop at Gaya where he knew about the recipe of *Shilao Ka Khaza*. But due to some conflict with the owner he left that shop and opened a new sweetmeat shop at Gaya in the year 1967 where he had been selling *Shilao Ka Khaza*. But due to some disturbance created by the landlord of that shop he again opened a sweetmeat shop at Kudra (near Sasaram) in the year 1976. But, unfortunately he had to close that shop due to scarcity of skilled *karigars* and finally he migrated to Ranchi.

At present, there are eleven *Shilao Ka Khaza* shops at Ranchi. Among them there are two such persons who have two shops each and in both the shops they prepare *Khaza*. They belong to village Shilao. The owner of rest of the shops (except one) are local persons who have borrowed the labour from Shilao. The owner of one shop has appointed the old labour who were previously working in other shops.

Similarly, *Shilao Kā Khāzā* was first prepared by Bachcha Babu at Dhanbad in the year 1980. Bachcha Babu got this training from Munimji's shop at Ranchi were he was previously working as a *karigar* in the year 1977-78. According to him, as Munimji did not pay him wages timely so he left that shop and went to Dhanbad where his father had a business of straw of paddy. As he was not interested in this business, he finally opened a sweetmeat shop at Dhanbad with the training in *Khaza* making which he had received earlier in Munimji's shop at Ranchi.

Sometimes the owner of a shop who is eager to prepare new sweetmeats has to pay heavy amount to the owner of the shop from where he wants to borrow the *karigar* for a limited period. For example, many expert makers of *Tilkut*, were taken to Bokaro, Jamshedpur, Ranchi and Dhanbad from Gaya on such conditions.

Similarly, according to Gora Chand Ghosh (M/s. Dwarika Ghosh & Sons, a famous sweetmeat organization of Calcutta), he gave some expert labour to his relatives who opened new sweetmeat shops at different places.

In this way we see that migration of a community and the

sweetmeat-makers play an important role in the diffusion of sweetmeats.

Initiative taken by Influential Persons

In some cases the acceptance of new cultural-traits connected with sweets have been due to the initiative of prestigious persons.[2] For example, Bengali sweets are of three basic kinds : using *Chhenā*, thickened milk, and wheat flour. Also there is a fourth kind, using powdered pulse, but most sweetmeat sellers said that it was specially developed to appeal to North Indian palates. Here it may be mentioned that at one stage Bengal was ruled from the north, and the *Nawabs* of Bengal and *Maharajas* of Cooch Bihar and Burdwan also originally came from North India.

North Indian sweets are primarily made of *besan*, *khoa* and *ghee*. They are by far the richest of sweets produced in India and under normal conditions cannot be eaten in large quantities. The pride of a sweetmeat maker was that his sweets would remain edible for a year or more, because if the better quality of *ghee*, milk and spices were used, it does not get spoiled (Akbar, 1984).

The use of dried fruits shows the influence of trade from Central Asia as well as its patronage by the Nawabs and kings of old days. *Badam Barfee* may constitute an example which is made of *khoā* and spiced with almonds. It is a delicacy. Sweets from North India have been in Calcutta for centuries and their makers came down the Ganga many centuries ago (Ibid). *Sohnpāpri, Mysore Pāk, Motichur Laḍḍu, Kaju Barfee* are all northern delicacies that have become very popular with the Bengalis.

The sweetmeat *Belgrāmi* is well-known in Bihar only due to residence of the well-known 'Bilgrami family', descendants of Nawab Nurul Hussain Khan, who came from the family home at Bilgram in Oudh after peace had been concluded with Shiya-ud-daula, when he received a large *Zamindari* at Koath (Bihar).

Diffusion of Sweetmeats Through Kinship Network

The bonds of marriage, parenthood and sibling which connect the members of the elementary family with one another result in a network of relationships by kinship and affinity. To show the diffusion of sweetmeats through kinship network, some cases collected are given below:

At Patna, there are about fifteen shops who prepare *Shilao Ka Khaza*. Among them, the shop of Ram Bishun Ram is one of the oldest ones. At present his shop is situated near Patna Science College. He has been preparing this sweetmeat since 1960. After some time his brother Doman Ram opened a separate shop at Bikhna Pahari, another *mohalla* of Patna. In the year 1980, the son-in-law of Ram Bishun Ram named Basant Kumar, opened a new shop just in front of the museum. In the year 1981, the *Shālā* (brother-in-law) of Doman Ram named Saryu Nand started a new shop at Patna City. All such persons got their training in the preparation of the *Khaza* from Ram Bishun Ram.

The sweetmeat *Raskadam* is famous of Kahalgaon and Dalsingsarai of Bihar State and Maldah and Aurangabad of West Bengal State. According to Sohan Sah (who owns the oldest shop of sweetmeats at Kahalgaon in Bhagalpur district) his father Baiju Sah got the training of preparing this sweetmeat at Pharkka in Maldah where the brother-in-law of his father had a famous sweetmeat shop. In early days, his father was residing with his brother-in-law at Pharkka where he received his training in the making of *Raskadam*. At Dalsingsarai, this sweetmeat was first introduced by Ishri Sah. According to Lalo Sah, his father, Ishri Sah got the training of making this sweetmeat from Kahalgaon. At Kahalgaon (in the house of Baiju Sah) the eldest sister of Lalo Sah was married in the year 1950.

After analysing the cases, we find the sweetmeats were diffused in many cases through affinal kinsmen.

Social Congregations at Market Place, Fairs, Festivals and Pilgrimage Centres

Social congregations at markets, fairs, festivals and pilgrimage centres also help in the diffusion of sweetmeats. Market is the place of exchange of goods. Here, the people come in contact with the various sections of people with their different styles of life, dress, customs and food habits which to some extent help in influencing the life of the people.

Besides these markets, the opportunity to have large social congregations is made possible by holding of the annual *Mela* at different places like Rajgir, Sonepur, Gaya, etc. In these *Melas* people from far and wide, from different strata of society come and meet. These markets and periodical fairs have proved to be of much importance with respect to culture contact and borrowings of cultural traits. Daily, weekly, and monthly markets provide the necessary things to the people which are brought by different merchants from different places, to sell in the markets.

Similarly at pilgrimage centres, the people of different communities live together either in *Dharamshalas* or in the house of their *Panda*. On such circumstances, the people belong to other community also know about the food habits of each others communities. Generally people prefer to bring more sweet things in comparison to salty things at the time of pilgrimage. At pilgrimage centre, the pilgrims also purchase some famous things of that area. When the people return to their homes they distribute those things among their neighbours. For example, if a person goes to Gaya for pilgrimage he also purchases *Tilkut* because this is one of the famous things of Gaya. When they go back to their homes, they distribute the *Tilkut* among their neighbours. In the long run on the one hand they learn the recipe of such sweetmeats and prepare it in their homes while on the other hand, they pursue the owner of their favourite sweet shop to prepare such sweetmeats. Gradually such sweetmeat is included as an important item of their casual food.

Maintenance of Livelihood and the Standard of Shop

There are some sweetmeats which are prepared only in their appropriate season, e.g. *Tilkut* of Gaya is prepared only in winter season. On such circumstances the people who are associated with this sweetmeat have to face economic difficulties in other seasons. Such persons prepare other sweetmeats to maintain their livelihood in other seasons. They prepare *Lai* and *Anarsa* in summer and rainy seasons respectively. But the sweetmeat *Lāi* is more famous of Barh. Here we see that *Lai* has been diffused from Barh to Gaya on large-scale.

Sometimes, for maintaining the standard and reputation of the shop, the owner of the sweetmeat shop has to prepare all the varieties of sweetmeats which are available in that locality. For example, the sweetmeat *Chhena Ka Belgrami* is famous of Udwantnagar. Nowadays this sweetmeat is also prepared at Maner, though *Maner Ka Laddu* is also one of the famous sweetmeats. According to Suresh Prasad Gupta a shopkeeper of Maner, as their customers insisted upon him to prepare the *Belgrāmi* he made it. Udwantnagar and Maner are situated on Patna-Buxar road. Some of his favourite customers purchased this sweetmeat and gave it to him, and said, "Try to prepare this type of sweetmeat". Ultimately he thought that if he did not prepares this sweetmeat, his customers may go to other shops. So he went to Udwantnagar and took the training for preparing the *Belgrāmi* sweetmeat. After that he frequently prepare this sweetmeat since 1978. In this way, we see that sweetmeats are also diffused for maintaining the livelihood and the reputation of shops.

Selling the Sweetmeats by Hawkers at Different Places

Generally we see that the hawkers sell the sweetmeats at bus stands, railway platforms, in running trains and by carrying the famous sweetmeats of different region at different places. This also helps in the diffusion of sweetmeats.

At the bus stand of Maner, Gaya, Pakri Barawan, Barh, and Siuri we see that the hawkers are selling the famous sweetmeats of their respective areas, such as *Maner Ka Laddu, Tilkut, Barra, Lai* and *Morabba* in packets. Similarly the sweetmeats such as *Mihidana, Sitabhog* (at Bardhman), *Manohara* (at

Beldanga), *Barh Ka Lai* (at Barh) and *Tilkut* (at Gaya) are frequently being sold by hawkers at railway platforms and in running trains. Generally, such types of sweetmeats belong to the category of dry sweetmeats. Due to this, it is easy for customers to carry it from one place to the other. Nowadays 'Dry *Mihidana*'[3] is being sold in polythene packets.

Besides, some hawkers are selling the sweetmeats of different regions such as *Mihidana* and *Sitabhog* of Bardhman, *Moa* of Jayanagar. For example, there are about seventy persons of 24-Pargana district of West Bengal who used to come to Ranchi every year since the last 16 years. They come here in the middle of *Magh* and stay up to whole of *Chait*. After that they go back. Again, they come in the month of *Jeth* and stay here up to Durga Puja. At Ranchi they stay in groups in the houses of milk-men near Birsa Chowk. They prepare *Mihidana* and *Sitābhog* and sell it in different areas of Ranchi.

Thus, the vendors and hawkers also contribute their mite to the diffusion of sweetmeats and traits connected with it and make a sweetmeat popular which is new to that area.

Overcrowding of Sweetmeat Shops at one Place

If the number of shops become overcrowded or reach saturation point at a particular place, there is a possibility of diffusion of sweetmeats. Here, the saturation point means, that the number of shops at a place are more than sufficient and there is no use of further expansion in the number of shops. For example, there are eight sweetmeat shops at Udwantnagar who prepare *Belgrāmi* sweetmeat. The first shop was established in the year 1965. Since 1965 to 1975 the number of shops were increased up to eight. After 1975, there is no further extension in the number of sweetmeat shops. Thus, it is seen that the number of sweetmeat shops at Udwantnagar reached up to the saturation point. After that gradually the sweetmeat diffused from Udwantnagar to Arrah in the year 1975. At Arrah, there are about six sweetmeat shops who prepare this sweetmeat. Since 1980, this sweetmeat is also prepared at Kasap and Piro. Kasap and Piro come under the same subdivision, i.e., Arrah of Bhojpur district and are located 3 and 7 km (approximately) away from Udwantnagar respectively.

Similarly, the *Shilao Ka Khaza* is diffused from Shilao to various other places particularly to Bihar Sharif, Rajgir and Bakhtiyarpur. At Shilao, there are about twenty sweetmeat shops. But due to maximum number of shops at Shilao, many people of Shilao opened their shops at Rajgir. At Rajgir, there are six shops of this sweetmeat. Out of them, four persons bring the *Sada Khaza* from Shilao. At Rajgir they only prepare the sugar syrup and coat the *Khaza* with it. So, the overcrowding of sweetmeat shops at a particular place also helps in the diffusion of sweetmeats and the traits connected with it.

Industrialization and Urbanization

One of the many effects of industrialization and urbanization in the social field is its heterogeneity. Ideas and ideologies, language and literature, food habits and dress pattern, behaviour and religious outlook all become heterogeneous as the people from different places enter in the industrial belt (Vidyarthi, 1970).

Industrialization and urbanization have also helped in the diffusion of sweetmeats from one area to the other. For example, due to industrialization of Hatia at Ranchi, shops developed step by step and most of them have come to exist after the commencement of the first phase of industrialization. These shops were established to meet the new demands of the migrants. The outsiders came here to establish shops of various kinds. Along with the migration of the people, demand for different commodities increased. Some of the migrants who came here to seek jobs is in the factory temporarily opened shops in the absence of a suitable job. Vidyarthi (Ibid) in his study mentioned that shops of 33 types (total number of shops were 289) were established in Hatia to meet the new needs of the migrants. Out of total number of shops 33 were hotels and 13 were tea and sweet shops.

Due to modernization, the facilities of communication have rapidly increased. In these days transportation is so fast that one can travel a longer distance within minutes and hours. One can travel from Ranchi to Calcutta even by bus within 8 hours. Besides air, train-express and passenger, state transport service, there are private bus çoaches due to which people can travel from Ranchi to Calcutta comfortably within a shorter period in comparison to earlier periods. Due to such facilities the sweetmeats such as *Mihidana, Jaynagar Ka Moa, Sponge Rassogollas* are diffused from West Bengal to Bihar.

While in rural areas we find the prevalence of joint family system, in urban areas specially in the industrial belts there are mostly nuclear type of families. In leisure period, the housewives either go to pay courtesy calls to their friend's house or remain busy in reading books and magazines readily available in the urban and industrial surroundings. Among them, novels, recipe books, magazines such as *Manorama* (Hindi, fortnightly), *Saptahika Hindustan* (Hindi, weekly), *Dharmyuga* (Hindi, weekly), *Grih Sobha* (Hindi, monthly), *Vama* (Hindi, monthly), *Desha* (Bangla, weekly), *Paribartan* (Bangla, weekly), *Femina* (English fortnightly) are common. In such magazines recipes of different types of dishes including sweet-dishes and sweetmeats are given frequently. As housewives are generally interested in cooking such dishes at their home, many of them learn these recipes and try them. Gradually, when it works, it becomes a part of their regular or casual food. Sometimes the male members also encourage and help their wives in preparation of new dishes.

Scientific and Technological Developments

The adoption of scientific and technological developments specially in the field of recipe of sweetmeats, not only free it from impurity but it also helps to some extent in the diffusion of sweetmeats. Nowadays, few sweetmeat-makers use machines in the preparation of some sweetmeats such as *Rassogolla* and *Sandesh.* The boiling and curdling of milk, grinding (to free the *Chhenā* from globules and thoroughly mixing it) and packing the *Rassogollā* in vacuum tins, all are done by machines. By packing the *Rassogollā* in vaccum tins we can preserve it for about one month and such sweetmeats could be also sent out by parcels.

Besides, the gradual replacement of old systems of recipes through improved modern scientific methods have also lead to greater popularity and diffusion of sweets in many circles.

The factors discussed above are not exclusive to a particular category.

Area of Diffusion

From the foregoing discussions we can say that the sweetmeats diffused from one place to the other. But the area of their diffusion varies from one sweetmeat to the other. The sweetmeats are diffused on (i) All India level; (ii) Zonal (Inter-State) level; (iii) State level; and (iv) Regional (cultural-linguistic zone within a State) levels. There are also some sweetmeats which did not diffuse from their original place. Now the question arises as to why some sweetmeats diffuse on these levels while some others did not? To elaborate such points the author has selected one case-study of each of the categories. These sweetmeats are *Rassogolla, Raskadam, Shilao Ka Khaza, Belgrami* and *Keshariya-Pera*.

(i) The sweetmeat *Rassogollā* has its diffusion on All-India level. This is the sweetmeat which was first prepared in syrup. According to N.N. Das, the factors like easy availability and low price of ingredients, easy preparation (except *Sponge Rassogolla*) helped in the diffusion of this sweetmeat on an all-India level. Besides, their liking by every community and all age groups, its superb taste and easily digestibility also helped in the extensive diffusion of this sweetmeat. Packings in vacuum tins and its long preservation value also were responsible to some extent in the diffusion of this sweetmeat. Migration of Bengali community including Moyra caste to Bihar and Orissa played an important role in making this sweetmeat more popular in these areas. Transportation is one of the important factors due to which it diffused on an all-India level.

(ii) The sweetmeat *Raskadam* has its diffusion on zonal level. This sweetmeat is famous of Kahalgaon and Dalsingsarai of Bihar and Maldah and Aurangabad of West Bengal. In Bihar, this sweetmeat was first prepared at Kahalgaon and from Kahalgaon it diffused to Dalsingsarai. Similarly, in West Bengal, it was first prepared at Maldah and subsequently it diffused to Aurangabad. The factors such as location of shop nearing state borders, transportation and kinship network played important roles in the diffusion of this sweetmeat.

(iii) The sweetmeat *Shilao Ka Khaza* has diffused on State level. The factors such as migration of labour, opening new branches by famous sweetmeat-makers, transportation facilities, overcrowding of shops at one place, and migration of community of sweet-makers helped in the diffusion of this sweetmeat on such level. This sweetmeat is prepared at Bhurkunda, Chaibasa, Jamshedpur, Dhanbad and Bakhtiyarpur. At Chaibasa and Jamshedpur it was observed that some labourers who were primarily working at Chaibasa left that shop and joined other sweetmeat shops at Jamshedpur on higher wages. Similarly the persons who were primarily working at Jamshedpur left that shop on the assurance given by the owner of other shops at Chaibasa that he would be paid better remuneration and other facilities there.

Some sweet-sellers who gained popularity opened their new branches at other places, e.g. two persons of the Shilao also opened their new branches at Dhanbad. Sometimes a sweet-seller just changes the name of his shop and opens his new branch at the same place and there are so many examples of it in different towns and cities.

Various types of transportation facilities also helped in diffusion of this sweetmeat from Shilao to Chaibasa, Jamshedpur, Hernauth and Bakhtiyarpur. Two persons who primarily opened their shops at Bihar Sharif also opened new shops at Bakhtiyarpur.

Due to overcrowding of shops at Shilao, this sweetmeat diffused to Gaya, Ranchi and Bihar Sharif.

Lastly, migration of sweetmeat maker's community from Shilao to Patna and Bakhtiyarpur also helped in diffusion of this sweetmeat to such places.

When we go into the details about the diffusion of this sweetmeat, it may also be said that sweetmeats diffuse easily to those places, which do not have any famous sweetmeat there.

(iv) There are some sweetmeats which are diffused on regional level, i.e., such sweetmeats are prepared only in one cultural-linguistic zone of a State and in some cases marginal area of its consecutive cultural-linguistic zone. And it is from this that they diffuse to other cultural-linguistic zones or areas. The sweetmeat *Belgrāmi* is mainly prepared in Bhojpur cultural-linguistic zone. It is famous of Koath in Rohtas district where it is prepared with *Maidā.* At Udwantnagar this sweetmeat is also prepared but here the basic ingredient is changed, i.e. instead of *Maidā* they use *Chhenā.* So we may say that this is one example of Stimulus Diffusion.[4] Two factors were mainly responsible for the diffusion of this sweetmeat on regional level. Firstly, the regular frequency of transportation and secondly, several marriages among the people of such villages also helped in growing the kinship network. So, affinal kinship was also responsible for the diffusion of this sweetmeat to some extent.

(v) *Keshariya Pera* is being prepared since last three centuries at Gaya. This is one of the oldest and famous sweetmeats which is not prepared at any other place of Bihar other than Gaya. Few years ago this sweetmeat was prepared at Patna. But after sometime the owner of that shop had to close the shop due to following reasons:

(a) *Climate:* In spite of giving all the necessary ingredients in proper quantity and preparing it carefully, the taste and flavour of this sweetmeat was not so effective in comparison to Gaya. It was attributed to climatic factors.

(b) *Rising Price of the Product:* As saffron that is used in *Keshariya Pera* is costly, the price of the sweet was also high and thus the selling of this sweetmeat was not up to the mark. As a result, the income was not sufficient to maintain the livelihood, and the shop at Patna had to be closed.

(c) *Karigar's Difficulties:* As the *karigars* were not ready to live at Patna as this place was costlier in comparison to Gaya, the shop had to be closed.

Similarly, *Maner Ka Laddu* also did not diffuse from their original place. The following reasons were attributed to it:

(a) The quality of gram in this area is very 'light' due to which it is possible to prepare such small size of *Bundia*.

(b) It requires a greater amount of concentration, patience and labour which does not get returned in terms of profit.

(c) It is not possible to prepare such type of sieve[5] at other places.

In spite of that, non-availability of the proper ingredients, lack of patience in the present generation and expert workers also discourage diffusion of such sweetmeats. For example, the sweetmeat *Motichur* which is famous of Bishnupur (West Bengal) is prepared by the seed of *Piyara* (the nut of *Chironjia sapida*) which is at first ground in a stone hand-mill, then fried in *ghee*. But due to non-availability of such seeds in proper quantity at other places and lack of patience involved in its making, this sweetmeat could not get diffused from its original place.

Affinity among Sweetmeats of different Places on the basis of W Formula

The characteristic features i.e., traits of sweetmeats have been divided into nine broad categories according to different basis such as on the basis of colour of sweetmeats, type of milk, contents of sweetmeats, quantity of syrup in the sweetmeats, sweetening agent, shape, size and basic ingredients. Such categories will be dealt with one by one in the following pages.

According to Colour of Sweetmeats

In olden periods, the sweetmeat makers used costly things

such as *pistā* (pistachio nut), *Kesar* (saffron), flavour of the twigs of the *Harsingar* (Weeping nyctanthes) flower for colouring the sweetmeats. But nowadays the sweetmeat makers of rural areas in particular and urban areas in general use different types of readymade colours such as green, red, yellow, *champai* for colouring the sweetmeats. In olden days if one had to go to their relatives such as in-law's house they had to carry at least five varieties of sweetmeats. But nowadays those varieties changed into different colours only. Besides, the sweetmeats have their own natural colours also, e.g., white colour of *Rassogolla,* black colour of *Kala Jamun,* yellow colour of *Keshariya Pera* and the like.

White: The sweetmeats mostly prepared with *chhena, khoa* and sugar come under this category, e.g., *Rassogolla, Barfee, Chhena Payes, Kalakand, Nariel Ka Laddu, Tilkut.*

Red: Light-red colour is also included in this group. Sweetmeat like *Gulāb Jāmun, Raskadam, Belgrāmi* come under this group. *Raskadam* is prepared in both the States, i.e., Bihar and West Bengal. This sweetmeat is of two types. One is prepared with *khoa*, *chhena* and *posta* which is of either yellow or white colour and the other is prepared with only *chhena* which is of light colour. The first type of sweetmeat is generally found in North West Bengal and Bihar whereas the second type is found in South West Bengal and Bihar.

Black: There are some sweetmeats which are fried in *vanaspati* for a long time as a result of which the upper layer becomes black. The sweetmeat *Kālā Jāmun* comes under this category.

Green: The *Barfee* and *Laddu* prepared with raw and green gram come under this category. At the season of green gram, i.e., in the months of January-March the sweetmeat makers prepared those sweetmeats with green gram. After that they just mix the green colour in *besan* and prepare this sweetmeat.

Yellow: The sweetmeats prepared with *besan,* e.g. *Bundiā Laḍḍu, Barfee, Jalebi, Chandrakalā* come under this category. Sometimes the yellow or orange colour is also mixed in the basic ingredients to make the sweetmeats more yellow. The sweetmeat *Imarti* is prepared with *Urad* pulse, but to make it yellow in colour they mix yellow colour in the basic ingredients. Similarly the sweetmeat *Kesar Bhog* is orange. It is very much similar with *Rassogollā* except that its colour is yellow.

Brown: Sweetmeats prepared with *Maida,* e.g., *Gaja, Balusahi, Piyao, Khaza, Barra, Inersa* and *Belgrāmi* (Koath) come under this category. Such type of sweetmeats are generally fried in *vanaspati* till their colour becomes brown. After that either syrup of sugar is poured or the sweetmeat is itself immersed into the syrup.

Saffron: In these days saffron is very costly, as a result most of the sweetmeat-makers are not in a position to use saffron in preparation of sweetmeats. But if they use it, it would not be possible for many customers to purchase the same. However, few sweetmeat-makers use it in very small quantity. *Kesariya Pera* is one of the examples of this type but nowadays instead to *Kesar* they use only the flavour and colour of *Kesar.*

Mixed Colour: Sometimes more than one layer (of different colours) of sweetmeats are pasted together. Such types of sweetmeats are *ChocolateBarfee* (chocolate +white colour), *Tirangā Barfee* (Kesariya + white + green colour), *Nariel Ka Barfee* (white + chocolate colour). Such sweetmeats of mixed colour are generally found in semi-urban, rural village and tribal areas.

According to Milk

Generally, the milk of cows and buffaloes are used in the preparation of sweetmeats. The milk of buffaloes contains more fat, as a result the *chhena* becomes coarse, hard and also contains harder fat globules. So in the preparation of *Rassogolla* people prefer the *chhena* of cow's milk for delicacy and sponginess for which it is famous. The sweetmeats of *khoa* are generally prepared with buffalo's milk. But all these things depend upon the availability of milk.

According to Contents

Plain: As its name signifies, only those sweetmeats come

under this category in which (a) neither anything is stuffed inside the basic ingredients, nor two layers are pasted by cream and (b) *chhena*, *khoa*, *besan* and *maida* are one of its basic ingredients, e.g., *Rassogolla, Kala Jamun, Pera, Kalakand, Laddu, Barfee, Khaza, Gaza, Balusahi, Sandesh* and the like.

Stuffed: There are some sweetmeats in which *khoā* or *chhenā* is stuffed inside the basic ingredients. The sweetmeats like *Chandrakalā, Raskadam, Kheer Kadam, Mitha-Singhara, Cream Roll, Jal Bhara Sandesh* are examples of this category.

Sandwich Type: Sometimes, two layers of sweetmeat are pasted with the help of *khoa* or cream and it looks like a sandwich or toast. The sweetmeats like *Chhena Toast, Cream Chop* come under this category.

Sweetmeats Covered with Cream: There are some sweetmeats which are totally covered by the coating of sugar or cream. The sweetmeat *Manohara* is the peculiar example of such category.

Sweetmeats Made of Vegetable: The sweetmeats like *Morabba,* and *Parval Kā Miṭhāi* are the popular examples of such category. Here it is interesting to note that at *Siuri* (West Bengal) *Morabba* is also prepared with fruits, e.g., *Aam Ka Morabba, Bel Ka Morabba* and *Ananas Ka Morabba*. Such type of sweetmeats are also included in this category.

According to Syrup

Syrup of sugar is also a complementary thing for sweetmeats. Most of the sweetmeats are made of syrup and this is one of the basic ingredients. The quantity of syrup varies from one type of sweetmeat to the other.

Sweetmeat in Syrup: There are many sweetmeats which are either immersed or remain floating in the syrup. The sweetmeats like *Rassogolla, Kala Jamun, Keshar Bhog, Rasawala Bundia* are few examples of this category.

Sweetmeat Soaked in Syrup: Besides the above category, there are other type of sweetmeats which are fully soaked in syrup. Firstly, the raw material is fried in the *vanaspati* and then it is immersed into the syrup. After sometime, when the sweetmeat soak-up the syrup according to their capacity, then it is taken out. The sweetmeats like *Bundiā, Jalebi, Imariti, Cham-cham, Piyao* come under this category.

Dry Sweetmeats: Sometimes the raw materials are fried in *vanaspati* and immersed into the syrup. But here, the quantity of syrup is comparatively lesser and the sweet harder in comparison to the sweet of the above category. Sometimes syrup is poured on the fried materials. In some cases sugar is itself fried with basic ingredients. In such category the whiteness of sugar appears on the upper layer of sweetmeats. The sweetmeats like *Khaza, Shakarpala, Gaja, Barfee, Pera* and *Batasa* come under this category.

Syrup at the Core: In this category, the upper layer of sweetmeat becomes hard as if it is a dry sweetmeat, but actually the inner layer of the sweetmeat is fully saturated with syrup. The sweetmeat like *Belgrami* is one of the peculiar examples of such category.

According to Sweetening Agent

Generally the sweetmeat-makers use sugar and jaggery as a sweetening agent in the preparation of sweetmeats. Recently, some shops have begun making sweets for diabetic patients using '*Sorbitol*'. It is supposed to be absolutely danger-free for those who have been forced to give up their passion for sweets, according to a little leaflet brought out by one of the manufacturers, i.e., K.C. Das Pvt. Ltd. of Calcutta which goes to quote medical studies on this sweetener. Such types of sweetmeats are exclusively meant for diabetic patients. In the winter season the sweetmeat like *Moa* and *Sandesh* are also prepared with jaggery popularly known as *Naler gura, Taler gura*. Some indigenous sweetmeat like *Latto* is prepared with simple jaggery. In rural areas the sweetmeats like *Tilkut, Lai,* and *Khaza* are also prepared with jaggery.

According to Shape

These days sweetmeats are prepared in various shapes. The number of shapes are increased on the occasion of fairs and festivals. Some of the shapes are discused as follows:

Round: The sweetmeat, whose shape is very much similar to a ball, comes under this category. The sweetmeats like *Rassogolla, Gulab Jamun, Kala Jamun, Kesar Bhog, Raskadam, Manohara, Kheer Kadam, Rasmalai, Lai* and *Laddu* may be noted in this connection.

Disk: The sweetmeat which looks like a round plate comes under this category. Here, the outer surface of the sweetmeat is circular. Regarding the inner surface it may be concave, convex, biconvex or parallel. The sweetmeats like *Tilkut, Babarsā* (concave), *Barh Ka Lai* (biconvex), *Pera, Cream chop, Sarpuriya, Inersa, Keshariya pera, Jalebi* and *Imariti* the inner surface of which are more or less parallel, come under this category.

Triangle: The sweetmeat whose shape is very much similar to a triangle comes under this category, e.g., *Mitha-Singhara, Chhena Toast, Dilruba* and the like.

Sweetmeat on Paper Dish: Sometimes the sweetmeats like *Sandesh* and *Barfee* are served on either plane or curve shaped small paper-dish. This paper-dish gives a beautiful look to the sweetmeat and in some cases acts as a support.

Small Pieces: The sweetmeats like *Ilaichi dana, Shakarpalas* and *Nikhuti* come under this category. The sweetmeat-maker sells such type of sweetmeats by weight instead of pieces.

Square: The sweetmeat which is formed with four equal sides and four right angles comes under this category, e.g., *Barfee, Sandesh, Kalakand, Sohnpapari* and the like.

Egg Shaped: There are some sweetmeats which are prepared with *chhenā* but their shape is very much similar to egg, i.e., the outer surface is bi-convex and upper and lower surface is flat. The sweetmeat *cham-cham* is one of the peculiar examples of such category.

Parallelogram: The sweetmeat with shape similar to parallelogram comes under this category. The name of some dry sweetmeats like various varieties of *barfee* may be mentioned in this connection.

Moulded: Some of the sweetmeats are moulded in various forms such as *shankh,* fish, apple, orange, banana and small animals. Generally such types of sweetmeats are made of *khoa* and sugar. On the occasion of Diwali such type of sweetmeats are found in abundance.

Barrel Shaped: The sweetmeats like *Lengcha, Lorha Mithai* and some of the *chhena* sweetmeats come under this category.

Amorphous: The sweetmeats which have no definite shape come under this category. The sweetmeat *Belgrāmi* is one of the examples of such category.

According to Size

With the exception of few sweetmeats, each type of sweetmeat is made in various sizes. The size of the sweetmeat varies according to price, e.g., the weight of one piece of *Rassogollā* varies from 20 gm to 200 gm and the price also varies. In big towns such as Calcutta, Patna and Ranchi, one can find sweetmeats of bigger size, whereas in smaller towns and rural areas one can find sweetmeats of only medium or small size. The size of sweetmeat also shows the status of the people in the respective areas. If in the of rural areas where by and large the people of low income groups reside, the sweetmeat-makers prepare big size of sweetmeats, they become costly and beyond the reach of the rural families. Here four sizes of sweetmeats may be mentioned.

Very Big Size: When the weight of one piece of sweetmeat is more than 100 gm, then such sweetmeats come under this category, e.g., *Belgrami, Rassogollā* and *Śarpuriya.*

Big Size: The sweetmeat whose weight (one piece) varies from 50 gm to 100 gm come under this category, e.g., *Belgrami, Śarpuriya* and *Lorha-Mithai.*

Middle Size: If the weight of one piece of sweetmeat varies from 25 gm to 50 gm, such type of sweetmeats come under this category. In other words if 1 kg sweetmeat contains 20-25 pieces, then such sweetmeats come under this category.

Small Size: The sweetmeat whose weight is less than 25

gm comes under this category.

According to Basic Ingredients of Sweetmeats

Generally the sweetmeats are prepared with *chhena, khoa, maida* and cereals. *Chhena* is the counterpart of cheese made in India and neighbouring countries from boiling milk by the addition of lemon juice, acid, whey or sometimes tartaric acid. The clot containing the milk fat is separated from the whey by draining and pressing. The product is used in cooking and for confectionery. *Khoa* forms a major ingredient of several Indian sweets.

Sweetmeat is also prepared by mixing more than one ingredients, e.g., *Kalakand* is prepared with *chhena* and *khoa*. It is not possible to prepare the sweetmeat with only *chhena* or khoa so either *maida* or *arrowroat* in little quantity is mixed with the *chhena* or *khoa*. This helps is binding the sweetmeats. Such combinations are not considered as a separate category. In some places sweetmeats are also prepared by mixing of intoxicant materials, e.g. *Bhang Ka Pera.*

(i) *Dry fruits*—There are some sweetmeats such as *Pinna, Sohan Halwa, Kaju ka Barfee* in which dry fruits are lavishly used. Such sweetmeats come under this category.

(ii) *Kesar*—These days *Kesar* is too costly to use it in the preparation of sweetmeats. However, some sweetmeats like *Keshariya Pera* are prepared with it. The sweetmeat in which saffron is used as a basic ingredients comes under this category.

Sweetmeat Traits and Their Occurrence

For the present analysis 45 traits connected with sweetmeat and 16 places of each State, i.e. Bihar and West Bengal were selected. The presence and absence of sweetmeat traits are recorded in Table 9.1 on the basis as discussed earlier in this chapter. From this table the author would like to show the (a) places where all types of traits are found, (b) traits found in all places, (c) where minimum number of traits are found, (d) traits exclusively found in Bihar and West Bengal and like. This enables the author to show the affinity among different places of Bihar and West Bengal on the basis of 'W' formula.

The following points emerge from the Table 9.1 showing the list of sweetmeat-traits and their occurrence. The figure within bracket shows the number of traits found in respective places:

(1) There is not a single place where sweetmeats of all types of traits are found. However, maximum number of traits connected with sweetmeats are found in Gaya (39),[6] Patna (28) and Ranchi (28) of Bihar State and Calcutta (239), Krishna Nagar (37) and Barddhaman (33) of West Bengal state.

(2) Out of 45 sweetmeat traits, there are only 11 such sweetmeat traits (viz., Sweetmeats of white and red colour, sweetmeats made of Buffalo's milk, plain sweetmeats, sweetmeats submerged in syrup and soaked in syrup, sweetmeats in which sugar is used as a sweetening agent, sweetmeats made of *chhena* and *khoa*, sweetmeats of round and disk shaped) which are found in all the places.

(3) There are some places such as Udwantnagar (22), Barh (24) and Koath (24) in Bihar State and Baharampore (22), Janai (22) and Jiyaganj (20) in West Bengal where minimum varieties of sweetmeats are found.

(4) Sweetmeats specially meant for diabetic patients are not prepared in Bihar State. In West Bengal such types of sweetmeats are found at Barddhaman, Medinapore and Calcutta. At Barddhaman and Medinapore the sweetmeat '*Chitraranjan*' is prepared with less quantity of sugar. Though this sweetmeat is not medically approved, however, as the quantity of sugar is comparatively less so the diabetic patients eat it frequently in those places. At Calcutta, N.N. Das, Messrs K.C. Das Pvt. Ltd. prepare the sweetmeats for diabetic patients with a special type of sweetening agent, i.e. '*Sorbitol*'. Such sweetmeats are comparatively costilier than other sweetmeats.

(5) There are some places in Bihar such as Deoghar, Gaya, Darbhanga (Darbhanga is not included in sample) where sweetmeats are also prepared with mixing of intoxicants viz., *Bhang*[7] (Cannabis sativa).

(6) In respect to West Bengal sweetmeats prepared with *Chhena* and *Khoa*, and cereals are found in all the places of Bihar, whereas the sweetmeats of following traits viz., middle size, big size, dry sweetmeats, sweetmeats of cow's milk are found in all the places of West Bengal in comparison to Bihar.

(7) Sweetmeats prepared with saffron, triangle shaped,

amorphous size, core type are found at few places only.

(8) Though the number of places (according to our sample) where sweetmeats of moulded form are found, are equal in both the States, here it is interesting to note that the varieties of moulded form of sweetmeats are comparatively more in number in West Bengal.

(9) The number of places where the sweetmeats of big size are found, are comparatively more in Bihar but at Krishna Nagar (West Bengal) biggest size of sweetmeat is found, popularly known as *'Sarpuriya'*. The weight of this sweetmeat varies from ½ kg. to 1 kg.

(10) Regarding the availability of 'sweetmeat of mixed colour', the number of places in Bihar and West Bengal are almost the same (5:6). But it is observed that the sweetmeat-makers of Bihar specially at Barh and Bihar sharif, use excess amount of colour and the number of colours are also comparatively greater, whereas in West Bengal especially at Aurangabad and Chandan Nagar, only the former is true.

(11) The number of places where sweetmeats prepared with jaggery are found, are comparatively more in Bihar. But as far as the quality of sweetmeat is concerned, it is found that in West Bengal the sweetmeat maker uses good quality of jaggery (Viz., *Naler gura, Taler gura*) as a result the taste of sweetmeat is much better than that of Bihar.

There are aslo some places in Bihar viz., Jamshedpur, Ranchi, Ghatshila, where such types of sweetmeats are prepared. But here it is again interesting to note that the places being comparatively closure to West Bengal, the sweetmeat-makers and the owner of the shops are Bengali by caste.

(12) The sweetmeat made of vegetable is commonly known as *Morabba* (with the exception of *Parval Ka Mithai* (Sweetmeat made of the fruit of the plant Trichathan thanses dioica. Though the number of places where *Morabba* is prepared are comparatively more in Bihar, but at *Siuri* (West Bengal) maximum varieties (15) of *Morabba* are prepared. Not only vegetables but fruits are also used in the preparation of *Morabba*.

(13) It is observed that in West Bengal the sweetmeats of small pieces are found at greater number of places in comparison

to Bihar. Sweetmeats such as *Nikhuti, Gujia* are not found in Bihar.

(14) It is usually said that the syrupy sweetmeats are characteristics of West Bengal and dry sweetmeats of Bihar. But after analysis it was found that the dry sweetmeats are also found in all the places of West Bengal as in Bihar.

(15) The sweetmeats prepared with saffron are found in equal number of places in both the States. But here it would not be out of place to mention that in the present time instead of saffron, the flavour of saffron is used in some sweetmeats, e.g. *Kesar Bhog*.

Affinity Among Sweetmeats of Different Places on the basis of 'W' formula

To show the relative affinity among different places of Bihar and West Bengal separately this section is divided into two parts, i.e. affinity among different places of Bihar and affinity among different places of West Bengal. For this purpose the sequences of sweetmeat traits and places as shown in Table 9.1 are rearranged on the basis of decreasing order. After that presence or absence of traits are recorded from the selected places of Bihar and West Bengal. Further, this data is analysed on the basis of 'W'formula. Finally, the classified answers have been finally computed in Table 9.2) to show the relative affinity among different places.

Affinity Among the Sweetmeats of Different Places of Bihar

For showing the affinity of sweetmeats of different places of Bihar the author selected sixteen places of Bihar, viz., Gaya, Patna, Ranchi, Bihar sharif, Dhanbad, Deoghar, Buxar, Munger, Bhagalpur, Jamshedpur, Kuru, Maner, Ghatshila, Koath, Barh and Udwantnagar, on sampling basis. However, at the time of sampling it was kept in mind that such places probably must have some famous sweetmeat and it also includes some places situated on the border of two states.

Table 9.2[8] different correlations among the sixteen places of Bihar has been prepared by omiting decimal points from the results of 'W' formula. To make it more simplified the results may be further explained with the help of Fig. 9.1. From the

Fig. 9.1 the following points emerge:

(i) The places such as Ranchi and Patna, Jamshedpur and Buxar, Ghatshila and Jamshedpur have the highest degree of relationship, i.e. of the first rank to show the correlations between two places on the basis of 'W' formula, the relationship or affinity is categorised into six ranks, i.e. if the relationship between two places lies between 90-100% it is treated as of First Rank relationship. Similarly the relationship between 80-89%, 70-79%, 60-69%, 50-59% and 40-49% are treated as Second, Third, Fourth, Fifth and Sixth Rank respectively.

TABLE 9.2

Affinity Among Sweetmeats of Different Places of Bihar on the Basis of 'W' Formula.

	Ga	*Pa*	*Ra*	*Bi*	*Dh*	*De*	*Bu*	*Mu*	*Bh*	*Ja*	*Ku*	*Ma*	*Gh*	*Ko*	*Ba*	*Ud*
Ga	XX	84	84	73	83	68	75	71	66	68	71	62	68	60	68	53
Pa	84	XX	91	84	84	71	73	77	73	71	73	64	71	57	68	55
Ra	84	91	XX	75	84	71	77	73	68	75	73	60	71	62	64	46
Bi	73	84	75	XX	77	82	80	80	75	73	80	71	73	64	71	62
Dh	83	84	84	77	XX	73	84	84	80	82	88	75	86	73	80	62
De	68	71	71	82	73	XX	80	80	80	82	84	75	82	73	75	66
Bu	75	73	77	80	84	80	XX	86	77	93	86	82	88	84	82	68
Mu	71	77	73	80	84	80	86	XX	82	84	86	82	84	75	82	68
Bh	66	73	68	75	80	80	77	82	XX	80	82	85	84	80	77	73
Ja	68	71	75	73	82	82	93	84	80	XX	88	84	91	86	80	71
Ku	71	73	73	80	88	84	86	86	82	88	XX	82	88	80	77	68
Ma	62	64	60	71	75	75	82	82	85	84	82	XX	88	88	73	82
Gh	68	71	71	73	86	82	88	84	84	91	88	88	XX	82	80	71
Ko	60	57	62	64	73	73	84	75	80	86	80	88	82	XX	75	84
Ba	68	68	64	71	80	75	82	82	77	80	77	73	80	75	XX	73
Ud	53	55	46	62	62	66	68	68	73	71	68	82	71	84	73	XX

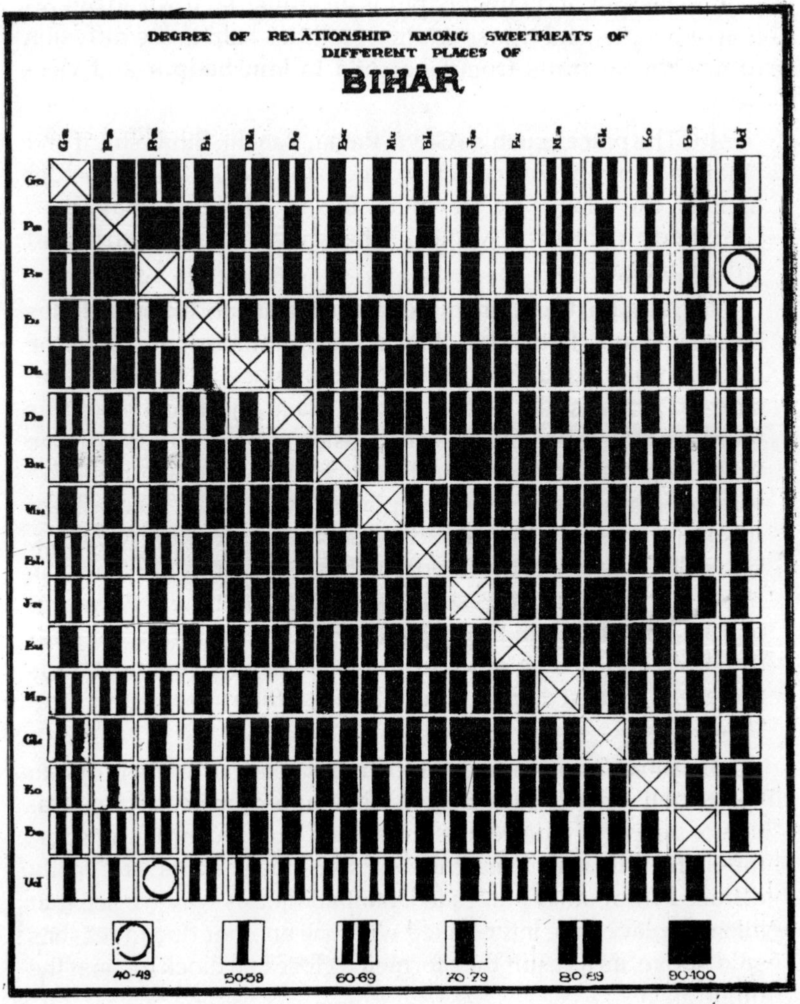

Fig. 9.1 : Degree of Relationship Among Sweetmeats of Different Places of Bihar

Due to direct and more frequent transportation facilities such as by train and State and private bus services between Ranchi and Patna, it plays an important role in the diffusion of sweetmeat-traits from one place to the other. Ghatshila is near to Jamshedpur and Jamshedpur is an industrial town so migration of people, and transportation facilities help in the diffusion of sweetmeat traits from Ghatshila to Jamshedpur and vice-versa.

(ii) The places such as Gaya, Patna, Ranchi, Bihar sharif and Dhanbad form a 'five cell close block' (of 70-100% relationship) against the places of Deoghar, Buxar, Munger, Bhagalpur, Jamshedpur, Kuru, Maner, Ghatshila, Koath, Barh and Udwantnagar.

Here again direct and more frequent transportation facilities between Gaya, Patna and Ranchi play an important role in the diffusion of sweetmeat traits from one place to the other. Besides, Gaya is an important sacred place and because of this there are maximum chances of diffusion of traits so it is also one of the important reasons due to which the sweetmeat traits are diffused from Gaya to other places. Regarding Bihar sharif firstly, it is one of the important sacred centres for Muslims. Secondly, it is one of the important business centres and also an important junction of bus services and lastly, it is near Pawapuri and Rajgir which are the important pilgrimage centres of Buddhist and Hindu religions. Due to such reasons sweetmeat traits are easily diffused from other places to Bihar sharif and vice-versa.

Dhanbad is an industrial town. As referred earlier, due to industrialisation of a town there is maximum chance of immigration of people of different communities, and secondly transportation facilities also increase so sweetmeat traits are easily diffused from other places to Dhanbad. In this way we see that all such places are inter-linked with one another due to reasons said above, as a result they formed a close cell block against the other places.

(iii) Jamshedpur is such a place which has higher rank of affinities with maximum number of places, i.e. with Buxar and Ghatshila of the first rank (90-100), with Dhanbad, Deoghar, Munger, Bhagalpur, Kurru, Maner, Koath and Barh of the second rank (80-89), with Gaya of the fourth rank (60-69) and with rest places of the third rank (70-79).

The important factors behind it are as follows:

Firstly, migration of several communities from other places to Jamshedpur, secondly, geographically Jamshedpur is situated on the border of two states, i.e. Bihar and West Bengal and is thus a marginal area between Bihar and West Bengal. Thirdly, direct and more frequent transportation facilities from Jamshedpur to other places, and lastly industrialisation of this town which play an important role in the diffusion of sweetmeat traits.

(iv) Buxar and Ghatshila are such places which have maximum number of affinities with other places, i.e. with one place of the first rank, with eight places of the second rank and again with one place of the third rank. It is also interesting to note that the correlation of these two places with the other places are almost of the same rank.

This is due to the marginal area of two States. Buxar is located on the border of two States, i.e. of Bihar and Uttar Pradesh and Ghatshila of Bihar and West Bengal. Due to impact of both the States there is maximum chance of diffusion of the sweetmeat traits.

(v) The correlation of Munger with Bhagalpur, Jamshedpur, Kuru, Maner and Ghatshila, Bhagalpur with Munger, Jamshedpur, Kuru, Maner and Ghatshila, Jamshedpur with Munger, Bhagalpur, Kuru, Maner and Ghatshila, and Ghatshila with Munger, Bhagalpur, Jamshedpur, Kuru and Maner are almost of the same rank.

From geographical point of view Munger and Bhagalpur are the two adjacent districts of Bihar, and Jamshedpur and Ghatshila are also the other adjacent places within the same district, i.e. Singhbhum due to which there is affinity in sweetmeat traits among such places. Secondly, due to historical importance there is similarity between the Munger and Maner (due to impact of Muslim emperors). Thirdly, as the Bhagalpur and Ghatshila are the marginal places between two States, i.e. Bihar and West Bengal, so due to impact of adjacent States, there is much similarity in both the places. After interviewing several persons of Bhagalpur and Kuru the could not be able to find out the reasons behind the similarity between these two places. So, we see that due to aforesaid reasons there are much similarities in sweetmeat traits among such places.

(vi) Udwantnagar is such a place which has minimum number of highest rank affinities with other places such as with Maner and Koath of the second rank, with Bhagalpur, Jamshedpur, Ghatshila and Barh of the third rank; with Ranchi of the sixth rank; and with other places of the fifth rank.

As one side Udwantnager is surrounded by Buxar and on the other side by Maner which have their own famous sweetmeats, so there is less possibility of diffusion of sweetmeats and traits connected with it. Due to this, we find that there is less similarity with other place. As the sweetmeat '*Belgrami*' is diffused from Koath to this place and Maner is on the way so there is affinity of the second rank among such places. Thirdly, as the basic ingredients of this sweetmeat is *Chhena* (for which Udwantnagar is famous) so other varieties of sweetmeats which are prepared with *Chhena* are not found at Udwantnagar.

Affinity Among Different Places of West Bengal

For this purpose the author has selected 16 places of West Bengal, such places are Calcutta, Krishnanagar, Bardhaman, Siuri, Chandannagar, Bankura, Medinipur, Beldanga, Aurangabad, Raghunathganj, Shantipur, Jaynagar, Shaktigarh, Bahrampur, Janai and Jiyaganj.

The Table 9.3 prepared by omitting decimal points from the results of 'W' formula shows different correlations among the sixteen places of West Bengal. To make it more simplified the results may be further explained by Fig. 9.3. From Fig. 9.3 it transpires that firstly the places such as Beldanga and Chandannagar, Medinipur and Bankura; and Beldanga and Medinipur have maximum degree of relationships of the first rank, i.e. (90-100).

Regarding the first rank of affinities between Medinipur and Bankura, this may be due to the adjacent districts of Best Bengal. As referred earlier due to adjacent districts there is maximum chance of migration of people which help in diffusion of sweetmeat traits from Medinipur to Bankura and vice-versa. It is interesting to note that Medinipur is such a place whose eastern part is surrounded by two States, i.e. Bihar and Orissa. Due to impact of Bihar State on both the districts viz., Medinipur and Murshidabad there is similarity of the first rank between Medinipur and Beldanga.

Table 9.3

Affinity among Sweetmeats of Different Places of West Bengal on the Basis of 'W' Formula

	Ca	*Kr*	*Bar*	*Si*	*Ch*	*Ban*	*Me*	*Be*	*Au*	*Rag*	*Sha*	*Jay*	*Sh*	*Bah*	*Jan*	*Ji*
Ca	XX	80	80	77	73	71	71	64	60	57	57	57	62	60	60	51
Kr	80	XX	77	71	80	73	77	75	71	64	68	73	68	62	66	57
Bar	80	77	XX	80	80	73	77	75	75	77	73	71	77	71	75	66
Si	77	71	80	XX	82	80	84	77	73	77	73	71	73	73	68	68
Ch	73	80	80	82	XX	84	88	91	82	71	71	57	75	73	73	73
Ban	71	73	73	80	84	XX	95	88	75	55	73	55	77	80	80	75
Me	71	77	77	84	88	95	XX	93	75	77	77	82	82	80	84	80
Be	64	75	75	77	91	88	93	XX	77	75	75	88	80	77	82	82
Au	60	71	75	73	82	75	75	77	XX	80	75	75	71	77	77	73
Rag	57	64	77	77	71	55	77	75	80	XX	77	77	86	84	75	84
Sha	57	68	73	73	71	73	77	75	75	77	XX	82	77	80	80	80
Jay	57	73	71	71	57	55	82	88	75	77	82	XX	73	80	75	80
Sh	62	68	77	75	75	77	82	80	71	86	77	73	XX	84	88	88
Bah	60	62	71	73	73	80	80	77	77	84	80	80	84	XX	82	82
Jan	60	66	75	68	73	80	84	82	77	75	80	75	88	82	XX	86
Ji	51	57	66	68	73	75	80	82	73	84	80	80	88	82	86	XX

Secondly, the places such as Calcutta, Krishnanagar, Bardhaman, Siuri, Chandannagar, Bankura, and Medinipur form a 'seven cell close block' (between 70-100) against the places of Beldanga, Aurangabad, Shaktigarh, Baharampur, Jani, Raghunathganj, Shantipur, Jaynagar and Jiyaganj.

Regarding the formation of 'seven cell close block' among aforesaid places, if we compare one place to others places we find that from geographical point of view the districts of such

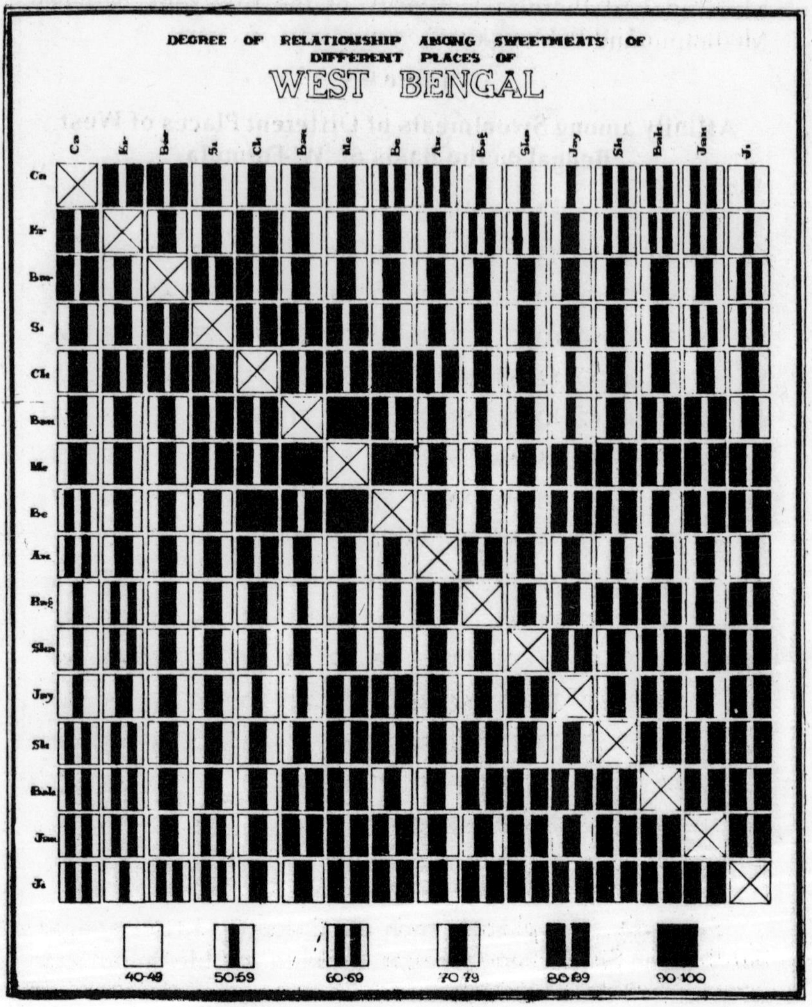

Fig. 9.2 : Degree of Relationship Among Sweetmeats of Different Places of West Bengal

places viz., Medinipur of Medinipur district, Bankura of Bankura district, Chandannagar of Hoogli district, Siuri of Birbhum district, Krishnanagar of Nadia district and Calcutta of 24-parganas district are inter-connected with one another in one way or the other. Frequent and regular transportation facilities, migration of people from one district to the other districts also play an important role in the formation of 'seven cell close block'.

(iii) The places such as Shaktigarh, Baharampur and Janai also form a 'three cell close block'(70-89). The correlation of this block with other places are almost of the same rank.

The places such as Shaktigarh, Janai and Baharampur belong to the districts of Bardhaman, Hoogli and Murshidabad respectively. These districts are adjacent to one another and more or less geographically situated in the centre of West Bengal. So on the one hand being adjacent districts, there is much similarities among such places and on the other hand, as such places are centrally located so there is the same rank of affinities with other places.

(iv) Jiaganj is such a place which has maximum number of affinities, i.e. with eight places of the second rank (80-89).

Jiaganj is an industrial town. This town is situated on the banks of the river Ganges. Its eastern side is surrounded by Bihar and western side by Bangladesh. So it has the second rank of affinities with maximum number of places.

(v) Medinipur is such a place which has the highest rank of affinities with maximum number of places, i.e. with Bankura and Beldanga of the first rank (90-100); with Siuri, Chandannagar, Jaynagar, Shantipur, Bahrampur, Janai and Jiaganj of the second rank (80-89); and of the third rank (70-79) with rest of the places.

As referred earlier, the eastern part of Medinipur is partly surrounded by Bihar State and partly by Orissa. This may be one of the reasons due to which it has the highest rank of affinity with maximum number of places. The first rank of affinities with Bankura is due to the adjacent district. Regarding Beldanga, the author could not able to find out the causes but it may be said that it is just a matter of chance due to which it has first rank of affinities with Medinipur.

(vi) The correlation of Baharampur with Shaktigarh, Janai

and Jiaganj; Janai with Shaktipur, Bararampur and Jiaganj; and Jiaganj with Shantipur, Bararampur and Janai are of the same rank, i.e. second rank (80-89).

Baharampur and Jiaganj come under Murshidabad district. The places such as Shantipur, Shaktigarh and Janai belong to the districts of Nadia, Bardhaman and Hoogli respectively. So the affinity among such places is due to the adjacent districts.

(vii) The places such as Raghunathganj, Shantipur, Jayanagar and Jiaganj with Calcutta; Jiaganj with Krishnanagar; Jaynagar with Chandannagar and Raghunathganj; and Jaynagar with Bankura have minimum degree of affinities, i.e. of the fifth rank (50-59).

References

1. The application of their formula was made Gifford and kroebar (1937), in their study of *Culture Elements Distribution* and by Saraswati (1978), in his study of pottery-making cultures and the Indian civilization.
2. Diwakar (1958: pp. 533–34) mentioned that the sweetmeats such as *Jalebi, burfee, gakuti* (miscalled makuti), *habshi halwa-i-sohan, savai, nankhatai* and *gulshakri* (rose conserves mixed with honey) were introduced into India by the Muslims during AD 1526–1707.
3. To prepare this sweetmeat, firstly one has to prepare the syrup of sugar according to weight of *Mihidānā* and after that dry *Mihidānā* is put into that syrup.
4. In many instances it is not the actual cultural–trait that is adopted by the borrowing people but merely the principle on which it is based. This process has been termed "Stimulus Diffusion" (Hiene–Geldern, 1968:170).
5. The sieve used at Maner contain unusual small holes not found elsewhere.
6. The figure within brackets shows the number of traits found in respective places.
7. It is surprising to note that such type of sweetmeats (usually called *Bhanga Ki Barfee* is also available in betel shops such as Deoghar, Darbhanga, Gaya and like.
8. (a) For the Table No. 9.2. At first the sixteen places as referred in Table No. 9.1, are rearranged on the basis of decreasing order of

traits found at respective places. Then on the basis of presence and absence of sweetmeats traits, affinity among different places has been established on the basic of 'W' formula. Here Table No. 9.2 has been prepared by omitting decimal points. For this table only appreciations of the names of places as in Table No. 9.1 has been used.

8. (b) As said, the sequence of sweetmeats traits and places as shown in Table 9.1 are rearranged on the basis of decreasing order i.e., traits are arranged in the following order. White, Red, Buffalo's Milk, Plain, Submerged in Syrup and the like. Similarly the places are rearranged like Gaya, Patna, Ranchi, Bihar-sharif, Dhanbad and the like. To calcute the 'W' formula between Gaya and Patna (a) i.e., + + = 35; (d) i.e., – – = 3; (b) i.e., + – = 4; (c) i.e., – + = 3.

$$\text{So } W = \frac{(a) + (d)}{(a + d + b + c)} = \frac{35 + 3}{35 + 3 + 4 + 3} = \frac{38}{45} = 0.84$$

10

Conclusion

After having carried out the detailed analysis of various aspects of the sweetmeats in India the author arrives at certain definite points.

Firstly, as regards the concept of sweetmeats and the Indian sweets, the following points emerge:

(i) In ancient and old times people used *Kheer, Payasa, Navnita, Kasar, Gujia, Ksaira* as 'sweetmeats' as mentioned in relevant texts. But actually speaking they are not sweetmeats. In many such texts there does not exist a clear cut difference between 'sweet-dishes' and 'sweetmeats'. However, technically speaking and in the present context they are different . A 'sweet-dish' is a broad term which includes any type of sweet preparation. Such preparation may or may not be sweet. The sweet-dishes which have not been deeply fried in *ghee,* cannot be preserved for more than one day. People prepare sweet-dishes in their house according to their own choice, convenience and need of consumption. Mixing of sweetening agent is essential for both, i.e., sweet-dish and sweetmeat but in some cases sweetening agent is not mixed in sweet-dishes but due to natural sweetness its taste becomes sweet. But it is not the case with sweetmeat. From religious point of view sweet-dishes are supposed to be more pure and non-adulterated in comparison to sweetmeats.

(ii) A sweetmeat must have five essential criteria like:

(a) *Sweetening agent* : Unless sweetness in the form of sugar or molasses or its substitute like sugar candy, sorbitol is added to it, it cannot be called a sweetmeat;

(b) *Preservation* : Is one of the important criteria of sweetmeat. Sweet items which cannot be preserved for at least few days, cannot be called as sweetmeat;

(c) *Fire treatment* : Without fire treatment it is not possible to prepare a sweetmeat. It makes the item easily eatable and enhances the flavour creating a new food;

(d) *Easy availability in market* : It is another important criteria of a sweetmeat. And the last one is

(e) *Manual preparation:* i.e. sweetmeats must be prepared by manual power. A sweet item which is exclusively prepared by a mechanical devise at least in the Indian context may not be considered as a sweetmeat. However, nowadays some sweetmakers like K.C. Das (private) Limited (Calcutta); Ganguram and Sons (Calcutta) use machines for preparing some basic ingredients and some stages of recipes of sweetmeats, i.e. curdling, grinding, mixing of *Chhena* and also packing of the sweetmeats in vacuum tins. The scientific development, labour problem, economy of time, uniformity, and improvement in quality of sweets are some important factors which have gone behind the mechanisation of the sweet-making. However, even after the mechanisation, operation of machine are usually done by hands. Besides, there is certain process in the sweet-making, i.e., giving of round shape to the sweets while in new form which can be done by hand only. Besides, the mechanisation works only in the making of *Rassogolla*. Again in case of Ganguram and Sons, mechanization of sweet is confined to the mixing of *Chhena* only.

(iii) As regards ingredients of sweetmeats, *khɔa*, *chhena*, *ghee*, sugar, jaggery, *bean*, *maida*, *safeda*, dry fruits, hot spices, flavouring, perfuming and colouring agents are the chief ingredients.

(iv) Some of the sweetmeats have also nutritional value as besides the basic ingredients like *Chhena* and *Khoa* of which it is made and which are itself wholesome, they contain other nutritional items like *kaju* (cashewnut), *Pista* (Pistachio), *Kesar* (Saffron strands), *Gond, Kismis* (Raisin) and the like. It makes such sweetmeats more appetizing and tasty.

(v) Some of the sweetmeats are also of medicinal value like *Sandesh, Jalebi, Petha* which are believed to cure some ailments of the body.

(vi) As regards naming of sweetmeat it is interesting that being prepared by almost the same ingredients, sweetmeats may have different names. In few cases, the names of sweetmeats are based on their shape or the name of inventor. Sometimes the names of sweetmeat are used as a simile to other things, viz., *Chandrapuli* which looks like moon. *Aam Sandesh* which looks like Mango and the like.

Secondly, regarding the genesis and development of Indian sweetmeats we find that:

(i) Sweetmeats form an integral part of food in many families. Since ancient times offering of sweetmeats have been considered to be auspicious. In words of love 'sweetness' stands as the symbol of lover or beloveds, their bond itself considered to be 'sweet' as reflected in the names like 'sweety', 'Honey', 'Madhu' and the like.

(ii) Honey was the earliest sweet thing that the Indians knew. Its use was profusely made during Vedic period as frequently referred to in the Vedas. Another earliest reference relates to chewing of sugar cane as given in the *Artharvaveda.* Proto-Australoids people knew about the preparation of *Guda* and the Aryans learnt it from the Proto-Australoids. At the time of Patanjali, people freely ate *Guda*. In Kautilya's *Arthashastra* the references of *Rab* (molasses), *Guda, Khar* and *Shakkar* are found which were made of sugar cane.

(iii) Sweetmeat of *Aryans* was *Apupa* and they are it with appetite. In *Satpatha Brahman* references of *Apupa* are made.

References of *Payas* is found in *Patanjali*. The principal sweets of Vedic Indians consisted of *Apupa, Odana, Pakri*. In Epic period (at the time of Ramayana and Mahabharat; B.C.1200-800 B.C.) the sweetmeats such as *Apupa, Peya, Krisara, Madaka, Khandava* were found. The names of sweetmeats mentioned in the *Ashtadhyayi* were as follows: *Yavaka, Pishtaka, Samyava, Apupa, Palala, Churna*. Panini mentioned the sweets like *Madhu, Guda, Phanita, Sarkara. Puva* was one of the favourite dishes at the time of Vinaya. *Madhupandika* and *Madhugolaka* were two other sweet-dishes. *Khajja* or *Khajjaka* is another special preparation. At the time of Vatsyayana the sweet-dishes such as *Guda, sarkara* (iksuras) and sweetmeat i.e., *Khanda, Khadyani* were found. The sweets such as *Ksira-bhaksyas, ghrtapuras, gandikas, madhumastakas, saynavas, pupas, modakas, sattakas, Visyandana Samita, phenaka* were found at the time of Susruta Samhita. Varieties of *Sandesh* like *Talsans, Kamranga, Aam, Sandesh, Ataphal, Kamlanebu, Sandesh* were also found. Of the sweet preparations *Madhutaja* and *Madhugolaka* or *Modaka* were in common use at the time of early Buddhist and Jains (C. 800 B.C.-C. 325 B.C.). Besides, other sweets such as *mandaka, Madhusirsaka, Gulalavaniya, Ghayapunna, Sihakesara* and *Morandaka* were also found. Some good quality of sweets at the time of Maurya and Sunga period (C. 325 B.C.-C.75 A.D) were known as *Khandava* and Uccavacabhaksya. The sweets such as *Madhusirsaka, Pupalika Mudga, Utkarita, Vartika* were found in Kusana and Saka Satvahana period (C.75 A.D.-C. 300 A.D.). Besides the sweets of the earlier periods as referred above, several new sweets such as *Morendaka, Vimardaka, Locika, Istaka, Vitanaka* and *Polika* were found at the time of Gupta period (C. 300 A.D.-C. 750 A.D). *Udumbara, Murmura, Varsopalagolakas, Sarkari Putrika* (dolls prepared with sugar), *Ghrtapura, Phenakas, Khajjakas* and *Laddukas* were popular at the time of Post Gupta Period. At the time of fifteenth century the sweets such as *Masaphenis* (modern *Imratis*), *Lapsi, Bhaimi, Gunjhiyas, Jalebis (Kundalika* or *Jalavallika*), *Dughamandakas, Dugha Karanjika, Ksiravatis, Ksigamodakas, Ksirasaka, Indurasa, Dedhivatikas* were found. The sweets such as *Amrita-Gutika, Ksherasa, Amrita Manda, Karpurkuli, Sarabhaja, Sarpulis, Haribhallavas, Sebatis, Karpuramalates, Dalima,*

Maricha_laru, Nabata, Amriti, Padmochini, Chandrakanta, Khaza, Khandesaka were found at the time of Sri Chaitanya Deva (16th and first half of the 17th centuries). The sweet-dishes such as *Kheer, Mitha, Petha, Payas, Kalabara, Mugsanti, Khiramanna, Khirpuli* were found mentioned in different sections of the *Kabi Kan-kan Chandi.* Different types of sweet-dishes such as *kheer, khiranaru, Pistaka, Payas, Gura, Khiri, Khivara, Manoharpuri, Dudhapuli* were mentioned in the book *Chaitanya-Mangala.*

Thirdly from the point of view of cultural significance:

(i) Sweetmeats have an important place in Indian culture. The Hindu sacred texts tell us about the importance of sweetmeats known as *Naivedya* and it is one of the essential requisities needed for religious performances. For thousands of years, the Hindus have sought to please the Gods and Goddesses by showing their devotion through the offerings of sweet-dishes and sweetmeats. It is necessary as part of the rituals connected with the worship of a deity to offer some kind of food. Even some specific sweetmeats are the favourite offerings of specific deities or Gods. Such offerings are usually called as *Bhoga,* that are constituted mainly of sweetmeats or other sweet items.

(ii) During every ritual, festival and rites-de-passage and occasions of hospitality sweetmeats play an important role. Fair and festivals have played an important part in the life of the Indian people. Hindus celebrate hundreds of sacred occasions with festive observances. During festivals sweetmeats are used in different ways viz, as *Prasad, Sargahi* and as *Phalahar.* There are some *Samaskaras* such as *Jatakarama, Annaprasana, Karnvedha* in which sweetmeats are must and without it a *Samaskara* can not be complete. Again, it is used on every social occasion but at some occasions viz., success of any type, *Chhati, Nayota, Puchhari,* its use is considered to be auspicious and it makes a good omen. It is also considered to be a status symbol for those who use it as a part of their regular diet.

Fourthly, regarding the sweetmeat-areas of Bihar and West Bengal and their traditions we find that:

(i) A sweetmeat popular in its locality has the following

characteristics:

(a) The people of a locality in general relish such sweetmeats.
(b) When we talk about the characteristics of a place, among other things, we also refer to the sweetmeat of that area.
(c) Usually, when the people go outside to their relatives and friends, they are keen to carry such sweetmeats with them as a gift to these people.
(d) When a guest comes from outside that particular sweet is most likely to be served or the guest may ask about it, and
(e) When a tourist or visitor happens to pass through that area, he is keen to take with him this sweetmeat.

(ii) When we go into the details of the popular sweetmeats of Bihar, we find that the sweetmeats such as *Barra* of Pakri Barawan (Nawada district), *Belgrami* of Koath and Udwantnagar (Rohtas and Bhojpur districts respectively), *Khaza* of Shilao and Pupri (Bihar sharif and Sitamarhi district respectively), *Lai* of Barh (Patna district), *Laddu* of Maner and Sarsopahi (Patna and Madhubani district respectively), *Lorha Mithai* of Kuru (Lohardaga district), *Pantoa* of Kasichak (Nawada district), *Pera* of Deoghar (Deoghar district), *Piyao* of Ichak and Sherghati (Hazaribagh and Gaya district respectively), *Raskadam* of Kahalgaon and Dalsingsarai (Bhagalpur and Samastipur district respectively), *Rasmalai* of Ghatshila (Singhbhum district), *Sohnpapdi* of Buxar (Bhojpur district), *Tilkut* and *Keshariya Pera* of Gaya (Gaya district) are popular sweetmeats of Bihar.

(iii) Coming to the sweetmeats of West Bengal, sweets such as *Adaitbhoga* of Bolpur (Birbhum district), *Babarsa* of Khirpoi (Medinipur district), *Chhena Barra* of Baharampur (Murshidabad district), *Jal Bhara Sandesh* of Chandannagar (Hoogli district), *Kachagulla* of Ranaghat (Nadia district), *Kheer Pantoa* of Raghunathganj (Murshidabad district), *Lengcha* of Shaktigarh (Barddhaman district), *Maicha* of Beliator (Bankura district), *Malpua* of Jiaganj (Murshidabad district), *Manohara* of Janai and Beldanga (Hoogli and Murshidabad district respectively), *Mihidana* of Barddhaman (Barddhaman district), *Moa* of Jaynagar (24-Pargana district), *Morabba* of Siuri (Birbhum district), *Nikhuti* of Shantipur (Nadia district), *Raghawasai* of Maldah (Maldah district), *Raskadam* of Aurangabad and Maldah (Murshidabad and Maldah district respectively), *Sandesh* of Calcutta (Calcutta district), *Sarpuriya* and *Sarbhaja* of Krishnanagar (Nadia district), *Sitabhoga* of Barddhaman (Barddhaman district), and *Sponge Rassogolla* of Calcutta (Calcutta district) are the popular sweetmeats.

(iv) It is interesting to note that on the one hand there are some places which have more than one popular sweetmeats, on the other, there are some sweetmeats which are famous at more than one place. For example, the sweetmeats like *Keshariya Pera* and *Tilkut* are famous at Gaya in Bihar and the sweetmeats like *Sarpuriya* and *Sarbhaja* of Krishnanagar and *Mihidana* and *Sitabhog* of Barddhaman are famous in West Bengal that constitute the example of the former. On the other hand, the sweetmeat *Piyao* is famous of Sherghati and Ichak, *Raskadam* is famous of Kahalgaon and Dalsingsarai, *Manohara* is famous of Janai and Beldanga which constitute the examples of the latter. There are some sweetmeats however, e.g., *Khaza* and *Raskadam* which are famous in both the States.

(v) The tradition of sweetmeat in the social life of Bihari and Bengali people gets reflected in the fact that on any social occasion no dish is believed to be complete without sweets. According to traditional ideal prevalent in Bengali culture, a full-fledged banquet requires a perfect and balanced menu in which besides the food items of pungent, bitter, sour, astringent and saline tastes, in the last course of meal a food of sweet taste, either a sweet-dish or sweetmeat, must be served. Here, it is interesting to note that though Bengalis are very well known as the lover of sweets, they have also a great love for fish. But this character is lacking among the Bihari people in general. Similarly, sweets are taken while making important social visits, during life-cycle rituals, on getting a success or while going to see an ailing person.

(vi) The factors behind the popularity of sweetmeats in an area are manifold viz., ecology, quality and combination of basic ingredients, experience and patience of *Karigars*, cooking medium and personal reputation.

(vii) There are some sweetmeats of which basic ingredients and recipes are the same but they are known by different names in different areas. For example, sweetmeat made of rice flour and clarified butter is known as *Kachwaniya* in Patna and Saran, while *Modak* in Gaya and Shahabad and *Kesar* in South Munger.

(viii) After analysing the sweet-dishes and sweetmeats of different zones of Bihar, i.e. Bhojpuri, Magahi, Maithili and tribal zones, we find that:

(a) Regarding subsidiary dietary items relating to sweet-dishes or sweetmeats among the four zones, Bhojpur region is numerically on the top. Sweetmeat such as *Jalebi* and sweet-dish *Khajoor* are found in all the three regions except the tribal. Similarly, sweetmeat like *Bundia* and sweet-dishes like *Halwa, Kheer* and *Tikari* are found in the Magahi and Bhojpur regions but which are not found in Mithila and tribal regions.

(b) There are some typical sweetmeats of each region, e.g. *Anarsa* and *Piyao* of Magahi region; *Barfee* and *Sohnpapri* of Bhojpur region; *Balusahi, Gulgulla, Makhana Ka Kheer* of Mithila region and and *Latto* and *Lorha Mithai* of tribal region.

(c) Maximum number of popular sweetmeats (at every place one may find several varieties of sweetmeats but all such sweetmeats may not be popular) are found in the Magahi zone which is followed by tribal zone. In the tribal zone, the sweetmeats such as *Lengcha, Raskadam, Pera, Inarsa, Kalakand, Lorha Mithai* are famous. But such sweetmeats are generally consumed by non-tribal people. When we talk about the sweetmeats generally consumed by the tribals, mention may be made of following sweetmeats which are dry, crude, poor in quality and indigenous in character, e.g. *Latto, Jalebi, Barfee, Laddu*. Minimum number of popular sweetmeats are found in the Bhojpur zone.

Fifthly, when we go into the details of the communities associated with sweetmeats and their associations and problems, the following points emerge:

(i) Two communities, i.e. *Halwais* in Bihar and *Mayra* in

West Bengal are actively associated with this profession. The name *Halwai* is derived from *Halwa* (a type of sweet-dish). In Sanskrit, the term *'Halwai'* is equivalent to *'Modaka'*. *Halwais* are also called *Mithaiyas* or 'makers of sweetmeats'. They form a very important caste in the Hindu society.

(ii) In the present time about 60 per cent of other castes are also entering into this profession. Economic backwardness on the one hand, and spread of education, market, employment opportunities on the other, are important factors due to which many *Halwais* and *Mayra* castes had to give up their traditional occupation and take to other more paying jobs.

(iii) The persons connected with this profession have also their own professional Associations on All-India and State levels. The name of such association on the All-India level is *Akhil Bhartiya Khadya Peya Mishthanna Vikreta Mahamandal* while that of the State levels of Bihar and West Bengal are *Bihar Rajya Mistan-Bhojan Vikreta Sangh* and *Paschimbanga Mistanna Babasayee Samity* respectively. The main purpose of these Associatons is to ensure a sense of unity among the Sweetmeat-makers, solve the various problems connected with this profession, and promote their business.

In West Bengal, the people connected with this profession have to face greater problems in comparison to Bihar. One of the major problems is taxation on sweetmeats which is not prevalent in Bihar.

Sixthly, in regard to the diffusion of sweetmeats and its factors, the following observations may be made:

(i) Sweetmeat is a diffusable trait. Eleven factors have been identified that are responsible for its diffusion in historical perspective which are location of shops nearing state borders, migration or immigration of a community and sweetmeat-makers, involvement of influential persons, kinship net-work, social congregations at market places, fairs, festivals and pilgrimage centres, maintenance of livelihood and the standard of shop, hawking and vending at different places, opening of branches at different places by famous sweetmeat-makers, overcrowding of sweetmeat shops at one place, industrialisation and urbanisation, and scientific and technological developments.

(ii) The sweetmeats are diffused from one place to the other, but the area of its diffusion may vary from one sweetmeat to the other. The sweetmeats are diffused on all-India level, zonal (inter-state) level, state level and regional (intra state or cultural-linguistic area) level. In spite of that there are some sweetmeats which did not diffuse from their original place.

The factors like easy availability and low price of ingredient, easy preparation, liking of sweetmeat by all age-groups of people and every community, long preservation, migration of community and transportation are some of the important factors due to which a sweetmeat is diffused on All-India level. The factors such as location of shops nearing state borders, transportation and kinship network play an important role in diffusion of a sweetmeat on zonal level. The factors behind a diffusion of sweetmeat on state level are migration of labour, opening of new branches by famous sweetmeat-maker, transportation facilities, overcrowding of shops at a place and migration of communities connected with sweet-making. The factors such as regular and frequency of transportation, and kinship-network help in the diffusion of sweetmeat on regional level. Similarly, non-availability of proper ingredients, and lack of patience, capacity for hard work and declining expertise in the present generations work as negative factors of diffusion for a particular sweetmeat. The factors discussed above are not exclusive to a particular category.

(iii) To show the affinity among sweetmeats of different places on the basis of 'W' formula, forty-five traits connected with sweetmeats were selected on the basis of colour of sweetmeats, type of milk, contents of sweetmeats, quantity of syrup in the sweetmeats, sweetening-agent, shape, size and basic ingredients.

Regarding the traits connected with sweetmeats we find that there is not a single place where all types of traits connected with sweetmeats as referred above, were found. However, maximum number of such traits were found at Gaya (39)[1], Patna (28) and Ranchi (28) of Bihar State and Calcutta (39), Krishnanagar (37) and Barddhaman (33) of West Bengal. On the other hand, there are some places like Udwantnagar (22), Barh (24) and Koath (24) in Bihar, and Baharampore (22), Janai (22) and Jaiganj (20) in West Bengal where minimum number of such traits were found.

(iv) The places such as Ranchi and Patna; Jamshedpur and Buxar; Ghastshila and Buxar in Bihar, and Beldanga and Chandannagar; Medinipur and Bankura; Beldanga and Medinipur in West Bengal have maximum degrees of affinities in sweetmeats. The factors such as direct and more frequent transportation facilities, migration of people, industrialisation, marginality of area, location of the two places in adjacent districts play an important role in this connection.

(v) It is usually said that the syrupy sweetmeats or sweetmeats soft in nature are the main characteristics of West Bengal while dry sweetmeats of Bihar, though there may be some exceptions.

(vi) There are some places in Bihar where sweetmeats are prepared by mixing intoxicants like *Bhanga.* But such sweetmeats are not found in West Bengal. The sweetmeats of Bihar are largely flour-based. Though Bihari sweetmeats are not so popular in comparison to West Bengal sweets, the former are also famous in their own areas for its delicious taste and quality. Bengali sweetmeats are well known all over the country and by and large, they are milk-based.

Reference

1. The number within bracket show the number of traits found in respective places.

Appendix-1

Sorbitol : A Natural Sugar

Sorbitol, $C_6H_8(OH)_6$, molecular weight 182.2, is closely akin to glucose, the latter's aldehyde group being reduced to alcohol. It is a sugar occurring naturally in a number of fruits like apples, pears, cherries and others. It appears to be involved in the metabolism of fruits wherein the production of CO_2 by respiration corresponds to loss of sorbitol among others[1] and[2] CO_2 radioactivity was traced to formation of sorbitol.[3] These two reactions are significant to show that fruits have both catabolic and anabolic reactions of sorbitol and hence it must be connected with fruit metabolism. Since it can be obtained by reduction of glucose and give rise to fructose by enzymatic oxidation, it possibly has a vital role in the biosynthesis of sugars or is an intermediate in the interconversion of glucose and fructose particularly conversion of glucose into fructose which occurs specially abundantly in fruits.

Sorbitol dehydrogenase (Ketose reductose) occurs in mammalian liver and other sites and catalyzes the conversion of sorbitol to fructose[4], which enters the normal carbohydrate metabolism. Sorbitol + NAD $\rightleftharpoons$ fructose = NADH + H^+. Coupled with aldose reductase it transforms glucose into fructose of seminal plasma.[5] 70 per cent of orally ingested sorbitol is converted to CO_2, without appearing as glucose in blood. It is claimed to be non-carcinogenic and in general non-toxic. Intravenous administration to normal man of as much as 80 gm. of sorbitol produced no acute toxic symptoms.[6]

In recognition of its normal expected metabolism and natural sweetness (60 per cent as sweet as glucose) it has a long history of use as an ingredient or constituent of prepared foods. It yields calories equal to glucose or any other carbohydrate. It is approved and occurs in the GRAS list of the Food and Drug Administration of the USA. It has been, and is, used in different types of confectioneries in western countries.[7] Government of India food laws have permitted use of sorbitol (without assigning any limit) as ingredient in toffees[8] and prescribed sorbitol (and its esters of fatty acids) as emulsifying and stabilizing agent which can be used in specified foods with declaration on labels.[9] Sorbitol is marketed as a substitute for sugar under the name Sionin[10] or Sionone.

Though sorbitol gives 4 calories per gm. as other sugars and carbohydrates its absorption after ingestion is slow and hence its net calories are appreciably lower than the calculated values. This property has been utilized in formulating low calories (slimming) foods-confectionery and beverages.[11] Incidentally, the slow absorption rate is responsible for mild purgative action of sorbitol taken in large amounts, which incapable of being absorbed seeks an outlet through faeces.

Sorbitol and its metabolite, fructose are known to be tolerated by diabetics.[12] Sorbitol is used in place of sugar in diabetic diets as it does not produce a rise in blood sugar level when taken by mouth.[13] A daily intake of 36 to 54 gm. of sorbitol as a sweetening agent had no significant effect on the blood-sugar concentration and insulin requirement in patients with controlled diabetes, except in a patient with advanced hepatic cirrhosis. In patients with uncontrolled diabetes it might aggravate the hyperglycaemia.[14]

Sorbitol has a number of pharmaceutical uses too; it is used as a sweetening agent and vehicle in elixirs, linctuses and mixtures[15] and a substitute for glycerine.[16]

Sorbitol has many advantages for its use as a constituent or additive in foods. It is a natural sweetner and has no unpleasant after-taste like saccharin. Apart from technological utility as crystallization modifier, humectant, softening or plasticizing agent, sweetness controller, solvent effect, viscosity effect, rehydration aids and antioxidant action, and apart from usefulness in special (dietetic) foods, it affords palatibility and desirable textural properties to foods.

Thus, sorbitol is a natural sweetner (sugar), has a long history of use in normal, low-caloric and diabetic foods recording no adverse epidemologic finding, has known energy-yielding metabolic path, has no known toxicologic symptoms (except mild purgative action when taken in excess of the prescribed limit) and affords technological advantages in preparation of selected foods. For all practical purposes and in all respects, it is a food or a constituent foods like any other food. However, it should advisedly have a limit of intake as of any other constituent of food according to the tolerance of the individual.

Davidson et. al.,[17] has nicely summedup the position in his authoritative monograph on *Human Nutrition and Dieteties*: "In recent years a large industry has grown-up marketing diabetic chocolate, fruit drinks and preserves in great variety. The sweetning agent used in their manufacture is sorbitol. This derivative of glucose is slowly absorbed from the gut and so produces no immediate or important increase in the level of glucose in the blood."

(Compiled by K.C. Das Private Limited, Calcutta)

References

1. Donnen, I., *Biochem, J.* 33, 1611, 1947 (1939).
2. Furia, T.E., *Handbook of Food Additives, Chemical Rubber Co.*, Cleveland, 1968, p. 457.
3. Webb, K.L. and Burley, J.W.A., *Science* 137, 766 (1962).
4. Blakley, R.L., *Biochem*, J. 19, 257 (1951).

Bemiller, J.N., *In Carbohydrates and their Roles*, Schultz et. al, ed., Avi Publishing, 1969, p. 192.

5. Liers, H.G., *Le Metabolisme dufructose*, 1957.
6. Smith et. al., *J. Biochem*., 125, 231 (1940).
7. Same as Reference No. 2.
8. Prevention of Food Adulteration Rules, 1955, Govt. of India, A. 25-102 of Appendix B, Rule 5.
9. Ibid., Rule 60.
10. *Thorpe's Dictionary of Applied Chemistry,* Vol. II, p. 296.
11. Same as Reference No. 2.
12. Food Industries Manual, Leonard Hill, 1962, p. 117.
13. British Pharmaceutical Codes, 1968, p. 1252.
14. C.R. Shuman et. al., *Am. J. Clin, Nutr;* 1956, 4, 61, Per Abstr. Wld. Med., 1956, 20, 213.
15. Same as Reference No. 2.
16. *Extra Pharmacopocia*, Vol. I, 1952, 479.
17. Davidson et. al., *Human Nutrition and Dietetics,* Living-Stone, London, 1959, p. 619.

Bibliography

Abubakar, G.M., (1985) : *'Rassogollar Bayas 117 Bachhar'* in *Bartaman* (Bengali, Daily Newspaper) dated July 14. Bartaman Printers and Publishers Pvt. Limited, Calcutta.

Achaya. K.T., (1994) : *Indian food, A historical companion*: Oxford University Press, Delhi.

Agnihotri, S.K., (1980) : *Prachina Bhartiyon Ki Khan Pan Vyavastha* (Hindi). Atma Ram and Sons, Delhi.

Agrawala, V.S., (1953) : *India as known to Panini*. Allahabad Law Journal Press, Allahabad.

(1970) : *India as described by Manu*, Prithvi Prakashan, Varanasi-5.

Akbar, M.J., (1984) : 'Sweets and Confectionery' (ed). In *The Telegraph* (Sunday Magazine), dated October 21, Anand Bazar Patrika Ltd., Calcutta.

Anderson, E.N., (1997) : "Traditional medical values in food" in *Food and Culture A Reader*. Edited by Carole Counihan and Penny Van Esterik. Routledge, London.

Apte, V.M., (1951) : 'The age of Upanishads and Sutras in History and Culture of the Indian

People' in *Vedic Age* Edited by R.C. Majumdar. George Allen & Unwin Ltd., London.

Archer, W.G. & Prasad, S., (1943) : *Bhojpuri Gramya Geet* (Hindi), Patna Law Press, Patna.

Aryani, Sampati, (1965) : *Magahi Loka Sahitya* (Hindi), Hindi Sahitya Samsar, Patna.

Auboyer, Jeannine, (1965) : *Daily Life in Ancient India*, Asia Publishing House, Bombay.

Banerjee, Gopijiban, (1979) : 'Shyam Bazar Life, A Panorama of Plurality'. In *The Hindustan Standard*, Anand Bazar Patrika Limited, Calcutta.

Banerji, Chitrita, (1993) : *Life and food in Bengal*. Rupa & Co., New Delhi.

Beverley, H, (1872) : *Report on the Census of Bengal*, Bengal Secretariat Press, Calcutta.

Bhagavata Purana, (1980) : Lord Krishna in Skanda x 1, as quoted in Maria, Jack Santa's *Indian Sweet Cookery*. B. I. Publications, Delhi.

Bhattacharya, Chiranjivi, (1984) : '*Rasarajer Rasakatha*'. In *Desh* (Bengali, Weekly Magazine), dated March 3, Anand Bazar Patrika Limited, Calcutta.

Bhattacharya, France, (1983) : *Les mets el la Cuisine dans Le Cande Mangala* (French) Puausartha-7.

Biswas, Govind, (1984A) : *Jayanagrera Moya : Payera Gurera Panchali*. In *Aajkal* (Bengali, Daily Newspaper), dated November 27. Pratap Kumar Rai, Composing and Printing, Calcutta Private Limited, Calcutta.

(1984B) : '*Jayanagrera Mona : Nayak Banam Khalnayak*'. In *Aajkal* (Bengali Daily Newspaper), dated December 18, Pratap Kumar Rai, Pvt. Ltd. Calcutta.

Blunt, E.A.H, (1969) : *The Caste System of Northern India*. S. Chand & Company, Delhi.

Bose, Nagendranath, (1905) : *Vishwakosh* (Bengla), (ed.). Bishwasti Kosh Publication, A Bose Company, Calcutta (1311 B.S.).

Bose, N.K., (1959) : *Modern Bengal*, Vidyodaya Library, Private Limited, Calcutta.

Brah, (Editor), (1992) : *Encyclopaedia of India, Vol. XXII, Meghalaya*, Rima Publishing House, New Delhi.

Chakrabarti, Mukundram, (1964) : *Kabi Kankan Chandi* (Bengali). Basumati edition. Edited by Bijit Kumar Dutta, (1370 B.S.).

Chakravarty, Taponath, (1956) : 'The Narayanpur Image of Vinayaka' In *The India Historical Quarterly*, Vol. XXXIII, June and September, Nos. 2 & 3.

(1959) : *Food and Drink in Ancient Bengal*, Gossain & Co. Private Limited, Calcutta.

Chaudhury, P.C. Roy, (1957A) : *Bihar District Gazetteer, Gaya*. The Superintendent Secretariat Press, Patna.

(1957B) : *Bihar District Gazetter, Hazari-bagh*, The Superintendent Secretariat Press, Patna.

(1962A) : *Bihar District Gazetteer, Bhagalpur*. The Superintendent Secretariat Press, Patna.

(1962B) : *Inside Bihar*, Book Land Pvt. Ltd., Calcutta.

(1964) : *Bihar District Gazetteer, Darbhanga*. The Superintendent Secretariat Press, Patna.

(1965) : *Bihar District Gazetteer, Santhal Pargana*. The Superintendent Secretariat Press, Patna.

(1966) : *Bihar District Gazetteer, Shababad*, The Superintendent Secretariat Press, Patna.

Chaudhury, Sanjib Kumar, (1940) : Sri Sri Chaitanya Charitamrita of Sri Sri Krishnadasa Kaviraja Gosvamin (Translated in English). Sri Chaitanya Charitamrita, Karyalaya, Dacca.

Chopra, P. N., (Editor), 1992 : *Encyclopaedia of India, Vol. I*, Rima Publishing House, New Delhi.

Clarendon Press, (1933) : *The Oxford English Dictionary*, Oxford.

Croft-Cooke, Rupert, (1969) : *Exotic Food*. George Allen and Unwin Ltd., Ruskin House, Museum Street, London.

Crooke, William, (1974) : *The Tribes and Castes of the North-Western India*. Vol. II. Cosmo Publications, Delhi.

Das, Kalipada, (1983) : *Murshidabad Ka Sahi Mithai*'. In *Paribartan* (Bengla Weekly Magazine) dated 27th July, Biblabi Anukul Chandra Street, Calcutta.

De, Sushil Kumar, (1946) : *Bangla Prabad (Chhora O Chalti Katha)* (Bengali). Ranjan Publication House, Calcutta.

Diwakar, R.R., (Editor), (1959) : *Bihar Through the Ages*. Orient Longmans, Calcutta.

Dresden, Mark Jan, (1941) : *Manavagrhyasutra* (Translated into English), Groningen, Batavia.

Durga, Bhagwat, (1965) : *The Riddle in Indian Life Lore and Literature*, Popular Prakashan, Bombay.

Dutta, Sukumar, (1983) : *Siurir Morabba Jemana Mukho-rochak Jemini Rogira Pathya Bate*. In *Paribartan* (Bengla) dated July 27. Biplabi Ankul Chandra Street, Calcutta.

Fund and Wagnalls, (1955) : *New Standard Dictionary*, New York.

Gait, E.A., (1902) : *Census of India 1901, Vol. IV*, Bengal, Part-I, Bengal Secretariat Press, Calcutta.

Garrett, J.H.E., (1910) : *Bengal District Gazetteers, Nadia*,

Bengal Secretariat Book Depot, Calcutta.

Ghosal, Shonu, (1983) : *Ranaghater Misthi : Prastuta Pranali.* In *Paribartan* (Bengla Weekly, Magazine), dated July 27, Biplabi Ankul Chandra Street, Calcutta.

Ghosh, Mahita, (1985) : *Tapura Tupura* (Bengla). Sri Bhumi Publishing Company, Mahatma Gandhi Road, Calcutta.

Ghoshal, S.N., (N.D.) : *Census of India, Series 23, West Bengal.* Director of Census Operation, West Bengal.

Ghosh, Tushar Kanti, (1981) : *Rasagollar Char Purusa* in *Jugantar* (Bengali Daily Newspaper) dated October 29, Jugantar Limited, Anand Chatterjee Lane, Calcutta.

Ghoshal, U.N., (1951) : 'The Age of Imperial Kanauj, Social Condition'. In *The History and Culture of Indian People*, Vols. III. & IV. George Allen & Unwin Ltd., London.

Ghulati, S. P., (Editor), 1992 : *Encyclopaedia of India, Vol. XXIX, Karnataka*, Rima Publishing House, New Delhi.

Ghurye, G.S., (1961) : *Caste, Class and Occupation.* Popular Book Depot, Bombay-7.

Ginsburg, Norton, (1972) : 'Area' in *International Encyclopaedia of Social Sciences*, Vol. I, David L. Sills (ed.), The Mac Millan Company & The Free Press, New York.

Girling, D.A., (1978) : 'Cookery' in *Everyman's Encyclopaedia* (ed.), Vol. 3, J.M. Dent & Son Ltd.

Gode, P.K., (1943) : 'Some notes on the History of Indian Dietetics with special reference to the History of Jalebi' in *New Indian Antiquary*, Vol. VI., pp. 169-87.

Gopalan, C. & S. C. Balasubramanian, (1968) : *The Nutritive Value of Indian Foods and the Planning of Satisfactory Diets,*

Nutrition Research Laboratories, Hyderabad.

Gopalan, C. et. al., (1980) : *Nutritive Value of Indian Foods.* National Institute of Nutrition, Indian Council of Medical Research, Hyderabad.

Goswami, B. and B.K. Ray, (1910) : *Manusamhita* (Translated into English), Buckland Press, Calcutta.

Government of India, (1982) : The Prevention of Food Adulteration Act, 1954 (37 of 1954). Ministry of Law, Justice and Company Affairs.

Grierson, G.A., (1968) : *Linguistic Survey of India.* Vol. V., Part-III, Motilal Banarsidas, Patna.

(1975) : *Bihar Peasant Life.* Cosmo Publications, Delhi-6.

Haldar, J., (1926) : *Bengal Sweets.* Chuckervertty, Chatterjee and Co. Ltd., Book Sellers and Publishers, Calcutta.

Hassnain, F. M., (Editor) 1992 : *Encyclopaedia of India, Vol. IX, Part II, Kashmir,* Rima Publishing House, New Delhi.

Heine-Geldern Robert, (1968) : 'Cultural Diffusion'. In *International Encyclopaedia of Social Sciences,* David L. Sills (ed.), Vol. 4. The Mac Millan Company & The Free Press, New York.

Helen, Hemingway Benton (1973-74) : *The New Encyclopaedia Britannica* Macropaedia, Vol. IV.

Herskovits, M.J., (1970) : *Man and His Works.* The Science of Cultural Anthropology, New York.

Hoey, W., (1880) : *A Monograph on Trade and Manufactures in Northern India.* The American Methodist Mission Press, Lucknow.

Hopkins, W., (Editor), (1972) : *Hindu Polity.* Trubner & Co., London.

Hunter, W.W., (1976) : *A Statistical Account of Bengal,* Vol. XIV, Concept Publishing Company,

Delhi.

: *Encyclopaedia of India, Vol. XIX, Nagaland*, Rima Publishing House, New Delhi.

Hussain, Majid, (Editor), 1992 : *Encyclopaedia of India, Vol. XXI, Manipur*, Rima Publishing House, New Delhi.

: *Encyclopaedia of India, Vol. XXVII, Andhra Pradesh*, Rima Publishing House, New Delhi.

Jarrett, H.S., (1978) : *The Aini Akbari*. Vol. III by Abul Fazl Allami. (Translator). Royal Asiatic Society, Calcutta.

Jayasi, M.M., (1934) : *Padmavata* (Hindi). Sahitya Sadan, Chirgaon, Jhansi (2012).

J.M. Dent & Sons Ltd., (1978) : *Everyman's Encyclopaedia*. Vol. 3. Toronto.

Kaimal, P.K.V., (Editor) (1992) : *Encyclopaedia of India, Vol. V., Orissa*, Rima Publishing House, New Delhi.

Kanhyaju, K., (1945) : *Vrata aur Tyohar* (Hindi). Navyuga Sahitya Sadan, Indore.

Kar, Taraknath, (Editor), (1964) : *Mistanna Bhojan* (Hindi). Adarsh Press, Patna-4.

Kashy, M. J., (Editor) (1992) : *Encyclopaedia of India, Vol. XX, Kerala*. Rima Publishing House, New Delhi.

Kon, S.K., (1959) : *Milk and Milk Products in Human Nutrition*. Food and Agriculture Organization of the United Nations, Italy.

Kroeber, A.L., (1948) : *Anthropology*. Oxford & IBH Publishing Company, New Delhi.

Kumar, N., (1970) : *Bihar District Gazetteer, Patna*. The Superintendent Secretariat Press, Gulzarbagh, Patna.

(1971) : *Image of Patna*. Government of Bihar, Gazetteer Branch, Revenue Department, Patna.

Lal, B.B., (1982) ; *Census of India 1981, Series 4, Bihar* Superintendent Secretariat Press, Patna, Bihar.

Lal, Tejnarayan Shastri, (1962) : *Maithili Lokgito Ka Adhyayana.* (Hindi). Vinod Pustak Mandir, Agra.

Linton, Ralph, (1936) : *The Study of Man : An Introduction*, New York, Appleton.

Maharishi, Valmiki. : *Sri Madvalmikiya Ramayana,* Parts I & II, Gita Press, Gorakhpur.

Majumdar, B. & S. Mukhopadhyay, (1971) : *Jayananda's Chaitanya Mangla* (Bengali). *Bibliothica Indica*, No. 293, Asiatic Society of Bengal.

Majumdar, Durgadas, (1978) : *Gazetteer of India, West Bengal, Nadia*, Government of West Bengal.

Majumdar, G.P., (1935) : 'Food (Man's Indebtedness to Plants)'. In *Indian Culture.* Vol. I. (January). No. 3.

Majumdar, R.C., (1971) : *History of Ancient Bengal.* G. Bharadwaj & Co., Calcutta-9.

Malik, Malti, (Editor) 1992 : *Encyclopaedia of India, Vol. II, Haryana.* Rima Publishing House, New Delhi.

Maria, Jack Santa, (1980) : *Indian Sweet Cookery*, B.I. Publication, Calcutta.

Mishra, G.S.P., (1969) : *The Age of Vinaya.* Munshiram Manoharlal, New Delhi.

Mishra, Jayakanta, (1949) : *A History of Maithili Literature*, Vol. I, Tirabhukti Publications, Allahabad.

Mishra, M. & Govind Jha, (1980): *Jyotirishwar Varna Ratnakar.* (Maithili). Maithili Academy, Patna.

Montagne, Prosper, (1961) : *The Encyclopaedia of Food, Wine and Cooking.* Paul Hamlyn, London.

Mookerjee, Pankaj, (1983) : 'Of Rasogollas and Rajbhogs' in *The Economic Times*, dated August 14.

Mujataba Ali, Saiyad, (1958) : *Dhupa Chhaya* (Bengla). Triveni Prakashan, Calcutta.

Mukhopadhyay, Shyamal, (1983) : *Barddhaman Sitabhog, Mihidana and Lengcha*. In *Paribartan* (Bengla; Weekly, Magazine) dated July 27. Biplabi Anukul Chandra Street, Calcutta.

Nepali, Gopal Singh, (1965) : *The Newars, An Ethno-sociological Study of a Himalayan Community*. United Asia Publications, Bombay.

Om Prakash, (1961) : *Food and Drinks in Ancient India*. Munshi Ram Manoharlal, Delhi.

(1968) : 'Food habits of Indians in the Fifteen Century as gleaned from Brhadyogatarangun of Trimala Bhatta'. In *Proceedings of the Twenty ninth Indian History Congress Session, Part-I, Patiala, 1967*. Gyanpeeth Private Ltd., Patna.

O' Malley, L.S.S., (1908) : *Bengal District Gazetteers, Bankura*. Bengal Secretariat Book Depot, Calcutta.

(1910) : *Bengal District Gazetteers, Birbhum*. Bengal Secretariat Book Depot, Calcutta.

(1911) : *Bengal District Gazetteers, Medinapore*. Bengal Secretariat Book Depot, Calcutta.

(1913) : *Census of India, 1911, Vol. VI*. City of Calcutta, Part-I. Bengal Secretariat Book Depot, Calcutta.

(1914A) : *Bengal District Gazetteers, Murshidabad*. Bengal Secretariat Book Depot, Calcutta.

(1914B) : *Bengal District Gazetteers 24-Pargana*. The Bengal Secretariat Book Depot, Calcutta.

(1919) : District Gazetteer Gaya, as quoted in Pandeya, R.B. 1980 : *Magahi Bhasa Ka Itihash* (Hindi). Lok Sahitya

Sangam, Gaya (p. 105).

Pandey, Rajbali, (1949) : *Hindu Samskaras*. Vikram Publications, Bhadaini, Banaras.

Pandey, Ras Bihari, (1980) : *Magahi Bhasa Ka Itihasa* (Hindi). Lok Sahitya Sangam, Gaya.

Pandeya, Induprakash, (1958) : *Awadhi Lok Geet Aur Prampara* (Hindi). Ram Narayanlal, Allahabad.

Pasricha, Swaran & L.M. Rebello, (1969) : *Some Common Indian Recipes and their Nutritional Values.* Nutrition Research Laboratories, Hyderabad-7.

Patwardhan, V.N., (1952) : *Nutrition in India*, Hind Kitabs Ltd., Bombay.

Peterson, J.C.K., (1910) : *Bengal District Gazetteers, Burdwan.* Bengal Secretariat Book Depot, Calcutta.

Prasad, H.K., (1970) : *The Political and Socio-religious Condition of Bihar in the Chowkhamba Sanskrit Studies*, Vol. LXXVIII. The Chowkhamba Sanskrit Series Office, Varanasi.

Prasad, Mahabir, (1964) : *Mistanna*. In *Mistanna Bhojan* (Hindi) dated March 16, Mistanna Bhojan Karyalaya, Arya Kumar Road, Patna-4.

(Editor), (1976) : *Mistanna Bhojan* (Hindi), dated April 26, Mistanna Bhojan Karyalaya, Arya Kumar Road, Patna-4.

Prasad, N., (1961) : *Land and The People of Tribal Bihar*, Bihar Tribal Research Institute, Ranchi.
Government of Bihar, Ranchi.

Prasad, Vishwanath, (1962) : *Magahi Samskara Geet* (Hindi). Bihar Rashtra Bhasa Parishad, Patna.

Puri, Baijnath, (1957) : *India in the time of Patanjali*. Bhartiya Vidya Bhawan, Bombay.

Rajyalakshmi, P., (1991) : *Tribal food habits*, Gian Publishing House, New Delhi.

Rakesh, Ram Ikbal Singh, (1966): '*Maithili Lokageet* (Hindi). Hindu Sahitya Sammelan, Prayag. (2012).

Ramanna, B.R., (1978) 'Indian Sweetmeats' in Souvenir. All India Hotels and Halwai's Federation, Bombay.

Ray, D.L., (1954) : *Hasir Gana* (Bengla). Gurudas Chattopadhyay & Sons, Calcutta.

Ray, Niharranjan (1994) : *History of the Bengali people (Ancient Period).* Orient Longman Limited, Calcutta.

Ray, Ras Bihari, (1979) : *Sandesh Vikale Va Aikale.* In *Purasree* (Bengla, Periodicals). Vol. 2. July. Journal of the Calcutta Corporation.

Ray, Sukumar, (1985) : *Khai Khai* (Bengla). Vishwanath Basaka Book Store, Calcutta.

Reejhsinghani, Aroona, (1979) : *Indian Sweets and Desserts.* Orient Paperbacks, New Delhi.

Renner, H.D., (1944) : *The Origin of Food Habits.* Faber & Faber Ltd., London.

Risley, H.H., (1891) : *The Tribes and Castes of Bengal.* Vols. I & II. Bengal Secretariat Press, Calcutta.

Russell, R.V., (1916) : *The Tribes and Castes of the Central Provinces of India*, Vol-III, Mac Millan and Co. Limited, London.

Sangar, S.P., (1969) : 'Food and Drinks in Mughal India, in *Proceedings of the Thirtieth Session of Indian History Congress, Bhagalpur 1968.* Bhargava Bhushan Press, Varanasi.

Santra, Tarapada, (1982) : *Chhora-Prabade Grama Bangla Samaja* (Bengla). Peoples Book Publishing Company, Calcutta.

Saraswati, Baidyanath, (1978) : *Pottery-Making Cultures and Indians Civilization.* Abhinav Publications, New Delhi.

Sarkar, J.N., (1976) : *Hansi Rashi* (Bengla). Sishu Sahitya Pvt. Limited, Calcutta.

Sen, Rajani Kant, (1924) : *Kalyani* (Bengla). Gurudas Chattopadhyay & Sons, Calcutta.

Sharma, B.N., (1978) : *Festivals of India.* Abhinav Publications, New Delhi.

Sharma, Man Mohan, (1978) : *Folklore of Nepal.* Vision Books Pvt. Ltd., New Delhi.

Sharma, M.P.N., (1973) : '*A Report on Techno-Economic Survey of Ranchi District.* Rural Industries Project. Department of Industry. Government of Bihar, Patna'. Superintendent Secretariat Press, Bihar, Ranchi.

Shastri, Ram Pratap Tripathi, (1966) : *Hinduo Ke Vrata, Parva aur Tyohara* (Hindi). Lok Bhartiya Prakashan, Allahabad.

Singh, Anima, (1968) : *Maithili Lokageet Me Sohar Aur Khelawana* (Hindi). Mithila Darshan Pvt. Ltd., Calcutta.

Singh, Durga Shanker Prasad, (1923) : *Bhojpuri Lokageet me Karun Rasa* (Hindi). Hindi Sahitya Sammelan, Prayag. (2001).

Singh, R.N., (N.D.) : The Comprehensive History of Bihar, Vol. III, Part II as quoted in Pandeya, R.B. 1980 : *Magahi Bhasa Ka Itihasa.* Lok Sahitya Sangam, Gaya (p. 103).

Singh, S.S., (1983) : *Pasa Se Dekhane Ka Sukha* (Hindi), Parijat Prakashan, Patna-1.

Singh, Vijendra Narayan, (1974): *Bhojpuri Samskar Geet* (Hindi). Bhojpuri Sansad, Varanasi.

Sinha, Maniklal, (1977) : *Paschim Radh Tatha Bankurar Samskṛiti* (Bengla). Kavirajpara, Bishnupur. (1384 B.S.).

Souvenir (1960) : The All India Hotels Halwais Federation, 3rd Annual Session. August.

Sri Hari Sriman Maharsi Vedvyasamnita. (N.D.) : *The Mahabharata* (Sanskrit), Part-V, *Shanti Parva.* Gita Press, Gorakhpur.

Srivastava, Hari Mohan Lal, (1954) : *Lokokti Tatha Muhavare* (Hindi). Lakshmi Book Centre, Mathura.

Sriyuta, Vaythitahsidaya, (1957): *Lokotiyam* (Hindi). Ram Narayanlal, Publishers and Book Sellers, Allahabad.

Statesman, The, (1981) : 'Sweet and Sour'. In *The Statesman*, dated April 22, From Correspondent.

Swaminathen, C.R., (1983) : *The Kurma Mahapuranam* (Sanskrit), Nag Publishers, Jawaharnagar, Delhi.

Thakur, Murmu Bhagavata (1975) : *Dona Serena* (Santhali). Santhal. Pahariya Seva Mandal, Baidyanath, Deoghar.

Thakur, Ravindranath, (1969) : *Sancavita* (Bengla). Visva Bharti Granthan-Vibhaga, Calcutta.

(1981) : *Jivansmriti* (Bangla). Visva-Bharti, Calcutta.

Thakur, Ritendranath, (1910) : *Modir Dokan* (Bengla). Punnya Jantra, Dwarikanath Tagore Lane, Calcutta, (1316 B.S.).

Thompson, W.H. (1923) : *Census of India, 1921*, Vol. V. Bengal, Part-I, Calcutta, Bengal Secretariat Book Depot, Calcutta.

Tiwari, Sashi Shekhar, (1970) : *Bhojpuri Lokoktiyam* (Hindi). Bihar Rashtra Bhasa Parishad, Patna.

Tripathi, Ram Naresh. (N.D.) : *Gram Sahitya* (Hindi); (ed.) Vol. I. Hindi Mandir, Sultanpur, Awadh.

(1940) : *Hamara Gram Sahitya* (Hindi). Hindi Mandir, Prayag.

(1952) : *Gram Sahitya* (Hindi), (ed). Vol. III, Atma Ram & Sons, Kashmiri Gate, Delhi.

Upadhyaya, B.S. (1947) : *India in Kalidasa*. Kitabistan, Allahabad.

Upadhyay, Krishnadeo. (1955) : *Bhojpuri Lokageet* (Hindi), Part-I. Hindi Sahitya Sammelan Prayag, (2011).

(1957) : *Loka Sahitya Ki Bhumika* (Hindi). Sahitya Bhavana (Pvt) Ltd, Allahabad.

(1960) : *Bhojpuri Loksahitya Ka Addhyayana* (Hindi). Hindi Pracharak Pustakalaya, Varanasi.

Varma, C.D.P. and P.T. Jha. (1967) : *Sanskrit Shabdarth Kaustubha* (Sanskrit). Ram Narayanlal Beni Prasad, Allahabad.

Index